Three
Spanish
Philosophers

SUNY series
in
Latin American and Iberian Thought and Culture

Jorge J. E. Gracia and Rosemary Geisdorfer Real, Editors

Three
Spanish Philosophers

Unamuno, Ortega, Ferrater Mora

José Ferrater Mora

Edited and with an Introduction by J. M. Terricabras

State University of New York Press

Published by
State University of New York Press, Albany

For information, address the State University of New York Press,
90 State Street, Suite 700, Albany, NY 12207

Production by Michael Haggett
Marketing by Fran Keneston

Library of Congress Cataloging-in-Publication Data

Ferrater Mora, José, 1912–
    [Selections. English. 2003]
    Three Spanish philosophers : Unamuno, Ortega, Ferrater Mora / José
Ferrater Mora ; edited and with an introduction by J. M. Terricabras.
        p. cm. — (SUNY series in Latin American and Iberian thought and culture)
    Includes bibliographical references and index.
    ISBN 0-7914-5713-3 (alk. paper) — ISBN 0-7914-5714-1 (pbk. : alk. paper)
    1. Unamuno, Miguel de, 1864–1936. 2. Ortega y Gasset, Josâ, 1883–1955.
3. Death. I. Terricabras, Josep-Maria, 1946– II. Title. III. Series.

B4568.U54 F3913 2003
196'.1—dc21   2002030967

10 9 8 7 6 5 4 3 2 1

At the end of the twentieth century and the beginning of the twenty-first, Latinos were the fastest growing ethnic group in the United States. I am sure that the children of many immigrants read and write Spanish fluently, but no doubt there are many who do not, and it is to those that this book is dedicated, so that they may have the opportunity to see that there is much that is written by Spanish-speaking people that has enriched contemporary culture, and of which they should be very proud. Ferrater Mora was born and educated in Spain, traveled to Cuba as a refugee from the Spanish Civil War, lived in Chile, lectured in Argentina, Uruguay, Mexico, Puerto Rico, and lived and taught for over forty years in the United States, later returning to Spain to give numerous lectures. His thought is thus the product of both the Spanish- and the English-speaking worlds.

Priscilla Cohn
(widow of Ferrater Mora)

Contents

Introduction   1

Part I   Unamuno: A Philosophy of Tragedy   9
Editor's note   11
Text   13
Biographical Note   105
Unamuno's Works   106
Selected Bibliography on Unamuno   114

Part II   Ortega y Gasset: An Outline of His Philosophy   123
Editor's note   125
Text   127
Biographical Note   191
Ortega y Gasset's Works   192
Selected Bibliography on Ortega y Gasset   201

Part III   Ferrater Mora: Chapter Three of Being and Death   209
Editor's Note   211
Text   213
Biographical Note   257
Ferrater Mora's Works   259
Selected Bibliography on Ferrater Mora   262

Index of Persons   263

Index of Subjects   267

Introduction

Twentieth-century Spanish philosophy lacks the significance and the international influence it might have had due, in part, to the fact that this century has been a particularly difficult one in Spain's history. On the one hand, Spain has suffered two dictatorships: that of General Primo de Rivera, from 1923 to 1930, and then that of General Franco, from 1939 to 1975. The latter was preceded by three years of civil war (from 1936 to 1939), the prelude to World War II. For decades afterward Spain suffered from poverty, division, and isolation. On the other hand, Spain is composed of territories that are highly diverse in culture, ways of life, and economic status. Not until the end of the twentieth century did some regions overcome their almost endemic underdevelopment and approach the more European standards of such territories as Catalonia and the Basque Country. Ideological repression and poor cultural development are then partly responsible for the fact that some of the most original Spanish philosophers have had to live abroad for long periods of their lives, and have had little relevance in their own country.

THREE PHILOSOPHERS

That is the case of the three philosophers presented in this book: Miguel de Unamuno (Bilbao, 1864–Salamanca, 1936), José Ortega y Gasset (Madrid, 1883–1955), and José Ferrater Mora (Barcelona, 1912–1991). Although belonging to three different generations, these three philosophers—who together with Xavier Zubiri, 1898–1983, are the most important Spanish philosophers of the century—suffered in the flesh some of the political vicissitudes of Spain's recent history and were forced into exile: Unamuno during the first dictatorship, Ortega and Ferrater Mora during the second one.

The value of the studies collected in this volume lies not only in the possibility for the reader to see these three philosophers all at once, but also in the fact that their thoughts are viewed through the eyes of the youngest

1

among them, Ferrater Mora, who was also the most attuned to modernity. While Spain was turning its back on the future, Ferrater spent most of his life in foreign countries: France, Cuba, Chile, and above all, the United States. This fact was no doubt decisive in allowing him to train his capacity to integrate tendencies, to promote dialogue, and to nurture his interest not only in philosophy but also in the most recent developments of art, science, and technology. With his perspicacious glance, he was able to consider various facts, and to interpret complex thoughts, which he unraveled with great expertise before his students' and readers' eyes.

This volume contains three of Ferrater Mora's fundamental works. On the one hand, we have selected two highly praised studies that soon became classical interpretations in their field: Ferrater's study of Unamuno *(Unamuno: A Philosophy of Tragedy)*, in its 1962 edition, and his study of Ortega *(Ortega y Gasset: An Outline of his Philosophy)*, in its 1963 edition. On the other hand, we have selected a third text by Ferrater to present some features of his own philosophical thought in a compact but adequate form. This is chapter three from *Being and Death: An Outline of Integrationist Philosophy*, which was published in English in the same period as the other two studies, when Ferrater was already in his fifties and at the height of his intellectual powers.

José Ferrater Mora was not a disciple of either Unamuno or Ortega, but he knew their works very well. As a matter of fact, Ferrater was a profound connoisseur not only of Spanish thought but also of the whole history of philosophy. His historical and systematic works, together with his well-known *Diccionario de filosofía*, corroborate this point. Let us remember that his four-volume *Diccionario* is the best and most praised dictionary of philosophy existing in Spanish, and one of the best dictionaries ever written by a single person in any language.

Ferrater used to say that in order to understand someone, it is necessary to consider not only that person's historical situation, but also his personal character, and even the role played by chance in that person's life. In his works Ferrater manages to combine a vast historical knowledge and a tremendous skill in selecting the main threads that allow us to develop the thought of a philosopher in a clear and coherent way. Indeed, Ferrater has two basic abilities as a philosopher: apart from being a systematic thinker capable of finding the important conceptual *relations* in a work, he also shows great skill in presenting, in an intelligible yet not simplistic way, matters which in someone else's hands would become unclear and confused. Ferrater's thought is both complex and clear.

In a very famous passage of his *Logic*, Kant wrote that the three main questions of philosophy, namely "What can I know?" "What ought I to do?," and "What may I hope?" in the end refer to the question "What is man?" because each of them is linked to this question. This is particularly true of the three texts in this book. These texts contain brilliant passages of philosophical anthropology. In these pages, Ferrater wittily shows what it means to be a human being, as these views were put forward by Unamuno, Ortega, and himself.

UNAMUNO'S THOUGHT

Ferrater presents Unamuno as a thinker of tragedy, that is, someone capable of discovering, explaining, and expounding the contradictions inherent in human life. The fundamental tragic feeling stems from a powerful source: the opposition between reason and faith. Unamuno is not a contradictory thinker, however, just for contradiction's sake. Nor does he show contradictions in order simply to suppress them. He wants to make them clear. Unamuno, who constantly disagrees with and dissents from other people both in politics and religion, always promotes fruitful discordance, wishing to remain true to himself. Because he does not accept the bifurcation between thought and action, his thought cannot be reduced to a simple definition. As Ferrater says, for Unamuno to live as a human being is to live tragically, in agony, in a permanent tension between opposed elements within ourselves, and particularly between, on the one hand, reason's commands and, on the other, the force of those irrational elements within ourselves that are so important for our lives.

Thus, Unamuno is not concerned with abstractions, but with people of flesh and blood, complex and concrete people who realize that no explanation explains everything, that what is really important always remains unexplained, and that in order to live authentically one has to live tragically. Unamuno doesn't view himself as a philosopher in the traditional sense, for philosophers are concerned with abstract concepts such as "truth," "humanity," "existence," and "life." According to Ferrater, Unamuno's thinking is better expressed as "poetic realism." Consequently, Ferrater points to Unamuno's novels as the place to find the best expression of concrete human beings. There individual characters become real because they are torn by the characteristic turbulence of life.

In 1914, at the beginning of World War I, Unamuno was already a very influential and highly reputed intellectual in Spain, despite his insurmountable skill in raising debate and controversy. Ferrater was just two years old in 1914, but Ortega and Eugeni d'Ors (1882–1954)—both of whom were then publishing their first books—soon became Unamuno's most serious competitors. After considering the three essays gathered in this volume, it becomes clear that Ferrater felt closer to Ortega and to Ors—the latter is not represented here—than to Unamuno, possibly because their style and themes were more closely connected to modern European thought.

ORTEGA'S THOUGHT

Ortega pays attention to Unamuno's work, both to criticize and to praise it. In his own work, Ortega borrows some of Unamuno's themes such as the distinction between "hispanizers" and "europeanizers." The main theme of Ortega's work, however, is the doctrine of human life.

From multiple perspectives, Ortega examines life as a problem, identifies insecurity as one of its main features, and persuasively shows that science, culture, and education are more important for life than technology. Ortega doesn't build a closed and circular system, but an open one. Ferrater acknowledges that Ortega is one of the few philosophers aware of the problematic character of philosophical activity. In this sense, Ferrater emphasizes Ortega's broad interests and versatile character as a writer who adopts a narrative way of approaching reality.

Ferrater distinguishes three phases in Ortega's work. The first one, which he calls *Objectivism* refers to the articles written in the period from 1902 to 1913; the second one, called *Perspectivism,* goes from 1914 to 1923; the third one, *Ratio-vitalism,* stretches from 1924 to Ortega's death. Ferrater neither defends nor criticizes Ortega's work. He succeeds in presenting Ortega's rich and diverse thought in a way that is at once instructive and rigorous. Ferrater's study enables us to understand why Ortega was first accused of being a rationalist, an intellectualist, and later, of being a vitalist. Ortega, who is aware of the fact that the problem of our times is to settle the dispute between rationalism and relativism, aims at making a contribution worthy of the twentieth century. In this respect the pages that Ferrater devotes to Ortega's concept of philosophy are highly thought-provoking. Ortega thinks that philosophy is bound to be a permanent failure, since it consists in nothing but the attempt to solve problems that continually change throughout history. Here Ortega is loyal to the historical character he attributes to knowledge and philosophy. In the final sentences of his study Ferrater emphasizes that "what philosophers can learn from Ortega is that 'the first principle of a philosophy is the justification of itself.' " He adds that "Ortega himself never lost sight of this necessity."

FERRATER MORA'S THOUGHT

Ferrater's first training in philosophy took place at the University of Barcelona in the thirties. At that time the two main figures in Spanish philosophy were precisely Unamuno and Ortega y Gasset. At the University Ferrater was taught above all continental philosophy, particularly phenomenological thought: Husserl, Scheler, and Heidegger. From 1947, when he went from Chile to the United States, and especially after his arrival at Bryn Mawr College in 1949, Ferrater was able to delve more deeply into the Anglo-American philosophical tradition. Thus he ended up being a thinker with an extraordinarily broad and balanced background.

The chapter we reprint here is an example of Ferrater's mature thinking. It consists of a text about human life and death, in which Ferrater provides us with the core of his later, more fully developed anthropology. Since the book, *Being and Death: An Outline of Integrationist Thought* contains fundamental elements of Ferrater's thought—as is clear from the subtitle—and since we have included only one chapter here, it may be helpful to outline some aspects of his thought, particularly those that can lead us to a better understanding of this chapter and of what he calls integrationism.

Death is a classical theme in European Philosophical thought. In reading this text we soon see that Ferrater exhibits a deep insight into phenomenological descriptions, an enormous skill and subtlety in his analysis of arguments, and an extreme rigor in presenting reasons. As a result, the very literary style of the text splendidly integrates the European and Anglo-American traditions. Thus, the author achieves an *integrationism of tendencies,* which is the first version of his integrationism. At this level, integrationism represents a general attitude rather than a philosophical method in any strict sense.

Ferrater, however, takes a further step and proposes an *integrationism of concepts* that amounts to the following insight: constant philosophical discords expressed in dualisms of all kinds characterize the history of thought. We have seen, for example, how Unamuno dealt with the opposition between faith and reason and how Ortega dealt with that between reason and life. There are innumerable oppositions like these in the history of philosophy. Let us mention some classical cases of dualism: realism and idealism, subjectivism and objectivism, rationalism and empiricism, internalism and externalism, being and nothingness, matter and spirit, body and soul. In his philosophy Ferrater does not neglect these dualisms but, on the contrary, takes them very seriously. The reason for this is clear: he does not want to lay the foundations of his philosophy on philosophical prejudices. He wants rather to take reality itself as his point of departure; he wants to start from what really happens, This is why he has to admit that what is really going on, what there really is, is above all philosophical discord.

Faced with philosophical dualisms, Ferrater does not adopt the quite common attitude of trying to overcome them in one way or another. He is aware that discord is practically unavoidable. He seeks, therefore, a way of making discord fruitful without having either to discredit it or accept it in a passive and uncritical way. Ferrater conceives of his integrationism as a way of making use of dualisms. According to him, opposed concepts do not express any reality: they are simply *limiting concepts,* or extreme limits. Each of them expresses an aspect of reality in an extreme way. In fact, dualisms are interesting not because they express a philosophical reality one needs to accept and interpret, but rather because they offer the framework for reflection within which we have to move when doing philosophy. Thus dualisms are there not to be reflected on, but rather to constitute the framework and the occasion of reflection. Though each term functions as a limit and shows its own insufficiency, at the same time each one counterbalances its opposite term's insufficiency. In this way philosophical oppositions are interpretable as reference points—like conceptual landmarks—for the understanding of reality. Basically this is what Ferrater's *integrationism of concepts* consists in. According to Ferrater himself it is a "philosophical methodology," a new way of doing philosophy.

Since Ferrater asserts that *Being and Death* outlines his integrationist philosophy, we can treat the very concepts "being" and "death" as examples of a paradigmatic application of the integrationist methodology. The objects of our world are very diverse: from stars, plants, animals, and human beings to ideas, projects, feelings, beliefs, and political regimes. We can reasonably say that all these beings or things exist; but we also have to admit that they have different kinds of existence. Clearly, any existing thing might cease to exist, but then we will also have to acknowledge that different kinds of things will have different ways of ceasing to exist, different ways of "dying." So "being" and "death" are concepts that do not apply to all beings univocally. When they stop existing, all beings *cease,* but it is not the case that all of them *die.* At least at first sight, it seems that *dying* applies to organic structures with certain biological functions. If that were always the case, the concept of *dying* would be included in that of *ceasing,* but the reverse would not be true.

Matters are usually more complicated than they look at first sight. Ferrater's philosophy commits itself precisely to a full respect for the multiple gradations and nuances of reality. In this case, even if it seems convenient to draw a distinction between "ceasing" and "dying," we have to admit that such a distinction will not solve our problems: actually, that distinction cannot be drawn on the basis of the distinction between "organic entities" and "inorganic entities," because these terms do not designate any watertight compartments, nor do they divide reality into two absolutely clear-cut parts. In the end, natural biological entities are organisms, but in a sense so are many social and cultural entities that have an independent life and undergo many different kinds of processes of growing and being transformed. Thus "cessation" and "death" are nothing but limiting concepts located at the extremes of a continuum: some beings cease when they stop existing; but other beings die; and there is still a very wide range of beings in the conceptual interval between death and cessation. This approach is also useful in understanding the different ways of viewing human death, which depend on the philosophical view one adopts, such as materialism, mechanism, spiritualism, and on the varying degrees in which it may be adopted.

Ferrater draws no radical, clear-cut distinction between "ceasing" and "dying"—or between any other concepts of our ordinary language—but rather tries to find the differences of degree between the concepts. The final reason for his doing so is that he accepts an ontology of continuity: he believes that there are no radical ruptures among the many beings which constitute reality; one cannot discover unconnected realities. Ferrater developed this train of thought further in *De la materia a la razón (From Matter to Reason)*, published in 1979. In his opinion, reality is a continuum organized in four hierarchical levels. These four levels are: physical, organic, social, and cultural. Each level is *autonomous*, because entities can only be explained in terms of the level to which they belong, each level being limited by the immediately superior level, which emerges from the inferior one and so constitutes a continuum with it. In this way we obtain three levels of the continuum: the physico-organic, the organic-social, and the socio-cultural. The result of all this is a splendid conceptual architecture—well-joined, but not at all rigid—that rejects two things at once: any absolute break within reality, and a monotonous continualism. So Ferrater's view is a continualist one—in order to guarantee the unity of what exists. But it is also emergentist—in order to guarantee the diversity and richness of the existing reality. Therefore, Ferrater's opposition to crude dualism coincides with his opposition to what gave birth to it, namely crude essentialism.

Like Ortega, but more rigorously systematic, Ferrater presents his philosophy as "an open system." This was precisely the title of his last series of lectures at the University of Girona in 1989, on occasion of the opening of the Càtedra that bears his name.

ABOUT THIS EDITION

This volume is, then, an introduction to the thought of three philosophers from three different generations who offer a deep, penetrating insight into human existence. It is not the least important merit of all three that they manage to express their thought convincingly in vivid language. Ferrater Mora—acting here as their interpreter—serves as a perfect example. He provides us with two synthetic and brilliant versions of Unamuno's and Ortega's rich and complex thought; that is, he produces two introductory and thought-provoking versions of their thought, without in the least reducing their substantial content. From his own work, he offers us a chapter which clearly reveals both his conceptual rigor in dealing with complex matters and his ability to express those matters in an extremely clear form.

The publication of this book corresponds to an old project, nearly as old as the Ferrater Mora Càtedra itself. One of the aims of the Ferrater Mora

Càtedra was to make accessible to a wider public Ferrater's thought and works, as well as all his private documents and papers. As it happened, the fact that he had to go into exile as a young man turned out to be a great opportunity for him: he had access to a philosophical world and to a freedom of expression which would have been totally denied him in Spain at that time. As a result of his exile, however, he suffered two handicaps: first, it prevented him from having students in his own country despite the fact that he had many readers; second, although he published five books in English, he did not become well-known in the United States. That is why this publication seems so appropriate.

Finally I would like to express my gratitude, above all to two friends who have been behind this publication ever since it was first planned: Professor George Kline, who was for many years a colleague of Ferrater Mora in the Department of Philosophy at Bryn Mawr College, Pennsylvania; and Professor Priscilla Cohn, Ferrater's widow, a philosopher herself, whom we have to thank, among many other things, for having made everything easy in the difficult process of moving Ferrater's library to the University of Girona. I am also grateful to Professor Philip Silver, who translated Ferrater Mora's book on Unamuno when it was first published in English, to the Editors of this SUNY series for their help and their willingness to publish this book, and to Mr. Joan Vergés, a scholar attached to the Ferrater Mora Càtedra, for his valuable help in updating the complementary information added as a corollary to each of the three essays published here.

In this volume one can see the truth in what Ferrater said at the end of the preface he wrote for the first American edition of *Being and Death:*

> I should add that the book makes no pretense of making easy things difficult. From the point of view of its possible appeal to the public, making easy things difficult may be occasionally a more effective procedure than making difficult things easy or simply letting things be what they are. I know of not a few cases of works whose authors have succeeded in making easy things very arduous, and have subsequently enjoyed a wide reputation. To be sure, few people have read such works, but fewer still have dared confess that they did not. I have myself nothing against success—indeed, I sincerely hope that the present book will attain some measure of it—but I feel that, if it comes, it should be the result of understanding rather than of misunderstanding. Since in the world in which we live we have already had a good share of the latter, it may not seem too unreasonable to claim some of the former.

Prof. Josep-Maria Terricabras
Girona, March 2000

Part I

Unamuno: A Philosophy of Tragedy

EDITOR'S NOTE

In 1944 Ferrater Mora published a book in Spanish called *Unamuno: Bosquejo de una filosofía.* He republished it, with some revision, in 1957. From that book, and with some new revisions, the English version that is republished here came out in 1962. Ferrater gave that book the title *Unamuno: A Philosophy of Tragedy,* and wrote a new preface for it. In 1985 a new Spanish edition of the book appeared. Constantly revising and improving his works in every new edition, Ferrater prepared this last Spanish edition on the basis of the English version. Therefore, there is good reason to think that in his opinion the English edition was an improvement over the earlier ones.

So we reproduce here exactly the same text of the English version of 1962. There are just a couple of additions at the end of the text: first, a biographical note on Unamuno; and second, we have completed the notes and the bibliography of works in English. So, apart from carefully respecting the text by Ferrater Mora, we have updated some information that might help those readers for whom Spanish philosophy is not a familiar subject.

Preface to the American Edition

There are at least three ways of studying the work of an author and, in particular, that of a philosopher: the erudite, the critical, and the interpretive.

Those who employ the erudite approach are, or claim to be, impartial. Their mission is to amass (and, whenever necessary, correct) facts and dates, edit texts, unearth documents, sort out epochs and phases, inventory themes and motifs, trace relationships, discover books read, and track down influences. The work of erudition is, of course, necessary; more than that, it is indispensable. Without it one runs the risk of committing pompous falsifications or pronouncing solemn nonsense. Without an existent apparatus of erudition, the honest study of any author is impossible.

Those who employ the critical approach begin by adopting positions from which they usually strike out at the writer being studied. When these positions are purely external to, or have little to do with, the system of thought that is their target they obtain success as showy as it is useless. One can criticize Plato, Aristotle, Descartes, Hume, and Hegel with considerable success—particularly if one has the good fortune to have been born much later than they. When the positions adopted by the critics are purely internal, their success is equally notable though less spectacular. To achieve their ends they have only to lay bare the internal contradictions of a system and show that the conclusions would have been otherwise if the author had been faithful to his premises.

Neither of these two variations on the critical approach seems to me acceptable. The first is based upon a falsification; the second, upon pedantry. There is, however, a third variety of the critical approach which is much more respectable. This is the criticism of another system of philosophy using one's own philosophy as a point of reference—if, of course, this latter is fully evolved, mature, and not simply a series of more or less arbitrary opinions. And even then one's own philosophy should in some way be related to the philosophy to be criticized.

Those who employ the interpretive approach begin by sympathizing with the author studied. Yet "sympathizing with the author" does not mean identification with all his opinions or the appropriation of all his feelings. If this were to occur, interpretation would be impossible, and the only result would be repetition or, at best, summary. "Sympathizing with the author" primarily means getting inside his work, bringing his attitudes to light, scrutinizing his suppositions, and, above all, understanding his intentions. All this can be carried out in a style of thought different from that of the author being studied. But one must never give way to the temptation of falsifying the author's thought. The sympathy of which I speak is not, therefore, that of adherence, but of comprehension.

My book does not use the erudite approach. It does not pretend to, for much of this work has already been accomplished. Although much is still to be done in the study of Unamuno's themes and motifs, and the analysis of his modes of expression, in the investigation of his changes and crises, we already possess a sufficient body of carefully edited texts and of studies on specific aspects of Unamuno's work so that any future study of him may now rest upon a solid foundation of erudition. Furthermore, although Unamuno said and wrote many things, all of them can be reduced to a relatively small nucleus of preoccupations that tormented him all his life and make his philosophy, in spite of its apparent diffuseness, a singularly well-mortised whole. Nor is my book critical in either of our first two acceptations of that term. I neither adopt external positions in order to refute Unamuno's ideas, nor try to expose his internal contradictions. I might, I hope, have set out my own philosophy and considered Unamuno's in the light of it, but I suspect that the reader is more interested in Unamuno's thought than in mine.

For these reasons, I have used the interpretive approach. This approach is all the more suitable since Unamuno was one of those philosophers with whom these is the danger of being unjust if he is measured by alien standards—standards that lead one all too readily into making the author think and say what would never have occurred to him. I have decided to measure Unamuno by his own standards, even though, by so doing, I have forsworn certain techniques that are particularly congenial to me. It seemed the reader would arrive at a better understanding of Unamuno's personality and thought if I made an effort to expound and interpret them "Unamunianly." And this book would not be faithful to Unamuno if it did not contain a certain amount of disquietude and tension.

It has often been said that Unamuno was an existentialist thinker, or at least one of the forerunners of existentialist philosophy. To the extent that labels and tags aid in the understanding of an author—and even help to make him more widely known—I see nothing wrong with agreeing to such a description. After all, Unamuno's philosophy is nearer to the existentialist or existential philosophies than to any others. Nevertheless, he cannot be adequately understood by merely affiliating him with a philosophical movement. Unamuno evolved a mode of thought into which various important philosophical movements entered in a conflicting way without this conflict ever being finally resolved. Thus, for example, Unamuno was not simply an irrationalist. But neither was he a rationalist. As I try to prove in this book, both irrationalism and rationalism were equal ingredients of his philosophy. The same might be said of other philosophical movements or trends and, therefore, of existentialism. Yet Unamuno was no less an essentialist than he was an existentialist. How reason and faith, essence and existence, heart and head, and even peace and conflict, harmonized and struggled with each other is primarily what I have undertaken to demonstrate in this book.

J. F. M.

Bryn Mawr College
Bryn Mawr, Pa.

Chapter One

Unamuno and His Generation

1 THE GENERATION OF 1898

Miguel de Unamuno was born in Bilbao, the spiritual and industrial capital of the Spanish Basque country, on September 29, 1864. He spent his childhood and a part of his youth there, and it left an indelible mark on the whole of his life. Unamuno was always profoundly aware of his "Basqueness," even throughout his struggle against the political nationalism prevailing in that region. Far from believing that being Basque and Spanish at the same time were incompatible, he often urged that the Basques become the substance and, as it were, the salt of Spain. By so doing, he ranged himself with a large group of modern Spanish writers who, though born in the peripheral provinces of Spain, have done their best to revive the seemingly lethargic center—Castile.

Unamuno passionately adopted this center, but instead of quietly surrendering to its charm, he tried desperately to rekindle its fire. Whereas for Unamuno the Basque land was "the land of his love," Castile must be called "the land of his pain." The two regions were constantly at war in Unamuno's heart, or, as he saw it, in an unending embrace.

Since Unamuno was born in 1864, it has long been customary to include him in the Spanish literary Generation of 1898. In fact, he has often been considered one of its leaders, and even its most prominent figure. I shall follow here an already well-established usage, but I shall not attempt to explain Unamuno's personality and work entirely on the basis of a generational scheme. For one thing, there are other factors that must be taken into account—the psychological, social, and political, to mention only a few. For another, there are many points on which a writer and his generation are at cross purposes. I would consider the generational approach useful, then, but with the proviso that some limits be placed upon it.

The existence of the Spanish literary Generation of 1898 raises a few questions, and at least two of them must be answered within the compass of this enquiry. The first concerns the members of the generation; the second, characteristics they reportedly had in common.

Answers to the first of these questions have been legion. Some critics have restricted the Generation of 1898 to a small group of writers whose literary achievements and ideological significance are assured—Unamuno, Antonio Machado (sometimes also his brother, Manuel Machado), Azorín, Pío Baroja, Jacinto Benavente, Ramiro de Maeztu, and Ramón del Valle-Inclán. Others have felt that although this restriction is qualitatively valid, it is not historically so. Azorín and Baroja have convincingly shown that several writers, once famous but now virtually forgotten (Ruiz Contreras, Ciro Bayo, and Silverio Lanza), contributed as much to the literary climate that allows critics to speak of a Generation of 1898 as those writers who have become a standard part of the history of Spanish literature. Vicente Blasco Ibáñez could also be added to those whom Azorín and Pío Baroja have mentioned. In principle there is no reason why a phenomenal literary success should be considered as sufficient reason for excluding an author from even the most sophisticated histories of literature.

As if this disagreement over the number of writers to be properly included in the Generation of 1898 were not enough, the question of whether or not there were subgroups within the generation has often been asked. Some critics maintain, for example, that very definite subgroups—shaped by personal, literary, or political attitudes—persisted for a long time. Other critics counter by saying that there was by no means any feeling of spiritual coordination among the members of the generation as a whole, or of any particular group within it. Connected with the above questions is another: whether, according to strict chronology, it is even legitimate to include Unamuno in a generation whose other important members were several years his junior—seven years for Valle-Inclán; ten, for Azorín and Baroja; and no less than thirteen, for Antonio Machado. Confronted with this last problem, some critics and historians of Spanish literature have suggested the following solution: to consider Unamuno and Angel Ganivet (his junior by one year) members of a generation or semigeneration immediately preceding that of 1898. This would make Unamuno a member of an influential intellectual dyarchy occupying an intermediate position between the leading representatives of the Generation of 1898, and that other group or, as it has sometimes been considered, generation of writers to which Joaquín Costa, Juan Valera, Francisco Giner de los Ríos, Marcelino Menéndez y Pelayo, and Benito Pérez Galdós belonged.

Answers to the question of common characteristics of the various members of the Generation of 1898 are equally numerous. According to some critics these characteristics were mainly political or, if one prefers, historicopolitical. To these critics the Generation of 1898 was symbolic of the so-called "Disaster" (the loss of the Spanish overseas colonies after the Spanish-American War) and of the desire to meet this political setback in new, or supposedly new, ways by an inner-directing of the entire nation and a rebellion against all the conventional interpretations of its history. Others thought it was a question of purely literary traits. They felt the Generation of 1898 represented one of the great revolutions in the history of Spanish literature. And lastly, others favored traits at once more personal and more general in nature. They spoke of a community of sentiment at first negatively oriented (a dislike of empty rhetoric, of the routinely official Spain, of spiritual narrowness); but gradually this orientation became more positive in intention and in the results achieved. The most positive aspects of this spiritual renewal consisted in a search for authenticity, a rediscovery of the "real country," and a new sensitivity to the beauty of the language. Such a community of sentiment becomes even more clearly defined when contrasted with the intellectual attitudes current in Spain up until this time. It is by no means certain that the members of the Generation of 1898 reacted in the same ways to all the views held by the leading representatives of preceding generations. But since they often considered themselves, for a time at least, as the sole promoters of the spiritual renewal of which I have spoken, it is reasonable to assume that they had at least one view in common: the conviction (soon shaken by Azorín's indefatigable reconstruction of the Spanish literary past) that what they were doing in the field of literature and literary sensibility was something that no one else had done in Spain since the end of the Golden Age.

Our task here is not to comment at length on the above opinions; it will suffice to point out that although all of them contain information of use to us, they also reveal an important shortcoming: their purely schematic character. Their proponents seem to overlook the fact that there is no such thing as an unchanging nucleus of ideas and attitudes in a literary generation. It would be more exact to surmise that for a time a cluster of ideas, attitudes, aspirations, and desires were condensed into a changing core. As a consequence, the relations between a writer and his generation display a great variety of forms. It is quite possible for a writer to be a member of a given generation while moving constantly in and out of it. It is possible for a writer to do his work in a direction that a generation will later adopt as its own. It is also possible for a writer to become a member of a generation that has almost completed its cycle. Under no circumstances can it be said, then, that a literary generation is a perfectly definable historical entity and that all the literary achievements of its members exactly reflect the same pattern of spiritual ideals and aesthetic norms. The idea of a literary generation is, in short, not one that we can blindly accept, nor is it one that we can completely do without.

If we now apply this more flexible view to the problem of the Spanish literary Generation of 1898, and to the relationship between Unamuno and this generation, we will be able to conclude (1) that no characterization of the traits of the generation will ever be completely satisfactory, and (2) that Unamuno can be said to have been, and not to have been, one of its members. Thus, for example, although Unamuno and Ganivet were several years older than the other writers already mentioned, they were quite close to the cluster of ideas and attitudes usually associated with the Generation of 1898; indeed, they prepared the way for those ideas and attitudes. To be sure, Unamuno's contact with them was intimate, whereas Ganivet's was only peripheral. Because they both championed certain mental attitudes later developed by the other writers, and especially because Unamuno was hailed (according to Azorín) as a highly respected elder master of the group, they cannot be considered apart from the generation that they so decisively molded. On the other hand, with respect to the controversial issues that occupied the most famous Spanish writers of the time (Europeanism versus Hispanism, renovation versus tradition, activity versus stagnation), Unamuno assumed attitudes on occasion widely at variance with those of the other members of his generation. Therefore, whenever we accept the conventional picture of the Generation of 1898 and of Unamuno as one of its charter members, we do so with a number of reservations. And the more we consider Unamuno's activities *en bloc* instead of limiting ourselves to his early work, the more important these reservations seem likely to become. For example, there is something to be said in favor of the existence of an "intermediate generation" between that of 1868 (Joaquín Costa, Juan Valera, etc.) and that of 1898, and in favor of considering Unamuno, because of his date of birth, as one of its members. But in view of the philosophical character of Unamuno's work, and because a substantial part of it developed contemporaneously with the work of Ortega y Gasset and Eugenio d'Ors— who were born almost twenty years after Unamuno—we may even lump these three together in a special group connected with, but in no way dependent upon, the ideals promoted by the great majority of members of the Generation of 1898. So it seems that Unamuno was right, after all, when he claimed that he was "unclassifiable." All this helps to explain an apparently cryptic statement by the Spanish sociologist and novelist, Francisco Ayala: that Unamuno, far from being a continuation or a simple hiatus of Spanish tradition, was a true "period and new paragraph"—an abrupt end as well as a radical departure.

2 THE APPRENTICESHIP YEARS

With all the above in mind I will now trace Unamuno's biography—in particular, his intellectual biography. Above all, I will chart some sectors of his public life. Of course, insistence upon the public aspects does not necessarily mean that they alone are pertinent to an understanding of this philosopher's mind. Unamuno's public life was always deeply rooted in the silence of his inner life, so much so that most of the actions of his public existence emerge as eruptions of that deeper inmost silence. It is unfortunate, moreover, that the profound inner life of a thinker is often beyond the critic's grasp. It is even possible that, like any genuinely private life, Unamuno's will forever remain that famous "secret of the heart" which theologians tell us is revealed only in God's presence. Only by examining what is expressed in his writing— his thoughts, his contradictions, his doubts, his outbursts of joy, of anguish, and of anger—will we be able to catch a glimpse of his secret and his silence.

During the years succeeding Unamuno's birth, Spain gave herself up to such frenzied activity that it was difficult to tell whether the acceleration of her traditionally irregular pulse signaled a new vitality or a new decay. They were years of rebellion and crisis—1868, 1869, and 1870. The various upheavals suffered by the country had not yet coalesced into what would later be called the Second Civil War, fought with extreme fanaticism in the north, particularly when the Carlist siege of Bilbao began in December, 1873. By this time Unamuno, fatherless since his sixth year, was nine. The "first significant event" of his life, he often recalled, was "the explosion of a Carlist bomb" (February 21, 1874) on the roof of an adjacent house. The explosion left that characteristic "smell of powder" in the air around which many of Unamuno's ideas and feelings on Spain were to crystallize. From that moment Unamuno was able to recognize the existence of a tension that was to make itself felt again and again during his life. He realized that it was possible for Spaniards to talk about "the others"—the ones belonging to another faction—while acknowledging that these "others" were no less Spanish than themselves. He observed factions waging a cruel war against one another, and it puzzled him that each one of these factions was composed of true Spaniards in spite of the ideas (or, at times, lack of them) for which they tried to dismember and destroy their enemies. We are today inclined to suspect that underlying these struggles was a complex pattern of social and economic problems. But to Unamuno they presented themselves as a series of obsessions. It was the oppressive and at the same time vitalizing nature of these obsessions that Unamuno sensed during the monotonous days at school, and in the childish tussles he describes in his early autobiography, *Memories of Childhood and Youth (Recuerdos de niñez y de mocedad)*: angry voices blended with sane words; fierce cruelty linked with deep charity, all the confused shreds of the anarchist and absolutist temperament of Spain's immemorial soul.

The basic experience behind his first novel, *Peace in War (Paz en la guerra)*, was that smell of powder experienced during the siege of Bilbao. Just as the *Iliad* had been the epic of the Trojan wars, Unamuno intended this novel to be an objective epic of Spain's civil struggles during the third quarter of the nineteenth century. But it is not only a historical moment that is narrated in *Peace in War;* it is, according to Unamuno's own confession, "the essence of his people." He does not confine himself to describing a chain of events; he means to develop all the implications of a collective experience. That is why this book remained for a long time the major source of Unamuno's later interpretations of the Spanish soul. It is also the first complete example of his search for peace in the midst of continual war. In fact, for Unamuno the explosion of the bomb in Bilbao was the first of a long series of Spanish explosions that he was to witness; and in the center of the last and most violent of them all—the 1936–1939 Civil War—he was to die.

A year after the explosion, his primary education finished, Unamuno entered the Instituto Vizcaíno of Bilbao. We know little about him during these "high-school" years (1875–1880), but it seems that the one experience that dwarfed all others was the discovery, in his fervid and random reading, of an entirely new world: the world of ideas. He began to love poetry—the poetry of poets and the poetry of philosophers. A detailed examination of the authors read by Unamuno in these years would be most enlightening; here I may only mention that he avidly read Jaime Balmes—one of the promoters of the nineteenth-century neoscholastic revival, and a writer whom he later attacked; Juan Donoso Cortés—the leading representative of a staunch traditionalism; Antonio Trueba, and a host of Spanish Romantic poets. I suspect that he spent a long time reading and rereading his own first poems, an activity he might have defended later by claiming that if they were not original (as most probably they were not at this age) from a literary point of view, they might be original from a personal point of view—originality being for him not a question of craftsmanship, but a question of strong feeling and sincere belief.

When the completion of his "high-school" years in 1880 ended his residence in Bilbao, he went on to Madrid for university studies, which occupied him until 1884. There he plunged feverishly into a turmoil of philosophical ideas and religious doubts; and there, like his hero, Pachico, in *Peace in War,* he passed his days "hatching dreams." It appears that Madrid was not much to his liking. Unamuno, the native son of a provincial town, at that time still more rural than urban, was probably ill at ease in a city like Madrid which, while already proud of her meager cosmopolitanism, was a thousand miles from that universality which Unamuno felt to be the exact opposite of cosmopolitanism. Nor was Unamuno as greatly influenced by university life as Spanish students were later to be when, with Ortega y Gasset and others, the universities and particularly the University of Madrid gained influence and prestige. Probably more significant and influential than Unamuno's university life was his own voracious and diverse reading and his contact with the writings and the personalities of some of the dominant intellectual figures in the Spanish capital. The intellectual personalities then in ascendancy, or long since firmly established, spanned several generations, from those who, like Francisco Pi y Margall—the highly respected left-wing historian and political writer—had been born in 1821, to men like Joaquín Costa—the versatile man of letters—born in 1846. The same time span also included a more compact generation, that is, one of men born about the year 1838. This so-called Generation of 1868 included those deans of Republicanism, Emilio Castelar and Nicolás Salmerón, the educators Francisco Giner de los Ríos and the writers Pedro Antonio de Alarcón, José María de Pereda, Juan Valera, and Benito Pérez Galdós. Most of these men shared a desire to rejuvenate Spain, a desire that was as apparent in the skeptical and somewhat snobbish accents of Valera as it was in the trenchant language of Costa. Numerous controversies took place in this connection. The "Krausists" and the "Catholics" opposed each other in the most important of these controversies, each side representing not only different ideological currents and worldviews, but also, and perhaps above all, different temperaments. Unamuno picked his way among the spiritual peaks of his day, now in sympathy with one, now with another. To be sure, some temperaments attracted him more than others. He chose at that time the liberal, europeanizing group, and sided with the enterprising renovators who, guided by Costa, meant to "locke the Cid's tomb with seven keys." These renovators intended to put a stop to Spain's quixotic antics and to her unchecked "Cidismo." All this was very far from Unamuno's later thoughts on Spain's past, but nevertheless it freed him from the conventional, shallow views held by the extreme "traditionalists." At any rate, this was the intellectual climate of Madrid between 1880 and 1884 which influenced Unamuno more than the university ever could.

After four years of study, of silence, of solitary meditation, "wrapped in one's own thoughts," of debates in student rooms, at the Círculo Vasconavarro and the Ateneo, of long walks (Unamuno was already, and remained until his death, an indefatigable stroller), he received his doctoral degree and returned to the Basque provinces and an outwardly uneventful life. With his return to Bilbao and his renewed residence in the Basque countryside between 1884 and 1891, past experiences began to arrange themselves meaningfully for him. He earned his living by giving private lessons, found time to read extensively, to participate in discussions at the Sociedad Bilbaína, and to walk for long hours through the streets. He soon became aware of a historical horizon that would serve perfectly as the setting for a narrative. He focused his interest on the Second Carlist War as symbolic of a chronic phase of Spanish life. While he gave lessons, wrote unsigned articles for a Socialist newspaper, and prepared for his professional competitive examinations, he collected an enormous fund of anecdotal information about the war from the lips of survivors and by a continual reëxamination of his own childhood memories. With this information at hand, he tried to reconstruct the climate of the war as faithfully as possible. As I have said, he wanted to write a truly novelistic epic. Outlined as early as 1890, *Peace in War,* at first a short story, was not published in book form until 1897. In order to write the book, which was to become a long novel, Unamuno needed a spiritual and economic tranquility that Bilbao, for all its "charm," could not offer. Unamuno's literary labors needed new soil for their fruition; this was to be Salamanca, in the very heart of Old Castile.

3 THE CRITICAL YEARS

Unamuno went then to Madrid, and spent several months taking various competitive examinations for a teaching position. After several attempts at various positions, he won a chair of Greek language and literature in Salamanca. Valera and Menéndez y Pelayo, the defenders of two opposing points of view—the "modern" and the "traditional"—were among his examiners. These examinations took place in the spring of 1891, and it was then that Unamuno met Ganivet in whom he recognized a restless spirit akin to his own. Both were deeply involved in a quest for an authentically Spanish system of thought unaffected by external europeanizing influences and untarnished by Spanish "traditionalism." If in Ganivet this concern was disguised beneath a mask of ironic bitterness, in Unamuno, a more positive and more vital person, the concern was readily visible, based as it was upon an aggressively polemical nature. Both, however, drew on similar experiences; both were convinced that a Spanish philosophy could be distilled from Spanish life, rather than culled from the books on library shelves; both felt that, as Ganivet had written, "the most important philosophy for any country is one native to it, even though inferior to the able imitations of foreign philosophies."

Later in 1891 Unamuno moved to Salamanca, an event that marked for him the beginning of a new epoch. Salamanca came to mean more than an administrative position to Unamuno. His residence in this quiet city helped him to discover himself, his possibilities, and, in a sense, his limitations. There were few cities that could have provided a more perfect setting for his type of thinking than Salamanca, so heavy with silence and history, its *agora* interlaced by fields, and its immense plains set under high mountains. Here was a city in which to discover immutable truths beneath the transitory anecdotes, the living bedrock of "eternal tradition" beneath the continual upheavals of history. In his life-long tenure at Salamanca there was, moreover, a decisive period for Unamuno; it came between the publication of *On Purism (En torno al casticismo)* in 1895 and *The Life of Don Quixote and Sancho (Vida de Don Quijote y Sancho)* in 1905. The zenith of this period was the year 1897. He had experienced a great intellectual crisis in Madrid, but the one in Salamanca was to be more profound, more emotional, more intimate, and more religious. Even assuming that Unamuno's religious crisis had been less profound or less sudden than Antonio Sánchez Barhudo has detailed it, there is little doubt that a profound experience, or series of experiences, gripped Unamuno's soul. At any rate, there is a definite change in tone in his writing before and after 1897. Before 1897, and particularly between 1895 and 1897, we find Unamuno in a pitched battle with "purism" and traditionalism, which he declared to be empty and conventional. Local tradition, he argued, must be discarded in favor of universality. Repetition must give way to renovation; Spain must be prodded from the bog that held it fast. After 1897, however, and especially between 1897 and 1905, we find Unamuno absorbed in a tense and painful attempt at innerdirection. Here the *Three Essays (Tres ensayos)* of 1900, with their passionate inquiry into the problem—or rather, mystery—of personality, individual and collective, is a salient landmark. Unamuno's "Inward!" replaces his cry of "Forward!" Don Quixote replaces Don Alonso Quijano; and the stuff of dreams, no longer a stumbling block, becomes the very substance of existence.

It is true that there seems to have been some preparation for these new views during the two or three years preceding the "great crisis." After all, though Unamuno defended—before 1897—the importance of forms and symbols, and the stuff of which, he said at that time, the world was constructed, he also maintained that the former possessed "feelings" and the latter, "life." Therefore, the name, the incarnation of a concept must "repossess itself in the permanent, eternal realm"; forms and symbols were no longer to be considered attributes of an intelligible world, but of a more substantial universe—a sensuous *and* an eternal one. That is why the universality, which Unamuno opposed to cosmopolitanism, belongs to the "eternal tradition" that exists beneath the surface of routine conventions. But his ideas on the same questions became much more trenchant, and in many ways more searching, after 1897. If Unamuno underwrote tradition at this time, it was as something quite unlike that seclusion-within-one's-self practiced and preached by the traditionalists. For Unamuno, "seclusion within one's self" *(encerrarse)* meant a definite "opening inward" *(abrirse hacia sí mismo)*. Already in a small way before 1897, but much more after this year, he felt the need to "accumulate continually in order continually to pour forth, to empty one's self," or, as he once described it, "draw in in order to expand" *(concentrarse para irradiar)*.

In the light of this process we can understand how Unamuno moved from an eager receptivity to outside forces to a ceaseless pouring out from within, from the apparent "realistic objectivity" and accumulation of detail in *Peace in War* to the "critical subjectivity," the spareness and whimsicality of the novel *Love and Pedagogy* (1902). This is an abrupt change in tone, but we must not forget that it is but a modulation of the same melody that permeated all of Unamuno's work and life.

4   UNIVERSITY AND POLITICS

During these years Unamuno's public life seemed a well-regulated routine of lectures at the university, conversations, discussions, and walks. These occupations were practice for the more resounding activities of the days and weeks he spent in Madrid, where he quickened the pulse of literary and political gatherings in cafés, in the newspaper and literary review offices, and at the Ateneo. Contact with the emotional atmosphere of Madrid soon drew him into politics, but from his first visits to Madrid as a respected writer until his death, his manner of participation in politics was ever characteristically his own. Unamuno never belonged to any one political party; he was too pleased and too proud of being a heretic to all parties—and all regimes. He felt the need continually to disagree, and he saw himself in the role of "spiritual agitator," for at that time he was convinced that what Spain, and Europe, needed most was a quickening of the pulse and a stirring of the soul.

He became still more of a political heretic in 1914, after his dismissal from the post of rector in the University of Salamanca. The government declared that politics and the teaching profession were incompatible. To this pronouncement Unamuno countered by saying that they were, in fact, the same thing; for whereas politics is teaching on a national level, teaching is talking politics on a personal level. And to those who thought that this was only a paradox, he replied that paradoxes could not be dispensed with when it was necessary to jolt an indolent nation awake.

It has often been said that Unamuno was an impassioned personalist in his philosophy as well as in his politics, and that whereas the first is acceptable, the second is intolerable. This view overlooks two points; first, that it is unfair to expect a complete divorce of thought and action in Unamuno; and second, that his concern with the personal element in politics had its strict counterpart in his philosophy. Both were manifestations of one and the same attitude. At all times this "personalistic" feeling pervaded Unamuno's political life. When he expressed, as he was often to do, antimonarchist sentiments, it was never as an attack on the concept of monarchy and the royal prerogative as such. He attacked one monarchy and one king only, and he felt that this was proof of his predilection for concrete realities. This explains why Unamuno was always considered (and often angrily denounced) as an unstable political element: he was not a Monarchist, but this did not make of him, strictly speaking, a Republican. He was at all times what he wished to be: the dissenting element of all political parties, the troublemaker in all political rallies.

After Unamuno's dismissal as rector of Salamanca, his political activity increased, and he undertook two violent campaigns: one against King Alfonso XIII; the other, against the Central Powers and in defense of the Allied cause in World War I. It is imperative to remember, however, that politics never occupied Unamuno entirely, and that beneath it—often nourishing it—his literary and spiritual life continued as before. Between the publication of *The Life of Don Quixote and Sancho* in 1905 and the publication of his profoundest work, *The Tragic Sense of Life*, in 1913, the channel of his personal inner life broadened and deepened. We have as proof the publication of *Poems* (1907), of *Memories of Childhood and Youth* (1911), of *Rosary of Lyric Sonnets (Rosario de Sonetos líricos)* (1911), and of the volume entitled *Through Portugal and Spain (Por tierras de Portugal y España)* (1911). This last book is characteristic of his manner of travel and observation, for he appears at once captivated by the circumstantial and seduced by the eternal. These trips through Portugal and Spain thrilled Unamuno to the point of ecstasy, and his myopic perusal of France, Italy, and Switzerland contrasts sharply with the penetration he leveled at his own country and that of his "Portuguese brothers." Baroja wrote that Unamuno saw little or nothing in his European travels because of his fierce intransigence and his intellectual blindness. Baroja's remark is true, but only in part. For Unamuno's blindness was largely fostered by a desire not to allow his observation of foreign lands to distract him from the passionate contemplation of his own. At any rate, although we may complain that Unamuno was not objective enough when he looked north of the Pyrenees, we must thank him for having discovered so much south of that mountain range.

By 1914, Unamuno had become the undisputed mentor of many young Spaniards. This does not mean that he was always listened to with reverence; indeed, he was often violently opposed. But his towering figure made itself felt in the arena of Spanish thought, and there vied for leadership with the other outstanding figures of his time. His chief competitors were Ortega y Gasset, who had been publishing in newspapers since 1902 and had sent his *Meditations on the "Quixote" (Meditaciones del Quijote)* to press by 1914; and Eugenio d'Ors, who began publishing his *Commentaries (Glosas)* in 1905. The writing of these two differed considerably from Unamuno's both in style and content. Ortega offered a continental manner that was more than a servile imitation of

Europe, and d'Ors a twentieth-century viewpoint that was infinitely more appealing than an irrational exaltation of our Age. Because of the order, lucidity, and harmony that they proffered, their work was more acceptable to many than Unamuno's. Small wonder that there were frequent displays of enmity among the three philosophers and their followers. But the enmity gradually subsided as it became apparent that where one was weak another was doubly strong and that, in all fairness, none of the three was expendable. If some signal issue had been overlooked by Unamuno it was certain to appear in an essay by Ortega or a commentary by d'Ors, or vice versa; thus, by supplementing his work with theirs, they exposed Unamuno's inevitable, yet fruitful, limitations.

5   THE EXILE

This routine of academic lectures, travels and domestic life, discussions and political sallies, continued until 1924 when Unamuno burst more loudly than ever upon the public's ear, acquiring a notoriety that enormously enlarged the number and variety of his readers. His opposition to Alfonso XIII reached new extremes as a result of the Primo de Rivera *coup d'état* in 1923. His audience with the king, interpreted by some as a desertion of the antimonarchist ranks, merely exemplified, as he pointed out in a tumultuous meeting at the Ateneo and in the *El Liberal* offices a few days after, his unswerving fixity of purpose. It had only served to reinforce an opposition that reached titanic proportions when the dictatorship of Primo de Rivera was sanctioned by royal decree. Since the physical annihilation of famous opponents was not yet customary in European politics, Primo de Rivera's reaction to this ideological insurrection was at first fumbling and in the end rather mild. For some time after the advent of Primo de Rivera's dictatorship, Unamuno continued to voice his protests, and after his exile to Fuerteventura, one of the Canary Islands, they reached an ever larger public. He came to feel that this exile was the most important event in the political life of twentieth-century Spain, and he swore to do his best to destroy his now deadly enemy—a personal and, therefore, according to one of his paradoxes, a universal one.

Unamuno's contrariness during his transfer to the place of exile would provide a book of anecdotes. The anecdotes, unimportant in themselves, are nevertheless a measure of his warlike attitude toward the dictatorship, and above all toward the dictator. He continued to write and speak against the king and Primo de Rivera from Fuerteventura, and when the editor of the French newspaper *Le Quotidien,* to which Unamuno had contributed, arranged his escape from the island, he went to France in voluntary exile, to continue there his implacable opposition. A pardon arrived, by coincidence or political calculation, on June 25, 1924, the same day that Unamuno left for

Paris after less than a year of residence in Fuerteventura. On his arrival in Cherbourg, his private war with the dictatorship assumed worldwide proportions for the first time; Max Scheler mentioned it as one event that helped blacken the spiritual countenance of Europe in the twenties. Unamuno's antagonism had several motives, but the foremost of these was the personal—and, again, according to his much-used formula, the universal—recuperation of Spain. He raised a persistent voice, speaking and writing in Spain's behalf and in his own.

Given certain inevitable differences, Number 2, rue de la Pérouse, in Paris, was not unlike the pension where Unamuno lived during his student days in Madrid. The occupant was a student of supreme caliber, receiving visits from noted or dull celebrities. But there was little satisfaction in it all. To Unamuno the Paris of the twenties seemed to be a curtain that blocked his view of the Sierra de Gredos, which towered over Salamanca. Neither the spirited gatherings at La Rotonde—the famous Montparnasse café recently demolished to provide room for a moving-picture theatre—nor the interminable walks through streets teeming with beauty and history lessened the feeling that Paris was an obstacle in his path. He continued to publish in the European and South American press, his fight against the dictatorship never wavered, but his displeasure with the Spanish political situation inhibited any full cultivation of his religious and poetic spirit for a number of years. But his true vocation returned when he moved south to Hendaye within sight of the Spanish countryside across the border. No doubt this authentic vocation was more central than his political outbursts and manifestoes, or the *Free Pages (Hojas libres)* he published in collaboration with Eduardo Ortega y Gasset and Vicente Blasco Ibáñez. To him his arrival in Hendaye was like the end of an exile. In *The Agony of Christianity (La agonía del cristianismo)* (1925) and in *How a Novel Is Made (Cómo se hace una novela)* (1927) there were cries of desperation; in Hendaye the desperation mingled with hope, and their union produced the experiences that with the advent of the Republic, were manifested in *Saint Emmanuel the Good, Martyr (San Manuel Bueno, mártir)* (1933) and *Brother Juan or The World Is a Stage (El hermano Juan o el mundo es teatro)* (1934). The stay in Hendaye was a genuine spiritual resurrection.

6   THE RETURN OF THE EXILE

Externally Unamuno's life in Hendaye was much like the one he had led in Paris. There were informal gatherings at the Grand Café, interviews, and many long walks. With the fall of the dictatorship, in 1930, Unamuno was finally at liberty to direct his steps toward Spain, and on the 9th of February he crossed the border and entered Irún. The nation was wild with jubilation now. Beside themselves, the vast majority of the Spaniards cheered the oncoming Republic, but not all with the same purity of intention. As often happens, many lay in ambush, intent upon its quick destruction and the proclamation of any of the politically extreme ideologies that must mean the eventual death of any truly democratic regime. In this period of exaltation and easy optimism, a bloodless revolution seemed possible. But not even the welcoming speeches on his arrival at Irún, the happiness and enthusiasm of the people, nor the whole pages dedicated in all the newspapers to the return of Spain's most famous exile, could make the hero of all their rejoicing forget the two points that had been his trademark: his concern with "eternal Spain" and his fundamentally heterodox approach to each idea and each person. The motto "God, Country, and Law" *(Dios, Patria y Ley)** which Unamuno uttered, once across the frontier, may have expressed antimonarchist feelings, but it was not yet, as many had expected, an assertion of Republican faith. Even before the Republic was proclaimed on April 14, 1931, Unamuno, who had done more than most to help realize that day, had begun his opposition, as much the political heretic as ever.

The return to Salamanca on February 11, 1930, was quite another matter. His home was there where the silence, which in the final analysis had nourished the best things of his existence, awaited his return. Any biography of Unamuno which presumes to investigate the core of his personality would do well to devote more space to his return to Salamanca than to either his entrance into Irún or the political demonstrations in Madrid in early May, 1930, on the occasion of his arrival in the capital and his famous address there to the Ateneo. In this speech he called the collaborators of the dictatorship to account, coined sharp phrases such as the well-known "Not *up* to the king, but from the king on down,"† and struggled to outline the political future. The cheers with which young members of other generations than his acclaimed him, and the homage of the press, gave the impression that Unamuno had become a full-fledged political leader. He seemed drawn along by the rapid, almost feverish succession of events. But in his heart he remained a poet and a thinker, an indefatigable seeker of the eternal. He raised his voice in Madrid, but only in the silence of Salamanca was he spiritually at home.

7   THE LAST YEARS

The proclamation of the Republic one year later found Unamuno unchanged: longing for the eternal and still a victim of the moment. As rector, Unamuno

---

* Trans. note: which echoed, unfaithfully, the traditional phrase: "God, Country, and King" (*Dios, Patria y Rey*).
† Trans. note: "No *hasta,* sino *desde* . . ."

opened the academic year of 1931–1932 at the University of Salamanca in the name of "Her Imperial and Catholic Majesty, Spain," thereby seeming to announce his opposition to the Republic, even if we take "Catholic" to mean here "universal" rather than a definite politico-religious attribute. What he really attacked, however, was the Republic's haggling over trivialities. The Republic was so absorbed with internecine struggles that it had neither the time nor the disposition for an examination of its own conscience. According to Unamuno this was the first, most important challenge of all—the key to all other problems. He felt it was even a key to the solution and management of what today has become the greatest single preoccupation of all governments, regardless of ideology: the national economy. From 1932 until his death, Unamuno's major preoccupations were the misgivings awakened by a growing willfulness in the masses, and the fear of a rapid spiritual and geographical disintegration of Spain. His articles in *El Sol* and *Ahora* became tinged with bitterness because now no one listened to him, or rather, because he thought that just when his work was beginning to bear fruit in the spirit of a new generation, his words fell on deaf ears. But in spite of deep concern and bitterness he did not lose hope. Repeatedly he exercised those same tactics that had served him well against the dictatorship. Times, however, had changed. He was accused by some of "selling out" to the enemy, he was curtly asked by almost all to define his position—the only thing he could not do. He had always felt it his mission to maintain an undefined—which by no means meant an eclectic—position, and to erase the boundaries between himself and his enemies. People who asked Unamuno to clarify his political position forgot that, as he had often said, he counted his own votes and they were never unanimous.

Finally Unamuno's merit was officially recognized. In 1934, at a magnificent celebration in his honor, he was formally retired from his chair and made "Perpetual Rector" of Salamanca. In 1935, he was made an honorary citizen of the Spanish Republic. These festivities marked the close of an animated era that had included his speeches, edged with grave injunctions and filled with incisive attack, before the Constitutional Congress. The tone of his farewell speech as university professor was more subdued. By now Unamuno realized that the agitation he had fostered, and the pain and strife he had decreed, had reached a danger point and needed modulation. At a time when all over Spain there were ominous signs of the impending Civil War and waves of violent disagreement, the renowned sower of fruitful discord began to preach harmony. In the first pages of *The Agony of Christianity* he had written: "My Spain, now mortally wounded, is perhaps destined to die a bloody death on a cross of swords." In *Life of Don Quixote and Sancho* he had written: "Yes, what we need is a civil war." But now Spain was threatened not by a civil war, a mere bloodletting, but by what Unamuno with great foresight had once called an "uncivil war"; one in which, unlike those he had imagined, there would never be peace in the combatants' hearts.

The life remaining to Unamuno, a towering solitary figure, will always be dwarfed by the magnitude of the war that had begun in July 1936. On the last day of this same year, Unamuno died amid communiqués of war, as did two of his great European contemporaries, Henri Bergson and Sigmund Freud, three years later.

For a time after his death he was called variously, traitor, weakling, and turncoat. He had hailed the military rebellion, then he had courageously challenged it; the most ardent supporters of the two factions had reasons to speak in anger against him. But those who have taken counsel with the man and his works will realize that he was always true to himself. To be sure, the little we know of his words and deeds during the last six months of his life is both baffling and distressing. But the question is whether it could be otherwise, for everything is baffling and distressing when it comes from the center of a maelstrom of cataclysmic violence. As if destroyed by lightning, Unamuno disappeared in the midst of this historical whirlwind. For a time, his voice was submerged. Some expected that is would remain so forever. They did not realize just how serious Unamuno had been in his intention to make each line he wrote vibrant with the life that was his own.

Chapter Two

The Man of Flesh and Blood—
The Idea of the World—The Idea of God

8 HOMO SUM

"Philosophy is the human product of each philosopher, and each philosopher
is a man of flesh and blood speaking to other men of flesh and blood." Thus
reads the opening sentence of Unamuno's *Tragic Sense of Life*. Never before
have the human condition of philosophy and the "earthly" constitution of the
philosopher been stated in such radical terms. To be sure, 'human condition'
and 'earthly constitution' are hardly expressions that Unamuno would have
used himself; he would have shunned both as bloodless abstractions. The
individual person, the substance that underlies both philosophy and the philosopher, was what mattered most to Unamuno. He often proclaimed that the
individual, concrete human being is the inescapable point of departure for all
philosophers worthy of the name.

A "point of departure" as clear and sweeping as Unamuno's implies first
the elimination of all idols—particularly the ideological ones. Thus, the first
step that Unamuno proposes—especially when writing in a strongly pragmatic vein—is the breaking of and with ideas. Now, Unamuno's pragmatism,
unlike the usual variety, is not just a philosophical tendency; it is, in fact, a
case of "ideophagy." What Unamuno means to do with ideas is to break them
in, "like a pair of shoes, using them and making them mine." As a system of
ideas, conventional pragmatism must (in its turn) be dealt with pragmatically;
it must be dismantled, used, and, as Hegel would say, "absorbed." Unamuno
is against any tyranny of ideas, even the tyranny of those ideas that pose as
guides to action. The conventional pragmatist holds that knowledge is meaningless unless its goal is the fostering of life; however, in his preoccupation

with life and its exigencies, he ends by bowing to a new idol. By so doing, he sacrifices what to Unamuno mattered most: our *own* life, pulsating beneath the jungle of ideas about it—that life made up of flesh and blood, but also of anguish, suffering, and hope.

The elimination of all idols is thus Unamuno's first step in the tireless search for himself and, through himself, for all human beings who like him enjoy or, in some instances, suffer an authentic life. Here we have the main motive for Unamuno's implacable blows against philosophies and "mere philosophers." Now, contrary to most of the "vitalist" and some of the "existentialist" philosophers, Unamuno did not think that the ideological idols were altogether useless. In his fight against "abstraction," Kierkegaard contended that anyone who thought as Hegel did, and identified being with thought, was less than human. Even more "existentialist" than Kierkegaard himself, Unamuno disagreed with this censure. For Unamuno, even the most abstract systems of thought were permeated with life. They were, in fact, one of man's ways of clinging to existence. Thus to Unamuno, Hegel seemed as human and as much concerned with his own concrete existence as those who expressed their concern more openly. Perhaps for Kierkegaard, living in solitude and anguish, only those who faced the fact of their own imminent annihilation could be saved, whereas for Unamuno, living in tragedy, fellowship, and hope, all could be saved, even those who insisted on substituting life and hope for thought.

Unamuno thoroughly criticized the philosophers' way of thinking, but only because this thinking frequently prevented the philosophers' recognizing what, irrevocably, they were, no matter how earnestly they might struggle to forget it: concrete, unique men of flesh and blood. Philosophers who attempt to reduce all realities to a single principle may try to account for the existence of human beings in purely rational terms, and in so doing they inevitably finish by turning concrete human beings into sheer abstractions. Although they often emphasize *the* life and *the* existence of men, they never succeed in reaching "*my* life" and "*my* existence." Unamuno could not help using formulas that are definitely impersonal in tone; he used language, and language cannot dispense with abstract terms. Thus, he wrote that the individual concrete life is "a principle of unity and a principle of continuity." But such words as 'principle' should not mislead us. Unamuno used the term 'principle,' but he never identified it with an abstract "postulate." A principle was for him a kind of "fountain" or "spring," apt enough to describe the "source" of a number of human attitudes that are invariably concrete: the instinct of self-preservation, that of self-perpetuation, the awareness of tragedy, the experience of ambiguity, the inextricable mixture of desperation and hope, and so on. He felt that the "classical" philosophies had paid little attention to these attitudes. At best they tried to explain their nature, without meeting them face to face. But explanation is of no avail here; when everything has been accounted for, men realize that the most important things still remain unexplained. Philosophers, Unamuno held, should begin by acknowledging that they are men, and so before they attempt to know "Truth" they ought to inquire about their own "truth."

The laborious search for that supreme reality, the man of flesh and blood, places Unamuno at a vantage point from which all vitalism and all existentialism seem mere theories about a reality that is so "pure" as to be hardly reality at all. But we must not imagine that in Unamuno's philosophical "point of departure" a "preoccupation with man" is at all synonymous with a "preoccupation with all that is human." In absolute contradistinction to Terence's famous dictum—*Homo sum et nihil humanum a me alienum puto*— Unamuno declared that humanity—the concept of humanity, that is—was foreign to him. Such a concept is as suspect as the concept of human existence with which philosophers attempt to disguise their lofty abstractions. That is why Unamuno, that tireless sapper of philosophies, began by proclaiming his desire to be the exact opposite of a philosopher in the classical or traditional sense of this word. This attitude was adopted as a consequence of his rather vague definition of "a philosopher." Unamuno defined "a philosopher" as "a man who above all else seeks truth," even when this truth forces him to acknowledge the lack of substantial, intimate reality in his own being—or the possibility of its final and complete annihilation in death. Because Unamuno refuses to be annihilated, he rebels against all the forces that contribute to man's destruction. One of these forces is reason, or rather the overemphasis on reason, which he defined, I am sorry to say, with the same lack of precision as the concept of philosopher. Nevertheless, it should be taken into account that Unamuno's rebellion against this supposed annihilation is nothing like a show of stubborn egocentrism. The man Unamuno speaks for is, of course, himself. Yet he also speaks for all men who are not— or cannot be—content with the fictitious comforts of rational philosophy. This includes, paradoxically, the rationalists themselves, for they are, along with everyone else, men of flesh and blood whose "being" cannot be compressed into any abstract concept, not even the concepts of "existence" and "life."

9 IDEAS AND IDEALS

Unamuno's pragmatic point of departure is thus so radical that it has often been misunderstood, occasionally even by Unamuno himself. He has insisted so much upon the predominance of the "concrete" as against the "abstract" that he has led his readers to believe that the "abstract"—ideas and reason— must be destroyed once and for all. Yet we must embrace pure ideas *as well,* provided that we do it as concretely existing beings for whom ideas are as necessary to life as life itself. As we shall see later on, men cannot dispense with the "reprisals against life" launched by ideas. For the worst of ideas is not what they really are—the opposites life clings to in order to exist—but what they often pretend to be: comforting explanation that conceal the pangs that accompanied their birth. Therefore, the man of flesh and blood, who thinks in order to live even when thinking confronts him with the fact that he must one day cease to exist, must not simply dismiss ideas and reasons as irrelevant and powerless. He must face these ideas; he must crack them open and penetrate them; he must above all discover the ideals that lie beneath them. In tune with some of Nietzsche's aphorisms, and perhaps influenced by them, Unamuno proclaimed that the substance of any idea is the ideal (the Desire, the Wish, the Will) held by the man who formulated it. Ideas possess an "essential truth," whereas ideals possess an "existential" truth. Even the most absurd of all ideals have a truth of their own that absurd ideas can never have. The brittle truth of a hundred birds on the wing belies the poor truth of a single bird in the hand. An idea may be declared to be true or false; an ideal is beyond the realm of truth and falsehood.

A series of startling paradoxes is the result of these reflections. To begin with, if ideals are the substance of ideas, it must be concluded that ideas have also, at bottom, an "existential" truth; otherwise, ideas could not even be conceived by men. Furthermore, a man of flesh and blood can more willingly accept (or rather, use) ideas than can some philosophers. Unamuno could not sympathize with the philosophers who importunately denounce the limitations of reason and of the ideas that reason produces.

The ideas that philosophers—including antirationalist philosophers—have circulated about man have ever been means of avoiding confrontation with this "man of flesh and blood," despite the fact that this "man" has given such ideas the only life they can ever possess. In defining "man" as "a rational being," "a thinking subject," "a historical reality," and so forth, philosophers have imagined themselves in touch with man's reality; actually, they have never been close to anything but a mere formal principle. And even if we define "man" as "an irrational creature," we will only succeed in laying down another principle, an abstract, philosophical postulate. Now, we should not concern ourselves just with the business of living, and leave sterile definitions to the philosophers. Notwithstanding his claims to the contrary, Unamuno's approach to man is still of a philosophical nature. It enters philosophy by the back door, but enters it nevertheless. In this respect Unamuno is indebted to a well-known tradition (the tradition of Saint Paul, Saint Augustine, Pascal, and Kierkegaard) which he himself has often acknowledged. The kinship exists, not because his philosophy is literally based on the works of these authors, but because it was in them that he discovered—most often, as with

Kierkegaard, after his own position had been formulated—his true "spiritual brothers." But unlike most of them, Unamuno did not want to enslave philosophy. Quite the contrary: he wanted to free it from all idols, those of "irrationality" and "life" no less than those of "reason" and "ideas." The motives for this double objective are at the very heart of his thought, and cast a vivid light on his conception of tragedy. For Unamuno it would be incorrect to speak of a man who existed authentically—in flesh and blood—if he did not also exist tragically, and it would be inadequate to say that he lived tragically if his life were not continually torn by the enmity—which acts through the coexistence—of two series of warring provocations: the will to be, and the suspicion that one can cease to be; feeling and thought; faith and doubt; certainty and uncertainty; hope and desperation; heart and head; or—in terms dear to some philosophers—life and logic.

10 REASON AND FAITH

This enmity is the single but powerful source of man's fundamental tragic feeling: the feeling that his hope and faith are incompatible with his reason, and yet cannot exist without it. For reason subsists only by virtue of its constant war—and therefore its continual embrace—with hope and faith. We must avoid the common error of supposing that Unamuno's thinking was entirely slanted in favor of a complete victory of irrationality over reason. Were this true neither could exist. Their warring coexistence is the substance of "tragedy," and the prime mover of the "tragic sense of life." If men could entirely escape the so-called "dictates of reason" to such an extent that they might then be defined as "irrational beings" hungering for eternal life, or blindly hopeful of it, there would be no tragedy in their existence. But Unamuno would then wonder whether they deserved to be called "human" at all. For Unamuno, to live as a human being and to live tragically were one and the same thing.

It may be argued here that the question before us is a purely semantic one; that the identification of "human life" with "tragic life" is a linguistic convention that we may take or leave. But Unamuno does not ask anyone to assent to a proposition; he wants everyone to yield to a fact: the fact that the permanent tension between opposites, and especially between reason and the irrational, is the very core of existence.

There is little doubt, at any rate, that Unamuno would not agree with Leo Chestov's passionate descriptions of man as an essentially irrational creature. According to the Russian philosopher, every authentic human being must renounce all ties with the objective world in favor of his own world of dreams. As a consequence, man's private universe is not disturbed by reason or by the universal and necessary truths—the so-called "eternal truths"—that reason uncovers and formulates. On the other hand, the human universe that Unamuno describes is one in which the victory of dreams over reason is no less precarious than the victory of reason over dreams. It is a universe that offers no final respite, no quietude, no peace. Even when man is most entirely and happily immersed in the irrationality of his dreams, reason comes forward to trouble his life. And thus man comes to realize that the world of reason—of ideas and abstractions—must be cultivated for the sake of life no less than the world of dreams. The man of flesh and blood is not a person who turns from unreason and the dream world to embrace the implacable yet comforting light of reason, nor the person who escapes the rational universe to hide in the warm, trembling cosmos of faith, but one who vacillates incessantly between one and the other; a person who is, in fact, *composed of these two elements.*

Instead of being principles from which to deduce and define a concrete existence, these two worlds are perfectly alive, active almost pulsating realities. Unamuno has at times called them metaphorically, "whirlpools." And the man of flesh and blood, who lives at war with himself and never relinquishes his desire for peace, appears astride them both, sinking out of sight between them only to rise uncertainly again.

To claim that man must philosophize in order to live is not, therefore, just another formula; it is the faithful description of an experience. Unamuno's pragmatism, his invocation of utility, his insistence that truth tends to become veracity and the idea, an ideal, are thus entirely compatible with his waging war against all things merely pragmatic. Though Unamuno wrote that "the so-called innate desire to know only awakens and becomes active after the desire to know-in-order-to-live is satisfied," he did so only to emphasize, against the rationalists, the importance of irrationality. He also wrote, and here against irrationalists, that "the demands of reason are fully as imperious as those of life."

11   A WORLD OF TENSIONS

Because he manifests a revolt of naturalism against the idealism of reason, and of the idealism of reason against pragmatical materialism, all attempts to pigeonhole Unamuno in one definite philosophical system are bound to fail. Unamuno does not advocate the union—which would entail a reconciliation, and eventually, a truce—of life and reason within the framework of a system where the idea of harmony would forever preclude any discord. There can be no harmony in that war which each human being wages against himself and his antagonists, but only perpetual strife, interminable contradiction, and continual—and fruitful—incivility. This is the only "formal principle," if that is the proper name for it, which permeates Unamuno's thinking. It may be stated as follows: To be, is to be against one's self.

Unamuno's emphasis on opposition, tension, and contradiction is obviously related to that type of thinking which since Hegel has been customarily called "dialectical." Nevertheless, there are two important differences between the conventional dialectical systems and Unamuno's.

On the one hand, dialectical systems attempt to describe and explain the attributes of the Cosmos as an impersonal being. In such systems, human reality follows the pattern of the cosmic reality. Sometimes "the Reality" is identified with "God," but even then the impersonal traits prevail over the personal ones. Unamuno's dialectic, however, is of an entirely personal nature. Unamuno refers mainly, if not exclusively, to human existence. And when the ideas of God and world are introduced, they are endowed with human characteristics. Even when he uses such abstract terms as 'reason' and 'the irrational,' they are to be understood as embodied in unique, concrete human beings.

On the other hand, all the philosophers who have tried to describe reality as a dialectical process of some sort—Nicholas of Cusa and Giordano Bruno no less than Hegel—have built conceptual systems in which the opposites end in reunification in the bosom of some ultimate and all-embracing principle. The war between particulars finds peace in the absolute generality of the essential One, so that the principle of identity overcomes, in the end, all contradictions. The dialectical method is one in which—as in Hegel—the total, "superior" truth (philosophical truth) reconciles the partial, "inferior" truths (mathematical and historical truth), one which purports to "save" all within the frame of the Absolute—the only realm in which peace is to be found. But in Unamuno's world, animated by the principle of perpetual civil war and unending strife, there is no place for any final harmony—and still less, any identity—which would be, in his opinion, the equivalent of death. Among those thinkers who defended the dialectical approach, there was something akin to a headlong rush toward the very identity they denounced, their attempts to dissemble their own longing for an ultimate unity by calling it an "identity of opposites" notwithstanding. In Unamuno there is not the slightest eagerness to be absorbed in this identity, nor the least desire to pour the past into the future; there is just an everlasting will to abide, "to prolong this sweet moment, to sleep in it, and in it become eternal *(eternizarse)*." Unamuno wishes to prolong his "eternal past" because only the moment most perfectly expresses what he seeks: a sense of being a man of flesh and blood among other men of flesh and blood, yet still longing to be all that one can long to be, to be "all in all and forever," a finite individual and an infinite reality at the same time.

All identity or even harmony of opposites, all mere submersion of the moment in an intemporal eternity, is undone in the perpetual battle between heart and head. So, for the authentic man, the correct spiritual disposition is not belief in the impossible simply because it is impossible (as some irrationalists would urge), nor yet disbelief because of its impossibility (as most rationalists would recommend), but its affirmation without believing it or, as Unamuno said, by creating it. This is the only means of arriving at that point where man is permitted to walk the floor of the abyss, that "terrible substructure of tragedy and faith," which is the common ground for both skeptics and believers, and where desperation ("the noblest, most profound, most human, and most fecund state of mind") meets and fraternally embraces hope. The embrace is a tragic one, and for Unamuno this means a vital one: a menace of death and a fountain of life. Desperation and doubt can never attain a complete victory over hope and belief, but the reverse is also true. At a time when sentiment and belief ride roughshod over reason and doubt, "there are reprisals," with "damned logic" clinging, at the same time, to what we may well call "damned feelings." And so the battle goes on forever: reason and faith, doubt and belief, thought and feeling, fact and desire, head and heart are united by an association in war, the only apposition in which they can survive since "each lives on the other," and feeds on the other, there being no third party to rejoice in or benefit from the struggle, no absolute unity or supreme harmony to lay peace between the antagonists. The only attainable peace lies in the eye of this powerful hurricane, but the eye subsists only because the hurricane moves on.

Thus the man of flesh and blood, who seemed to be so plain, simple, and straightforward, becomes a most complex reality seething with confusion and contradiction. No sooner had the philosopher asserted the concrete character of this creature than he injects it with what appears to be infinitely removed from any concrete reality: the pursuit of the impossible, the life of wish and dream. But even though the boundaries of personal unity seem thus to be broken, man never surrenders himself to any absolute being or to any transcendent realm of values. The man of flesh and blood strives to be all in all, while he fights to remain within the limits of his personal unity. He wishes to preserve his own nontransferable self, for being all in all means an infinite expansion of one's own personality rather than ceasing to be what one is.

At any rate, it would be a mistake to enlist Unamuno in the ranks of classical idealism, as it would be inadequate to consider him a naturalist or a realist. To be sure, Unamuno speaks often of "realism," but at such times it is to be understood as an injunction to create reality rather than as an invitation to describe it faithfully and accurately. Also he seems sometimes on the brink of naturalism and even materialism, but it is only because he wishes to emphasize what is concrete in man's existence. Realism, naturalism, and materialism define man in terms of what he is, which nearly always means, in terms of what he has been. Idealism, on the other hand, defines man in terms of what he ought to be. Unamuno prefers to "define" him in terms of what he will become, or more exactly, in terms of what he wants to become, since "we are lost or saved on the basis of what we wanted to be, and not for what we have been." If a name could be given to Unamuno's philosophical anthropology, "poetic realism" would perhaps be the least inadequate of all.

12 MAN AS A DREAMER

In view of the above, it is only too natural that Unamuno's notion of man should be drawn more successfully in his novels than in his philosophical essays. In Unamuno's novels there is frequent use of such expressions as 'living, suffering, flesh,' 'the marrow of bone,' and 'the painting of the soul.' There is frequent mention of dreams, since it is through dreams that the creatures we imagine, exist. We may say, then, that in the characters of these novels Unamuno's conception of man is truly given flesh. And this, as he writes, "without recourse to theatrical scenery, or other tidbits of realism which invariably lack the true, eternal reality, that of personality." All the "characters" thus described—or, more correctly speaking, created—struggle in order to exist. They fight against everybody, including their author, in order to be men of flesh and blood, for only in the course of such a struggle can they achieve their greatest reality.

Like their creator, all are "men of contradictions," and their goal in life is to "carve themselves a soul." *Mist's* (*Niebla*) Augusto Pérez goes so far as to threaten his author. He cannot do it, as the latter can, "with a stroke of his pen"—after all, the character is not an author. But he can menace the author by reminding him that God—a sort of supreme author—may stop dreaming him. As we shall see later on, the so-called fictitious characters in the novels possess a reality of their own. To be sure, they are the consequence of their author's "dreams." But their creator depends on his characters as much as they depend on him. Thus, Unamuno wants to make clear that although each man—"real" or "fictitious"—is truly himself, he cannot live without the others. Unamuno's repeated insistence on the notions of the "dream" and "being dreamed" may be grounded, of course, in his undeniable fondness for paradox; it is indeed a paradox to say that real persons and fictitious characters in novels are equally "men of flesh and blood." But underlying Unamuno's witticisms and puns there is a serious attempt to show that personality is more basic to men—real or fictitious—than any of the other characteristics of human existence thus far devised by philosophers. There is, and most important, the wish to show that all men of flesh and blood are closely interrelated. The so-called "independence" of the solitary man—again, "real" or "fictitious"—is deceptive. "A solitary dream," Unamuno writes, "is illusion, appearance; a dream shared is truth and reality." As Augusto Pérez says to his dog, Orfeo, "The world is the dream we all have in common, the 'communal dream.'"

If we say that the fictitious characters in novels are, in a sense, real, we can also say that real men are fictitious creatures—characters in a kind of cosmic novel. They too are the products of a dream: God's dream. This is the origin of the anguish felt by man as he becomes aware of the vast dream in which he is immersed, and of the possibility that some day he will awaken; that is, become convinced of the ephemeral nature of his dream, thereby sinking into the "twilight of logic and ratiocination," which can offer no consolation to "the hearts of those condemned to the dream of life." Because the awakening from this dream means that we cease to exist, we implore our Author not to stop dreaming us with a strange prayer: "Dream us, Our Lord!" Now, just as faith lacks vigor without doubt, and hope becomes sterile without desperation, so we are here confronted with the breathtaking paradox that dream lacks substance without the possibility of awakening from it and rebelling against it. When we rebel against the fact that God is constantly dreaming us, we assist God in His everlastingly creative task—dreaming.

The assistance we render God, analogous to that rendered us by our fictional heroes, makes it possible that just as we are God's children, He is, as Unamuno proclaimed, our child, the child "of poor anguished humanity, since in us the eternal, infinite, Universal Consciousness manifests itself, exists incarnate." As a consequence, the relationship between God and His creations is not one of cause and effect and even less one of action and consequence, but a peculiar relationship best described as "that of dreamer and dreamed." Perhaps this explains why Unamuno surmised that far from being products of a necessary emanation or an arbitrary creation, we are products of a dream. We are not, however, entirely at the mercy of the Dreamer, for we have the power of changing His dreams. We thus dream while awake, being both the object of those dreams in which we are the "creatures" and the subject of those dreams in which the world of what we call "fiction" comes alive.

13   GOD AND THE WORLD

Should we say, then, that we have in the notion—or rather, the metaphor—of the dream the unifying principle of the man of flesh and blood, the meeting point of all tensions and all oppositions, the "absolute essence" of human reality and, for that matter, of all reality? If we are God's dreams, and God himself is our dream, can we not conclude that dream is the universal stuff of which all things are made?

It goes without saying that Unamuno does not answer these questions as a philosopher would. He does not use argument, let alone any sort of rigorous proof. He uses a confusing but stimulating method in which bold assertions are blended with series of interrogations. As an example of bold assertion, let me quote the following: "It is not my fragile and transitory self, which feeds upon the earth and upon which the earth will one day feed that must be victorious, but my true eternal self, my archetype and form since before and until after time, the idea that God, the Universal Consciousness, has of me"— a rather surprising statement, excessively Platonic for one who has so often argued against "ideas," "forms," and "archetypes." The examples of interrogations are so numerous that I need cite no example. But it is illuminating to see that many of them refer to the question of dreams—in the aforementioned sense—and the relationship between "a dreamer" and "that which he dreams." This shows that Unamuno was certain about the real nature of this universal tissue of dreams, and in particular about the role that the Greater Dreamer plays in the economy of the universe. If, on the one hand, everything seems to move, in his opinion, toward the Dreamer, on the other hand he maintains that even in His bosom there is conflict, tension, and contradiction—or, to use Unamuno's own terms, strife, struggle, and war.

Since God is the perpetrator of all fecund war, He could be truly called "The Eternalizer," rather than "The Eternal." The war in which all things live has also its roots in the divine reality. Unamuno opposes, then, both rationalists who worship the principle of identity and rationalists who rejoice in contradiction, so far as all of them agree that God is the Reality in which all opposition is reconciled and all diversity unified. He also opposes those Platonic—and Neoplatonic—philosophies that reduce the sensible world to the status of a copy and reflection of the intelligible world. According to these philosophies, the authentic life consists in a contemplation of the divine world of the Idea. But since such a life would of necessity be a disembodied existence—or, more exactly, would mean living *as though* one led a disembodied existence—the Platonic emphasis on intelligibility and unity always ends by sacrificing the concrete man who formulated—and longed for—it. An analogous situation occurs, by the way, in those philosophies that, while apparently hostile to the idea of a static intelligible world, are no less eager to set the torch to the particular and the concrete, even though they concoct theories about a supposedly dynamic unity of opposites. Unamuno called these philosophies "monistic catchpennies," because although their main premise is the existence of diversity, in the end (as with Nicholas of Cusa, Giordano Bruno, and Hegel), this same diversity is seen to be the stuff of which unity is made. The proponents of these pseudomonistic systems hailed the idea of contradiction, but soon allowed their thoughts to be permeated by a principle of identity. All that is not identity, claimed Giordano Bruno, is vanity, nothingness, illusion, and void. All oppositions, proclaimed Hegel, must be reconciled. The absolute One, the absolute Idea, the pure Identity, thus emerge victorious over all opposition, so much so that in the end all struggles to win an eternal peace are resolved. Peace is at last attained, but with it, Unamuno agreed, life itself comes to an end.

There is no reconciliation and no peace in Unamuno's truly dynamic universe, whether it includes only the minds of men or also that of God. Here war plays the part of the Heraclitean "father of all things." But although Heraclitus admitted the existence of a certain cosmic rhythm—the rhythmic alternation according to which the universe travels an Upward and Downward Way—Unamuno dissociates existence from anything that might for so much as an instant diminish its unbending "fury." What we term "peace" is found only in war. Thus unity and identity are both present in Unamuno's universe. But they exist, as much as anything does, within the framework of an unending battle. They struggle to hold their ground, and they push forward—though unsuccessfully—toward ultimate domination. If God can be called the "Universal Consciousness," as Unamuno has sometimes named Him, it is not because He is the World's Reason, but only because He wages an unending struggle to merge with the world—and at the same time to free Himself from it.

It would of course be impertinent to ask Unamuno for any rational elucidation of a theme that, more than any other, he has always left adrift in a sea of indefiniteness and paradox. If, on the one hand, Unamuno surmised that this Universal Consciousness is trapped in matter, thus seeming to adhere to a pantheistic and even materialistic monism, on the other hand he declared that God—the eternal and infinite consciousness of the world—is something transcendent. In either event it can be said that He is *in* the battle. Could we not even say that He *is* the battle—or the very symbol of it? At any rate, as soon as we try to divorce Him from any struggle we are in danger of depriving Him of His existence. Then too, this battle presupposes a constant suffering after the manner of Schopenhauer—who probably influenced Unamuno more than the latter would have been willing to admit. It presupposes that anguish that is the "only truly mysterious mystery" and seems to rise as if it were a cosmic sap from inorganic matter through man to that Person submerged in matter who is its eternal and infinite consciousness. We might almost conclude that each man, each thing, each activity, and even each concept is a member of a sort of "body mystic" tormented by that anguish that is an essential part of the "God who suffers" and is as much a consolation to His creatures as it is to Himself. We are here confronted with a symbiosis of a very particular type—a cosmic symbiosis that concepts such as "interaction," "reciprocal action," and "mutual dependence" can never adequately describe. And yet we are in touch with something quite like an "organic symbiosis" when we read that "in God's bosom consciousnesses are born and die—die?—their births and deaths constituting His life," and especially when we read that "when we say God eternally produces things, and things eternally produce God, we are repeating ourselves."

Are we justified in saying that after all Unamuno returns to those very same definitions and formulae which the panentheists of all periods circulated so monotonously? Only if we fail to notice that he at once weakens his definitions and formulae by voicing them in a series of unanswered questions. The method of interrogation of which I spoke before now gains an upper hand. Might not matter itself, Unamuno asks, be the beginning of the unconscious God? Is not God the end rather than the beginning of the universe? Is there a difference in terms of eternity between beginning and end? Are things ideas of the Master Consciousness? Does God the Eternalizer ever forget what He has once thought? Questions of this kind result from a natural dissatisfaction with any definite solution, and show again how pointless is any attempt to contain Unamuno in a single intellectual pigeonhole. Monism, pantheism, materialism, spiritualism, and personalism are some of the best-known responses to the above questions. Not one of them is, however, entirely acceptable to Unamuno. God is "the ideal of humanity," "man projected to the infinite power and eternalized in it," but He is also that Highest Person who transcends this human projection, who affirms Himself over and against it. He is the reason of the world and its unreason, its consciousness and unconsciousness, its anguish and pleasure, its spirit and matter. Thus the only really apt name for God is what Unamuno was finally to give Him: "my heretic God." So much a heretic that He looks upon Himself with an heretical eye. God, like man, doubts Himself and in the process of doubting creates both Himself and man. This seems to be the meaning implied in "Atheism" and "The Atheist's Prayer," two of Unamuno's sonnets which best reveal his sense of the Divine. If in the first he says that:

> God is the unattainable
> desire we have to be Him; Who
> knows? Perhaps God Himself
> is an atheist;

in the second the atheist prays to a God in whom he cannot rationally believe, but whose existence he must affirm unless he wishes to deny his own. That is why this strange atheist exclaims:

Because of You I suffer,
Inexistent God, since if You existed
I too would really exist.

This is the God who denies and affirms Himself, who desires and fears, who pulsates in the heart of mankind and hovers above it. A God who defies rational proof but welcomes those who approach Him armed with the tools of belief and love. This last point is all-important, since a "belief in God begins with the desire that there be a God, with the inability to live without Him." Such a longing for God is no mere desire—at least, not one that thought can assuage; it is more in the nature of an anguish, a yearning for Him. He who dreams the world is in turn its dream; the Eternalizer is Himself eternalized. Without man and the world, God would not exist. But without God, man and the world would founder in the nightmare of the void from which the only salvation is an unending dream, the perennial memory of the "Master Dreamer." Nietzsche had proclaimed that "God is dead." Unamuno maintains that even the death of God is the life of man.

Chapter Three

Immortality—The Tragedy of Christianity—
The Idea of History

14 THE HUNGER FOR IMMORTALITY

By any standards of religious or philosophical orthodoxy Unamuno's idea of
God was a "heretical" one. He refused to apply any of the conventional
philosophical categories—"actuality" and "potentiality," "being" and "nonbeing,"
or "essence" and "existence"—to God. The reasons for this theological and
philosophical "heresy" are deeply embedded in his view that all beings tend
to sink into the vortex of an unending polemic, a permanent struggle. Since
tragedy stirs in the depths of everything, it is also active in the depths of God,
whose life is as full of tension and conflict as the life of man and that of
the universe.

On this grandiose and turbulent stage, and subject to the same dynamic
impulse, Unamuno's other major themes unfold—his other major obsessions;
and the most insistent of them all is that of immortality. Its role is such a
central one that at times it threatens to obscure all the rest. Faced with the
question, "What is the most important problem for man?" Unamuno would
have declared, in all likelihood, that it was the question of the soul's ultimate
destiny, that is, whether or not the soul is immortal. Although, in phrasing the
question, he often used the vocabulary of the Platonic-Christian tradition, his
purpose was not the same. In fact, it is misleading to speak of Unamuno's idea
of the soul in any terms that suggest an entity separate, or separable, from the
body. Even though we shall be obliged to use this same terminology, as Unamuno
was—the "Soul," "immortality," and "immortality of the soul"—it must be remembered that the real problem that concerned Unamuno was that of the

47

individual human death. Was each man doomed to an eternal death, or could one hope to survive it? This was the obsessive question in Unamuno's concern with the problem of the immortality of the soul.

Unamuno could not avoid thinking of death as both inevitable and frightening. His struggle against the fear of death was so impassioned that in dealing with the problem of immortality he seems to have halted the incessant pendulum movement of his thought at one of its extremes. If in speaking of God and man, negation unfailingly accompanied affirmation, doubt, faith, and despair, hope, in Unamuno's talk of immortality, assent often triumphed over denial. We are tempted to conclude that his desire for immortality blinded him to the misery of death, and that in this instance his heart won its only victory over the mind.

But such a conclusion would be premature, for to the degree that it was authentic—and it most probably was, Unamuno's belief in immortality was also beset by doubt. There can be no other explanation for his frequent use of the expression 'hunger for immortality' instead of 'belief in immortality'—'hunger' being an obviously much less intellectual term than 'belief.' We believe in immortality, Unamuno surmised, primarily because we desire it. Our desire to be immortal, to survive, is even stronger than our desire that there be a God. The hunger for immortality is an almost physiological impulse. Reason teaches us that immortality is highly problematical, if not absurd. Or, to be more exact, reason teaches us nothing in this connection, and thus leaves us in a state of perplexity. That is more disturbing than the certainty of our death. We can accept the Platonic proofs of the immortality of the soul only when we blindly accept their premises—if all that is "simple" does not perish, and if the soul is simple, then the soul does not perish. The premises themselves cannot be proved, either rationally or empirically. Therefore, although reason is in this instance "neutral," if often leads us into skepticism. It is a very peculiar kind of skepticism, one that acts as a stimulant rather than as a palliative. The stronger the conviction that immortality cannot be proved, the more deeply belief in immortality penetrates our minds. But the hunger for survival is tied to the anxiety caused by the imaginative anticipation of death as a complete extinction of our being.

Although Unamuno's thought on the problem of immortality was largely dependent upon Christian theological notions, it was not subservient to them. He struggled against these notions as much as, if not more than, he accepted them. Therefore, let us analyze the meaning of 'immortality' in Unamuno's thought and compare and contrast it with the "immortalities" of the theological and philosophical systems.

To begin with, Unamuno's "definition" of immortality is extremely vague: a thing is immortal when it is limitless in both time and being. 'To be immortal' means to be—or perhaps rather to wish to be—all in all *per omnia saecula saeculorum.* Unamuno's conception of immortality is related to the notion of impetus, or *conatus,* which, according to Spinoza (frequently cited by Unamuno in this respect), "impels" all things to the conservation of their own being. The essence of immortality seems to be, therefore, the struggle to perpetuate one's self. But although Unamuno was extremely sympathetic to the Spinozian notion of *conatus,* he disagreed with Spinoza in one important respect. Spinoza maintained that *nos experimur aeternos esse,* that "we feel that we are eternal." As François Meyer has pointed out, however, Unamuno adopts only Spinoza's verbal expression, and makes it serve his own end, quite unlike Spinoza's. As Meyer says, this end is a kind of "ontological greediness." Immortality is not only a *conatus* directed toward one's own being; it is an impetus to participate in all the other beings while remaining one and the same. Furthermore, immortality must be understood in its widest connotation and not limited to the desire felt by one human individual to survive. All things, and not only human beings, "long" to endure by absorbing the entire universe into themselves. And when this proves impossible, they "prefer" to be absorbed by the whole rather than remain confined within their own being.

Immortality is, then, a universal "desire" and one that never limits itself in any way. Being immortal means being both one's self and all that is not the self at the same time and forever. It can easily be seen that this "definition" of immortality is based upon the refusal to sacrifice anything. Properly speaking, for Unamuno, to be immortal is to be God. But the impossibility of any finite being's attaining this end leads Unamuno to place the following implicit "restrictions" upon the idea of immortality: (1) immortality is considered to be predominantly "human immortality"; (2) emphasis is placed more and more upon the survival of the human individual as individual, even if this means a diminishing, rather than an expansion of his being; (3) all possible forms of survival are explored, even the most "unsatisfactory" ones if these are found to be more "verifiable" than others. Thus, the "ontological greediness" originally ascribed to every being is so severely curtailed that we may wonder why Unamuno considered this "greediness" the basic metaphysical drive of all realities. It is still possible, however, to see in this "greediness" at least a general tendency—perhaps a "limiting concept." The innermost core of Unamuno's longing for immortality is still the impetus toward an ontological amplification of individuality and particularity, with each thing in the universe "longing" to become "all in all" and forever. But if a thing cannot be all things for all time, let it be at least itself most of the time. And if man cannot be God, let him at least share in imagination the eternality and omnipresence of God.

The longing for immortality itself oscillates perpetually between a maximum and a minimum. The maximum is "to be all in all while being one's self." The minimum is to subsist and survive, no matter how. This minimum plays an important role in Unamuno's thinking on immortality. Very often he seems to conceive of immortality as man's longing to endure and nothing more; it need only help him to overcome the fear of death. Thus, when no other alternative seems available, Unamuno is willing to accept an idea of immortality which presupposes a sacrifice of individuality and a submersion in a single (ubiquitous) existence. Faced with a choice between a simple annihilation and absorption by a universal reality (God, Nature, Mankind), Unamuno would certainly favor the latter. He would resign himself to a "survival" in the undifferentiated reservoir of an Absolute, even if this Absolute were, like the Buddhist Nirvana, the nearest thing to "Nothingness." For the Buddhistic idea of "Nothingness"—similar to the ideas of absolute Will and pure Unconsciousness proposed by Schopenhauer or Eduard von Hartmann—implies some kind of existence; in fact, for those who believe in it, or dream of it, it is true existence as opposed to the falsehood of the individual self, which always dissolves into transitory elements. We may, for the sake of universal Life, sacrifice our private life; we may, for the sake of the Absolute, abandon the relative. To be sure, Nirvana is a lesser evil with which Unamuno could only begrudgingly content himself. But it would still be something. "Something is better than nothing" is Unamuno's commonsensical recommendation when the question of the survival of human beings is at stake.

15   THE FORMS OF IMMORTALITY

Unamuno agrees, then, with all those who long for, or preach, immortality, but he disagrees with the specific content of any of the innumerable doctrines of survival outlined by religious thinkers and philosophers. The doctrines of Buddha, of Schopenhauer, and of Eduard von Hartmann are, in a way, soothing. They are not, however, sufficient, and least of all, convincing. A detailed analysis of Unamuno's feelings about the various Greek doctrines of "immortality" (Orphic, Platonic, Aristotelian, etc.) would result in similar instances of agreement followed immediately by confessions of dissatisfaction. As an illustration, let us select one such doctrine, and imagine Unamuno's reaction to it.

This is the doctrine—or rather, eclectic combination of doctrines—according to which 'to be immortal' means both "to be actual" and "to be eternal." To be actual is, properly speaking, to be what one essentially is, to fulfill all of one's own potentialities. To be eternal is to transcend time, or rather, to contain in one's bosom all possible time. Not all beings are immortal to the same degree. Some come into existence and then pass away, in accordance with the "law" of generation and corruption; others come close to immortality in that their movements approach the perfect circular movement; other beings—some would say only the Prime Mover—are truly immortal, because they are purely actual. From potentiality to actuality, from temporality to eternity, from imperfection to perfection, there is a hierarchy of being that is also a hierarchy of value. In one sense it can be said that each being in such a universe "desires" to be itself, to occupy its place in the ontological and axiological hierarchy, each partaking of immortality according to its degree of actuality and perfection. It is a beautiful and well-ordered cosmos, and one that is likely to assuage some philosophers' fears of annihilation. So far as this doctrine promotes the idea of immortality, and is even based upon it, it would be acceptable to Unamuno. But as soon as he had found a modicum of consolation in it, he would rebel against the many limitations it implied. For the immortality hinted at in this seemingly perfect universe lacks anguish, anxiety, and drama. Furthermore, this immortality is given, not won. If no other immortality were available, Unamuno would say, we may accept this one. But not without protest, for if it sometimes appeals to our minds, it can never seduce our hearts.

There is, then, no concept of immortality which completely satisfied Unamuno. But there is at least one concept of immortality near which he seems to linger: the Christian one. As a matter of fact, he often tackled the problem of immortality and the problem of Christianity simultaneously, as if they were interchangeable. "The hunger for immortality" and "the agony of Christianity" are two dimensions of the same *magna quaestio.*

True enough, Christian thinkers—if I may be permitted a few quick passes at such a complex subject—have often treated the question of immortality in a way that elicited particular reservations from Unamuno. So far as they followed certain intellectual patterns outlined by some Greek philosophers—above all, the Platonists—Christian thinkers have always severely limited the idea of immortality. These limitations concern not only time, but also being; instead of claiming that "the man of flesh and blood" is immortal, these thinkers claimed that the soul is immortal. This viewpoint is already apparent in some of the "eleventh-hour" Greek philosophies, particularly those which, like Neoplatonism, can be shown to have emphasized the central role of the soul in the economy of the universe. The philosophers of these schools provided so many arguments for it that many of the conceptual instruments later employed by Christian authors in dealing with immortality were drawn from these late Greek sources. Consequently, one may wonder why Unamuno was more satisfied with the Christian concept of immortality than with the Hellenic one. Yet, there is one point in the Christian concept—and even when most influenced by Greek philosophy—which probably attracted Unamuno's interest, and that was the fact that this concept is not at all a Christian elaboration of a series of Greek arguments, but rather a dynamic symbiosis of the two. The relation between Greek philosophy and Christianity was, Unamuno declared again and again, one of struggle: "Christianity, that irrational faith in which Christ came to life in order to give us new life, was saved by the rationalistic culture of Greece, which was in turn saved by Christianity." This is, in Unamuno's vocabulary, an "agonizing relationship," and one that cannot be avoided, for "a purely rationalistic tradition is as impossible as a purely religious tradition." Because of this struggle, the Christian concept of the immortality of the soul must have appeared to Unamuno, on closer consideration, considerably less "limited" than the Hellenic concept. It is still concerned, to a large degree, with the immortality of the "soul," but this soul is no longer comparable to an idea; it is the soul of a person—of a "man of flesh and blood," who wants to perpetuate himself not only with his mind, but with all his being.

To be sure, a few Greek thinkers—in particular, those influenced by Neoplatonism—had some inkling of a more "dynamic" immortality than the pure actuality and eternality of ideas would allow. They defined the soul as the only outstanding dynamic reality in motion upon the basically motionless stage of the universe, the only substance able to ascend—and descend—the ladder that leads through the various elements of the great cosmic hierarchy known as the "Great Chain of Being." For the soul to be immortal, these thinkers argued, it had only to strive to be so. This soul finds rest only in the world of ideas. But it is not itself an idea, an impassive entity; it moves ceaselessly upward or downward, always anxious to live a God-like life, but never attaining it. Therefore, in this idea of the soul, Unamuno found a mode of being which greatly attracted him: a state of tension, a permanent undercurrent of anxiety. Unfortunately, as soon as the soul had been "defined" in this way, the everpresent intellectualism of the Greek philosophical tradition gained the upper hand. The life of the soul was considered basically "theoretical," and "contemplative," even though the soul's continual state of contemplation—or its aspiration toward it—was disguised with the misleading name of "activity." Therefore, the Hellenic idea of immortality (and the Christian idea so far as it was influenced by the former) was, in Unamuno's word, a "caricature" of the "true immortality." If the man of flesh and blood is identified with the soul, and if the soul is defined in terms of such predicates as "rational" and "contemplative," then the immortality of the soul will be little more than an immortality of reason. This was, incidentally, what some Greek thinkers came to believe when they declared that only the so-called "Active Intellect"—or "Universal Reason"—was truly immortal. We are immortal not as individuals, but only as participants in the one and only Active Intelligence whose infinite rays of light permeate everything that is rational in this world.

Christian thinkers have never subscribed to an idea of immortality that goes so far as to deny personal immortality; the Alexandrian and Averroistic doctrines of the "Active Intellect" as the only immortal "soul" have always encountered the bitterest opposition among Christian philosophers. Yet, the concept of a suprapersonal immortality is one of the two extremes toward which Christian thought was forced by the Hellenic intellectual tradition. Unamuno emphasized this point again and again. Since Christian thinkers cannot dispense with reason, they must acknowledge some of the consequences that a rational approach to the problem would produce. One such consequence is that whenever a thing is immortal it must at the same time be universal and rational. On the other hand, Christian thinkers are committed to the doctrine of personal immortality, whether rational or not. They have to affirm what their reason may deny; they must struggle against reason while they are obliged to embrace it. They cannot use reason to prove immortality, but they can use it to strengthen hope and faith through doubt.

This is why Unamuno sharply opposed both the rational "proofs" of immortality and the idea that immortality is restricted to the "immaterial soul." He found support for his views in a very influential "tradition" of Christian thinkers; the theologians and philosophers he preferred in this connection were not Saint Thomas Aquinas or Cardinal Cajetan, but Saint Paul and Saint Augustine (and those laymen, Pascal and Kierkegaard, and perhaps Kant). The soul they spoke of was not an impassive entity, but just the contrary: a purely personal, radically intimate being, capable of possessing—of enjoying or suffering—experiences, an entity that stumbled and regained its feet, sinned and repented, and, above all, hated and loved. Instead of simply detaching itself from the body, freeing itself, in a Platonic manner, as if from a prison, or living in the body as if it were outside of it, this soul dragged the body after it toward eternal life, making the body a "spiritual" and not exclusively a rational one. These theologians and philosophers believed in something that Greek thinkers would have refused to admit for fear of betraying the rational spirit—namely, the resurrection of the dead, what Saint Paul called divine madness before the curious, but skeptical, Athenians in the Areopage. These were the things Unamuno delighted in underlining and tossed, like bones of contention, in the teeth of all manner of Pharisees. As a consequence, Unamuno completely rejected the "scholastic tradition"— which, incidentally, he misinterpreted and misjudged, for he identified it with Thomism, and Thomism with the doctrine of the modern Scholastics who had diluted the theology of Thomas Aquinas with large doses of Wolffianism. Unamuno's vehement forays against what he called "the theology of jurisprudence" (Thomism) were based upon this misinterpretation and oversimplification. Instead of denouncing Unamuno's historical errors, however, it would be better to understand what truths they were meant to reveal. One of these is quite obvious. Unamuno claimed that conceptualization and reason were necessary if the hunger for immortality was to perpetuate itself. The right type of reason could serve as both curb and goad. But this sort of reason was not to be found in Thomistic philosophy, not evident in Thomistic "proofs." Although Thomistic reason promoted a kind of fictitious security, it was only "an impotent Christianity," a "cathedral of adobe." That is why Unamuno was so vehement in his rejection of Thomistic conceptualization in favor of belief *and* reason, *and* the permanent war between them.

16　IMMORTALITY AS A STRUGGLE

What, then, was the variety of immortality which Unamuno espoused? Nothing less than an "absolute immortality" firmly anchored in the depths of all things and unbounded by any qualifications. But the immortality that concerned him most was that of the human beings who longed for it. Thus the hunger for immortality becomes a "private hunger for survival" that causes each human to cry out in anguish: "I will not die!"—or at least to live as if he cried out so. Into this framework, reacting against the naïve believers and the mere reasoners, Unamuno reintroduced the tragic sense that he had discovered in connection with man and God. There is in the concept of immortality too a perpetual contradiction. For example, deep within the concept of immortality there is the "sense of mortality." It may be argued that this is a derivative sensation, since it is the result of reflection rather than instinct. But once the "sense of mortality" attaches itself to our life, there is no escaping it. The sense of our own mortality becomes then a common-sense truth. It shows us, as Vladimir Nabokov has pointedly written, that "our existence is but a brief crack of light between two eternities of existence"—a "personal glitter in the impersonal darkness" on both sides of one's life. The "sense of mortality" is, furthermore, strengthened by our reason, which can never definitively prove mortality or immortality, but which usually finds the former more probable and "reasonable" than the latter. When experience and common sense join forces with reason, the conclusion is inescapable: human death is a certainty, and immortality at best an illusion. The denial of immortality, or the impossibility of proving it is, therefore, the virtual equivalent of the affirmation of death. But, as Unamuno says, the "yes" lives on the "no." Or, more accurately, man's life swings between the "yes" and the "no." This oscillation of judgment does not, however, lead us to a skeptical "suspension of all judgment"; but rather leads us to a permanent restlessness. It is another manifestation of the perpetual struggle of opposites which touches off the cosmic "civil war" in the midst of which all things live.

If he realizes the deep meaning of this "ontological oscillation," man can neither completely despair when faced with the certainty of his death, nor have absolute confidence in the security of his survival. "The immortal origin of the longing for immortality," Unamuno has written, "is a despairing resignation and a resigned despair." Therefore, to live is "to agonize"— in the etymological sense of 'to agonize' so insistently emphasized by Unamuno: "to fight against death." Although we are "in agony," we are never completely overcome by death. To be sure, we are never completely victorious either. But that is precisely what we want, Unamuno surmises, and what prevents us from dying once and for all. Even if there actually were a survival after death, it would be a continuation of the struggle against the threat of death. Without this "agony," the idea of immortality would be unbearable—if at all conceivable. The very idea of survival in Hell is less distressing to Unamuno than the idea of an eternal death disguised as an eternal and soporific bliss: "It is better to live in pain," he writes, "than to continue to live in peace." Unamuno's ideal of survival and immortality seems a kind of eternal purgatory where suffering and anxiety mingle with bliss and hope. Life on earth, incidentally, is just such a purgatory; it is the best possible exemplification of the aforementioned "agony." For, ultimately, the true life is *this* life; the rest is silence—or perhaps "mere literature." It is only too deplorable that this life is not eternal. Accordingly, "the immortality we crave is a phenomenal immortality"; we want the "bulk and not the shadow of immortality." We want, Unamuno concludes, to survive as we are, and as we wish to be, with our body, our home, our friends, our familiar landscapes, with all the things we love and hate, and to be sure, with our own past.

Unamuno never ceased to emphasize the "agonizing" nature of life and, therefore, the "agonizing" nature of any possible survival. "A life without any death in it, without incessant deterioration," he writes, "would be nothing but perpetual death, a stony rest. Those who do not die, do not live; those who do not die each instant, who are not resurrected in the same instant, do not live, and those who do not doubt do not live." The beatific vision we are promised as a reward would soon become a punishment if it did not entail "a labor, a continual and never-ending conquest of the Supreme and Infinite Truth, a hungry diving and delving ever more deeply into the bottomless depths of Eternal Life." Here Unamuno coincides with Lessing (and perhaps with most Romantics): the unceasing conquest of Truth is better than Truth itself. The Kingdom of God "endures force"; we must abandon the pseudo-tranquilizing certainty that it will simply be given us, whether for merit or through grace. If such a Kingdom were not always on the verge of being lost it would be a kingdom of the dead and not of the living. "Not to die" means to struggle in order to escape death, to live restlessly, fully aware of the danger that God may stop thinking us—no longer dream us. Unamuno does not ask for beatitude or for the complete fulfillment of hope; he asks for a Kingdom of "hopeful dissatisfaction, or of dissatisfied hope." "My soul, at least," he wrote, "yearns for something else, not absorption, nor quiet, nor peace, nor extinction, but an eternal drawing closer without ever arriving, an endless longing, an eternal hope eternally renewed"—in short, "an eternal Purgatory rather than a Celestial bliss; an eternal ascension." For "he who achieves Supreme Truth will be absorbed by it and cease to exist." And to avoid this cessation of existence—the worst of all evils, the supreme evil—we must stand guard and work, instead of resting in Paradise; we must "use eternity to conquer the bottomless abyss of the bosom of God, hand over hand, eternally."

17   THE ETERNAL PRESENT

"Bosom of God," "Supreme Truth," "eternal ascension"—these expressions recur often in Unamuno's writings. Nevertheless, it would be a mistake to suppose that his longings for immortality are always expressed in this lofty language. Immortality can have many forms, and Unamuno is not willing to sacrifice any of them. He has described two of these forms with particular care: the survival of one's past, and the survival of one's self in the memory of others.

Most doctrines of immortality are geared to the future; they assert that man will go on living for ever, but say little, or nothing, about how man should face his past. The reason for this silence about the past is the supposedly beatific character of human survival; a complete state of bliss seems to entail absolute forgetfulness. But Unamuno finds such doctrines not to his liking. To be sure, he insists on continuation, but cannot conceive it without "recuperation." A living immortality, he thinks, is one that allows us to relive the experiences of the past—if not all experiences, at least the ones that constitute the basic stratum of our personality. Since no rational account can be given of this recovery of the past, Unamuno expresses the wish for it mainly in poetic discourse. In one of his poems he cried out for "the days of yesterday," and asked the "Father of Life" that the past for which "he longs" be returned to him "all gathered up in the end," and as alive as when it first took place. He wants to relive what he once lived. The end of the sonnet "My Heaven" is quite explicit on this point; gentle melancholy and willful longing mingle together in these lines:

> Toward an eternal yesterday direct my flight
> But do not let it arrive for, Lord, you have
> No other heaven that would half so fill me with joy.

It may seem surprising that Unamuno should emphasize "the past" when we take into account his condemnation of the "dead crust" of the past, and his insistence on "intralife" and "intrahistory" (see chapter 4). There may be some inconsistency here, and I will not try to remove it merely to show that Unamuno was more logical than he seemed. Perhaps he thought there was an authentic and an unauthentic past, and that only the former was worth recovering and worth being relived. Perhaps he merely wanted to express the wish that all that is—and, therefore, has been—should become "eternized" (a wish also expressed in his longing to "perpetuate the moment"). I think Unamuno's insistence on "recovery" and "reliving" has its origin in his desire not to confuse immortality with purely atemporal bliss. If immortality means temporal survival, it must not destroy time, but continually relive and reshape it. It is also possible that since experience and reason alike show that survival as indefinite continuation of one's self is highly improbable, Unamuno wanted to make certain that there was at least a possibility of "immortalization" through one's memory.

As to survival in others, Unamuno claimed that it was the prime motor of production and creation. It is, for instance, the basic drive behind sexual love (as Schopenhauer had already pointed out) and, to be sure, behind carnal paternity. Although Unamuno also wrote that "the longing for immortality is nothing but a flower of the longing for descendants," he most often emphasized the primacy of the former over the latter. Human beings aspire to perpetuate themselves, consciously or not, by begetting children who will carry on into the future some of the characteristics of their progenitors. And since the children of the flesh are, according to Unamuno, the prototype of the children of the spirit, it may be said that artists, heroes, and saints pursue the same end as parents: to perpetuate themselves—by means of their works, their deeds, and their actions. Thus, if Don Quixote wishes to be famous "not only in this age, but in the centuries to come," not only throughout La Mancha, but in all Spain and to the ends of the earth, it is because he will not resign himself to perishing. Survival is also, therefore, survival through descendants, through works, and through memory. The problem here is to know whether the works of man will last forever. And as these works, and mankind itself, seem doomed to extinction, we must consider this kind of immortality—in the event it deserves the name— a most unsatisfactory one. Of course, Unamuno acknowledged this, but he proclaimed that, satisfactory or not, this kind of survival—or the hope of it—made it possible for men to go on living without completely despairing. If our lives were confined within too narrow limits, and were not reflected in the mind and in the memory of others, we would probably lose the will to live.

18   THE "AGONY" OF CHRISTIANITY

Although Unamuno looked everywhere for hints of survival and immortality, and welcomed them at the same time that he doubted them, there is every reason to suppose that his thoughts on immortality reached a dramatic climax when he was confronted with the way in which Christian authors treated this same problem. Basically, the decisive motives of which Unamuno availed himself for his concepts and his dreams of eternization, were predominantly Christian. At any rate, whenever he wanted to probe deeply into the question of immortality, he also inquired about the question of the nature and meaning of Christianity. He surveyed the agony of immortality—and of life—and "the agony of Christianity" with the same anguished hope. The Christianity from which Unamuno's thinking on immortality springs is of the conflicting and tragic type. He saw a perpetual contradiction in the heart of Christianity which both tears it apart and revitalizes it. This contradiction reveals itself in a series of conflicts in the course of which the very notion of Christianity perishes only to come alive again with renewed vigor.

One of these conflicts emerges as soon as we try to define Christianity. Unamuno proposed a formula that was strangely reminiscent of the definitions outlined by some German neo-Kantian philosophers: Christianity, he wrote, "is a value of the universal spirit." It would seem that Unamuno abandoned his impassioned vocabulary just as he was about to deal with one of his greatest themes. But when we place his definition in its context we are again on familiar ground. The complete definition reads: "Christianity is a value of the universal spirit with its roots in the intimate core of human individuality." In one single sentence the first contradiction in Christianity in clearly revealed: the contradiction of intemporal values with human experience. As a consequence we have the conflict between the universal and the individual elements, between the so-called "objective spirit" and the radical subjectivity of human life. Perhaps these conflicts might be ironed out by declaring that Christianity as a universal value exists only to the degree that it is rooted in experience. But since Unamuno believed that the reverse was equally true, that the world of experience exists only when encased in objectivity, in values, and in universality, the conflict persists. The personal and the universal components of Christianity coexist in a state of war. Christianity must be true—and hence be universal—and must be experienced—and hence be personal. We cannot do away with one of these elements merely to enhance the other, because then Christianity would lose its *raison d'être*. Christianity, in short, is a series of dogmas *and* a series of personal experiences. The paradox is obvious: one destroys the other, but cannot live without it. Accordingly, there is no "essence of Christianity," and the efforts of German theologians and philosophers to unearth it only exemplify that typically Teutonic intellectual wastefulness. Unamuno's "definition" is not a definition; it is an "invitation" to penetrate the mystery of Christianity. Perhaps, after all, Christianity has no essence; it simply exists, and, as all existences, wrestles with itself.

There are many contradictions and antitheses in Christianity which Unamuno points out. Three of them deserve special attention: the antithesis of Evangelism and Church dogmas; the conflict between the intemporal character of a religious doctrine and the temporal character of life; and the contrast between social and individual Christianity—a contrast similar to, if not the same as, that treated by Kierkegaard under the heading "Christianity versus Christendom." There seems to be little doubt that "Christianity must be defined agonizingly, polemically, by analogy with war." After all, Unamuno reminds his readers, Christ came to earth to bring war, and not peace.

I shall consider for a moment a conflict that was much discussed when Unamuno wrote his book, *The Agony of Christianity:* the conflict between the social and the individual (or rather, personal) components of Christian doctrine. Social Christianity is an attempt to cure the ills and evils of society by reforming it according to Christian norms. These norms are sometimes based on the Gospels, which are supposed to contain in capsule form principles whose application may help to "resolve the socioeconomic problem, that of poverty, of wealth, and the distribution of things in this life." At times they are based on social principles developed by Christian Churches—and in particular by the Catholic Church—in order to cope with the increasingly acute social problems of the modern age; a "just order" is then put forward as the indispensable basis of Christian society. On the other hand, individual (or personal) Christianity proposes to solve no other problem than that of the individual consciousness. This type of Christianity may appear as an ethical attitude or as a purely religious one—this last consisting in an effort to "imitate" Christ. It would seem that personal Christianity is more authentic than social Christianity, and Unamuno certainly began by favoring the former when he declared that Christianity—as social Christianity—"kills Christendom, which is a thing for solitary men." As soon as we focus our attention on the completely "solitary" character of Christianity, however, we notice that Christianity cannot endure; only a society of Christians—and a solidly organized one at that—can perpetuate the Christian attitude. We are thus confronted with a hopeless situation: social Christianity kills Christendom, and Christendom dissolves Christianity. Some would say that there is no need to push the conflict to this extreme, and that a more reasonable course would be to reconcile the personal and the social components of Christianity. But by now it should not be necessary to note that Unamuno would have fiercely denounced this eclecticism as Philistine. Not, therefore, "either one or the other"—and not "one *and* the other"—but "one *against* the other—and *vice versa.*" It is only insofar as Christianity and Christendom embrace in a struggle that the Christian attitude can become a vital one. We have here an example of "the agony of Christianity." Christianity must continually struggle with itself in order to survive.

19   THE "AGONY" OF HISTORY

"The agony of Christianity" is, in a way, similar to "the agony of history." Unamuno never used this last expression, but there is every reason to suppose that he would have accepted it as an adequate description of his feelings on the nature of "historical reality." For Unamuno history was what remains and what passes away, and most important of all, that insoluble dialectics between the two. Unamuno would agree with those who have viewed history—human history, that is—as meaningless, but he would also agree with those who have considered human history the greatest and the most meaningful of all realities. To be sure, in Unamuno's writings we do not find a fully developed philosophy of history. His thoughts on history are often vague and at times excessively apocalyptic. "History," as "God's train of thought on man's earth," he writes, "has no final human goal, it moves toward oblivion, toward unconsciousness." At the same time he claimed that history was "the only living thing, the eternal present, the fleeting moment that in passing away remains, and in remaining passes away." Furthermore, he occasionally emphasized the importance of tradition—essentially historical—but he also hailed the significance of what he called "the eternal present"—essentially ahistorical and atemporal. All this would seem to indicate that, although human history exists in its own right, it cannot be explained by itself, and needs some reality that transcends it.

These contradictions can be understood in the light of the Unamunian conception of "intrahistory," to which we have already referred and which we shall treat in greater detail later. The essence of human history is for Unamuno what lies within history—the so-called "eternal tradition." Therefore, Unamuno did not maintain that human history must be explained by something extrahistorical—by the unfolding of God's spirit, or by the evolution of nature, to give only two examples. He also rejected the idea of history as a collection of political, social, economic, cultural facts having no other foundation than themselves—even when arranged in a certain order that provides a satisfactorily causal explanation. The notions of "intrahistory" and of "eternal tradition," on the other hand, seemed more promising to him because they gave human history a meaning in terms of itself. Unamuno's views in this connection were probably conditioned by two assumptions: one, that the essence of history is personal in character; and two, that there is always something eternal in the "moment." The first assumption means simply that it is human beings who make history, so that history is, ultimately, the "history of men's souls." The second assumption is intended to mean that although historical events are unique and, as such, cannot be repeated, the eternal in them persists forever. This second assumption is, of course, the more Unamunian of the two and, in a sense, the more original. At any rate, it seems that Unamuno's views—or more exactly, feelings—on history were intimately related to his speculations on the problem of immortality. This is why we have entered them here as a conclusion of our analysis of the problem. Just as Unamuno wanted to pause in each moment, not merely to enjoy it, but rather to make it eternal, he also wanted to see in each one of the events of history a possibility or, at least, a glimpse of that eternity he dreamed of for himself. Thus he could say that to live eternally was to live within history—by no means, therefore, outside of it, in the bosom of God, of Nature, or of some Hegelian Universal Spirit. As so often in his writings, Unamuno does not provide any proof for this contention; instead, he invites us to "feel" the touch of eternity in historical events. Yet this eternity is in no way a pure intemporality: it is an eternity made up of—piled high with—time.

Chapter Four

Spain—Quixotism

20 EUROPEANIZERS AND HISPANIZERS

With agony and tragedy everywhere, it is no surprise to rediscover them in connection with Spain, Unamuno's permanent obsession. However, Unamuno did not apply his philosophy of tragedy to "the problem of Spain." On the contrary, it was his intuition of the conflictive nature of Spain and of all things Spanish which enabled him to evolve his philosophy of tragedy.

At any rate, we must not think that Unamuno's preoccupation with Spain was the result of a narrow-minded and outmoded nationalism. And this because, first, "Spain" may designate a vast and complex cultural area comprising not only continental Spain but also Portugal, and Spanish and Portuguese America. And second, because although Unamuno was a Spaniard par excellence, he was also a "universal man." An exclusively Spanish point of view would not do justice to Unamuno's ideas on, and ideals for, Spain. His treatment of "the problem of Spain" also included a number of opinions about the relations between Spain and Europe, and others on "the problem of Europe." Thus, unless we are aware of the inclusiveness of Unamuno's concern, we cannot understand his most original contributions to the problems here discussed, nor grasp the meaning of his search for "the eternal Spain" beneath the transient events of Spanish history. As we shall discover, "the eternal Spain" is ultimately an "intravital" and "intrahistoric," not a lifeless and ahistoric, Spain.

Unamuno developed his views on the subject in ever more personal reactions to the long and bitter debate between Europeanizers—those who favored, and wanted "to catch up with," Europe—and the Hispanizers—those who proclaimed that Spaniards needed to maintain their own tradition at all costs; if necessary, against Europe. This debate was particularly lively in the years of Unamuno's youth, and to a great extent conditioned the literary "rediscovery of Spain" by the members of the Generation of 1898. The Europeanizers were goaded to action by their acute discomfort at being obliged to compare the political, social, economic, and intellectual conditions of Spain and Europe. By "Europe" they meant Germany, France, England—sometimes Italy, and occasionally Switzerland and the Scandinavian countries. They meant to prove to all complacent Spaniards that there was a deplorable material and cultural lag in their country, and to warn their compatriots that this lag had increased with the passing years. Europe, they felt, had been making continual progress—political democracy, economic expansion, and scientific creation—whereas Spain had been, at least since the seventeenth century, or perhaps earlier, in a continual decline.

A list of the reasons suggested to explain this decline on Spain's part would fill an entire book. Nevertheless, these reasons can be reduced to seven basic types: (1) psychological reasons—a constitutional incapacity for fulfilling the demands of the modern era, a sharp sense of inferiority coupled with an excessive feeling of pride; (2) religious reasons—dogmatism, the Inquisitional spirit, intolerance; (3) demographic reasons—depopulation caused by continual wars and by the conquest of America; (4) economic reasons—the upset caused by the introduction of the "American gold," the destruction of farming by the Mesta, the crushing of incipient industry by the oppressive regulations of the state, and later, the myopic protectionism offered to a still shaky industry; (5) social reasons—the demise of a promising middle class at Villalar; (6) political reasons—misrule, ineffectual administration, the continued and ineradicable "Philipization" (or, in the words of Ortega y Gasset, "Tibetanization") of Spain; (7) educational reasons—illiteracy, insufficient attention to scientific research and technological ingenuity.

Although it was not always easy to substantiate these reasons (state administration, for instance, was far from being badly organized or ineffectual), this overall picture seemed close to the truth. And in order to shake off this burdensome heritage, the Europeanizers (Juan Valera in a subdued manner; Joaquín Costa with a roaring voice) proposed to follow the "European" example and introduce a greater amount of religious tolerance, increase political liberties, and reform the social and economic structure. Since it was felt (and is still felt nowadays, although with much less rhetoric and more attention to concrete developments than before) that attention to the European example would provide a solution for many of Spain's ills, an "open door" policy toward Europe—and a corresponding "deafricanization" of Spain—was considered an absolute necessity. Spain must be "regenerated" materially and spiritually (indeed, some of the Europeanizers were called "Regenerationists"). A few even thought that the achievement of this goal would inevitably entail, at least for a transitional period, a certain amount of what the Hispanizers declared to be the greatest of all evils for a country: imitation of foreign ways of life.

The tenets of the Hispanizers were at the other extreme. There were many things, they argued, that were wrong with Spain, but not those with which the Europeanizers concerned themselves. On the contrary, the chief trouble was that Spain had blindly adopted all the modern European vices: disbelief, skepticism, rationalism, the overevaluation of material rather than spiritual things, of science rather than belief, and of reason rather than faith. Therefore, the solution was a simple one: return to the "authentic tradition" of Spain, which the Europeanizers profaned, and recover the "lost virtues of past epochs." The origin of these "virtues" was sometimes traced to a single primeval source, but more often they were believed to have been molded during certain well-defined historical periods—under the Catholic kings, under Philip II, and during the Counter Reformation. It was not the differences between Europe and Spain which should give cause for alarm, but their increasing similarities. In agreement with the Europeanizers on one point at least, the Hispanizers proclaimed that Spain must be "regenerated," but instead of proceeding with an eye to the future they felt it would be more beneficial to return to the "past."

We have outlined the two extreme positions because they throw light on the background of the debate; but it must also be remembered that a good number of the attitudes toward the problem were infinitely more subtle. Menéndez y Pelayo, for example, although convinced of the need for a resurrection of the "true greatness" of Spain and a recapturing of the "virtues of the past," now obscured by mere imitation and "heterodoxy," suspected that the "spirit of the Enlightenment," responsible for much of Europe's advance, could not be discarded with a single stroke of the pen. On the contrary, the task was to discover to what degree Spain had helped in the formation of this spirit of enlightenment—and thereby, in the creation of science, philosophy, and technology—in many cases anticipating Europe's most highly acknowledged achievements. Spain, Menéndez y Pelayo concluded, need not imitate Europe because it had been, and still was, fundamentally European, although many Spaniards persisted in ignoring the fact. Did not the "Black Legend" of Spanish "colonization" lose much of its dark hue when the historical truth was examined with a degree of care? Could not much of the cruelty, authoritarianism, and fanaticism thought to be so characteristically Spanish, be found in equal abundance in Europe as well? Hence, one must beware of those who drew an excessively sharp dividing line between Spain and Europe. If there was any difference, Menéndez y Pelayo felt it was due to Europe's having always followed the "straight path," whereas Spain had more often followed a "crooked" one that had caused her to confuse the development of science with the destruction of faith, and the fostering of liberalism with the production of anarchy. The spirit of tolerance must be upheld, though never so as to sanction "error"—anyone who, like Menéndez y Pelayo, considered himself a "hammer of heretics" could not go that far—against stupidity, lack of culture, and bad taste. Juan Valera, on the other hand, felt differently. A Europeanizer with few equals, an enemy of arrogance, disdain, and fanaticism—in which he saw the principal causes of Spain's alienation from modern Europe—he was equally strong in his desire to help make Spain more truly herself. As the critic Guillermo de Torre has noted, this self-styled skeptic would react vehemently whenever any foreigner arrogantly presumed to judge anything Spanish. To rant for the sake of ranting was pernicious, intolerable; one must try to understand, smooth over, rectify. In short, all fanaticism, all exaltation and delirium, all extremes—no matter what faction sponsored them—must be discarded. Only in this way would Spain cease to swim against the European current. Then there was Pérez Galdós' point of view. Firmly convinced that there was much in modern Europe which Spaniards would do well to consider carefully, and seduced by political institutions and social customs best exemplified in the area north of the Pyrenees, and even on the other side of the English Channel, he was at the same time a patient rediscoverer, and a passionate lover of every corner—human and urban—of Spain. His profound appraisal of the history and life of his country was almost unequaled; few of his contemporaries knew how to extract, as he did, the permanent lessons in the lives and gestures most deeply embedded in the historical tradition of his country. And finally, let us recall Francisco Giner de los Ríos, who taught students to see and love Europe, but also to understand Spain, her villages, her people, and her countryside. Thus, it is apparent that there was an abundance of intermediate positions of all shades, and that, consequently, the extremes I have mentioned and the conflict referred to between Europeanizers and Hispanizers must be taken *cum grano salis.* This would seem to suggest the conclusion that certain syncopated rhythms, certain outrageous posturings, certain overly abrupt modes of action, were the exception in Spanish life, owing, quite simply, to external pressures of unfortunate lapses.

21   SPAIN AS A CONFLICT

The above is a difficult conclusion to accept if one is intent upon a profound examination of that life, and determined to come up with all that it contains of value. This conclusion was never Unamuno's. Does this mean that he considered it more important to approve one of the extreme attitudes that we began by listing rather than the other? Some have felt this to be true. They notice that he not only spoke out for Europeanization and, more often, for

Hispanization, but seemed to jump from one to the other as well. Accordingly, Unamuno would have been a Europeanizer when he proposed to "lock the sepulcher of the Cid," shortly before 1897, becoming a diehard Hispanizer when he proclaimed, both in the *Life of Don Quixote and Sancho* and at the end of *Tragic Sense of Life,* that Spain had never followed the "economic" methods of modern Europe: that the only "economy" to which she had been faithful was that "eternal and divine economy" of which the Counter Reformation had been the outstanding historical example; that (like Don Quixote) "Spain was demented"; that there was no need to worry about strengthening democratic institutions, producing technological wonders, or inventing abstruse philosophical systems (for, he said, if it was a question of inventing, "let Europe do that!"); and, finally, that it was useless to be annoyed by a Europe that was nothing but a "shibboleth"—a deception, a mirage, a fetish. On superficial evidence, therefore, Unamuno seemed to be not just one Hispanizer among many, but the most outspoken of them all. Going to the other extreme, he seemed to have become (as Ortega y Gasset so bitterly complained) a staunch defender of "Africanism," a standard-bearer of "barbarianism." And it is perfectly true that for a while Unamuno shunned all moderation, so much so that the traditionalism of the Hispanizers seemed tainted with "modernism" when contrasted with his own.

We must not, however, read Unamuno too literally, nor forget that he sincerely enjoyed reducing doctrines to absurdity by wrapping them in startling paradoxes. We recognize that Unamuno's frequently brash exclamations lend weight to the idea that he became an uncompromising "Hispanizer." But this idea is in conflict with all that we know of him. Unamuno would find little satisfaction in a conventional traditionalism, which he always judged vain, pompous, and shallow. And since, finally, it would be embarrassing to admit that he could have felt any profound sympathy for any one of the moderate (and, he would probably say, "hybrid") attitudes of which we have given some examples, it will be necessary to strike out in a new direction, in order to discover what Unamuno really felt about Spain—and in what way this feeling can be dovetailed into the permanent structure of his thought.

The term 'adentramiento' ('inner-directing,' literally), already examined with another purpose in mind, provides an illuminating indication in this respect. It would seem, at first, to suggest a retreat—quite appropriate in view of Spain's having suffered innumerable setbacks in the course of her history. Having failed so many times—or, rather, having never realized all of her overambitious projects—she would be foolish to try once more for success. There were, then, two alternatives: to adopt a policy adjusted to her means and to her diminished power; or to direct her efforts inward and initiate an untiring self-exploration. The first course of action is the business of statesmen; the second one, the task of poets and thinkers. This was the substance of Ganivet's "thesis." To a degree it was also the "thesis" of Unamuno. But he was less concerned than Ganivet with an "agonizing reappraisal" in the field of political action; he emphasized the spiritual side of inner-direction. Now, the motion described by the term 'adentramiento' must not be considered a retrograde one. Ganivet proclaimed that a "withdrawal toward the self" (*"retirarse hacia sí"*) did not necessarily imply a lessening of the force and vigor of national life. Unamuno was even more outspoken on this point. After all, solitude had never seemed to him more than a preliminary step in the search for companionship. "Only loneliness," he wrote, "can melt away this thick layer of shame that isolates us one from another; only in loneliness can we find ourselves; and when we do so, we discover we are all brothers in loneliness. And if we are unable to love each other, it is only because we are unable to remain alone." Therefore, once we reach the man within we are able to act out what we have already seen to be one of Unamuno's major obsessions: to flow, to abound, to pour out. Only well water is contained; spring water always overflows. Here also, "draw in in order to expand" (*"concentrarse para irradiar"*) was deemed by him the only fruitful norm, and it was precisely this injunction that neither "Europeanizers" nor "Hispanizers," "progressives" nor "traditionalists" were able to follow. Won by outward appearances—or by false essentials—they all neglected to notice that the salvation of a country can come only from the heart of the country itself, and that only by plunging down into its own "vital dwelling place" (*"morada vital"*)—to use a term whose meaning Américo Castro has so thoroughly explored—could a country touch solid bottom and move forward again without weakening or falsifying its existence.

But moving forward again did not mean reviving past glories or building up political and military power. Unamuno's point of view must not be confused with that of the traditionalists. The defenders of a so-called glorious tradition were, in fact, prisoners of a quite limited tradition, for instead of breathing life into the community they managed to retard, paralyze, swamp, and, finally, ruin it. Traditionalists were as blind to the real powers of a human community as the "progressives." "Progressives" were so haunted by the future that eventually they could only dream of utopias. The traditionalists were haunted by the past and inevitably became reactionaries. Despite their claims to the contrary, both were concerned exclusively with dreams, and not with that real fountain of spiritual power which always can be heard by anyone who is able to decipher its hidden harmonies.

Thus it was natural that Unamuno should have resolutely struggled against that variety of shallow patriotism which consisted of coddling the "stubble and chaff"; natural that he should have proclaimed the need to escape "that great pagan subject": history. History was to Unamuno essentially "the history of death"; Spaniards must therefore do all they could in order to rid themselves of that "damnable history that oppressed and suffocated" them. The Spain for which Unamuno searched was "not of this world"; it was to be found, as he wrote in one of his poems, "in the depths of the blue above it." He thus proposed the idea of an "eternal and celestial Spain"—with equal justification we could say "the idea of an eternal and subterranean Spain"—which scandalized traditionalists and progressives alike.

Let us not misinterpret Unamuno's impassioned vocabulary. This "eternal Spain" is not a pure Platonic idea transcending all tangible realities. Nor is it the dream of a megalomaniac—a thing of splendor and grandeur which reflects only ridicule on the dreamer. Unamuno has said that his "eternal Spain" was not extratemporal, but intratemporal, nor extrahistoric, but intrahistoric. He also wrote that we must plunge into "the eternal tradition, the mother of the ideal, which is nothing but tradition itself projected into the future." With these cryptic words he expressed as well as he could the intuition that Spain's authentic being was to be found above and beyond the petty attractions of glory and power, whether past or future. The true life of Spain was to be found in the hearts of the Spaniards themselves if they could only do away with historical tradition and the fallacies of traditionalism and progressivism, and direct their exploration inward to the core of the innermost self and there discover the permanent substructure underlying all historical events. For history, past or future, was the outer covering of the soul's purely internal rhythm.

Needless to say, the innermost self of a human community does not live in quiet and peace; like all else, it thrives on conflict—and conflict with itself. "Spanish existence consists of a polemic," Américo Castro has written in a quite Unamunian vein. A polemic in which Europeanizers and Hispanizers, progressives and traditionalists take part—and this is their justification; even the "extremists" and the "moderates" can be said to participate in the conflict. There may be "two Spains," but they are united; not by intellectual compromise, but in a vital dialectic. Like the man of flesh and blood, Spain lives in order to "forge itself a soul," and this even when its history proves to be only a process of self-destruction ("desvivirse").

"Like the man of flesh and blood"—this means that Unamuno believes he can discern the precise substance of the human being in the innermost core of what seems to be only a particular "national community." This is the meaning of Unamuno's injunction: "Let us Hispanize Europe!"—a step toward a "Hispanization of the world." This "Hispanization" does not entail any political or ideological imposition, or any kind of influence or domination—things of a "rotten past." It means simply a "display" of what may be called "the humanity of man." This is why Unamuno's preoccupation with Spain had little, if anything, to do with nationalism or patriotism. It was not a question of marking time in that "enraged or doleful replevin" which, according to the Argentine writer Jorge Luis Borges, was the single, monotonous entertainment of too many Spanish writers of the nineteenth century. Nor was it a question of dreaming, more or less lazily, of a hypothetical and future magnificence. Unamuno was very clear on this point: if Spaniards—and, in general, all human beings—wanted to fulfill themselves, they must remove the crust of the past, and avoid the mirage of the future. They must not live according to tradition, or according to reason, or according to tradition corrected by reason, or even reason seconded by tradition. Their life must be based on their own powers, on their own possibilities. Once they learned to disregard what *others* wanted them to be, they must strive to be what *they themselves* wanted to be.

It will be argued that all this is vague (or metaphorical), and that the much-praised "intrahistory" is either history itself reduced to a few essentials, or means nothing at all. This objection is reasonable. But we must be careful not to miss the important point in this Unamunian intuition: that in all history there is much that is alien to the "internal life" of a community and much that might very well "not have happened" without basically modifying this life. Behind this intuition was the idea that the values, toward the achievement of which human existence is directed, can help us to a better understanding of that human existence than even history itself. In fact, Unamuno's ideas on history may serve in any attempt to understand life, whether it be human existence in general, or certain features of Spanish life.

"Spanish life" is thus a symbol of "human existence," but it is more easily detected in all those communities that participate directly in the Spanish tradition: the Hispano-Portuguese, the Hispano-American, and the Ibero-American. With the "Portuguese brothers," Unamuno included the South American and the "Ibero-American brothers" in his speculations about the Spanish soul. On the surface, Unamuno's phraseology appears to be another example of the outmoded political rhetoric that some Spanish statesmen still use in toasts at Columbus Day banquets, but it is really the result of a vital, constant interest in the ways of life and feeling particular to Spanish and Ibero-Americans. Unlike those who ignored the existence of Spanish and Portuguese America, or those who considered them little more than an intellectual colony, Unamuno took them into his heart, even though at times he lectured them very severely. He believed that Americans of Spanish and Portuguese descent lived exactly as did their European counterparts, even when they fought the latter for political or intellectual independence. Their life, he felt, was a polemic; they too felt the heartbeat of their intrahistory beneath the crust of historical events; and, finally, they too sensed that they were a symbol of "pure humanity."

22 THE QUIXOTIC SOUL

Let us also add: sensed that they were the symbol of pure Quixotism; for the Spanish spirit, the human spirit, and the Quixotic spirit were but three manifestations of the same reality according to Unamuno. His "philosophy of Quixotism" is as much an essential ingredient of his philosophy of the Spanish soul, as the latter is of his philosophy of human existence. Unamuno worshiped Don Quixote, and often took Cervantes to task for failing to understand his own hero. Unamuno's weakness for the use of paradox was never more evident than in his speculations on the nature and meaning of "Quixotism." He considered Don Quixote and Sancho men of flesh and blood, more real than Cervantes himself. He made a "religion" of Quixotism. He considered it the natural one for Spaniards and, for that matter, for all human beings who were guided by ideals. He proposed a "crusade" to rescue Don Quixote from the hands of those who saw nothing in Cervantes' work but a "literary masterpiece." There is no need to take this proposal of Unamuno's too literally, but the fireworks of his paradoxes must not keep us from recognizing his serious attempt to describe the nature of the "Spanish soul" and the soul of all mankind. At the heart of this soul is the longing for that immortality that Unamuno considered the trademark of humanity.

Like the "Spanish soul," the "Quixote soul" does not exhaust its capacity for activity by going out into the world to make history. To be sure, Quixotic deeds took place in history—they were located in a definite geographical area and permeated by the customs and ideals of a certain historical age—but they were always nourished by that profound "dream" that pulsated beneath all historical and circumstantial events. "The adventures of our knight," Unamuno wrote, "flower in time and on earth, but their roots are in eternity." As a symbol of what Spain and the Spanish community on both sides of the Atlantic offered the world, Don Quixote possessed "a soul," and only by taking it into consideration could his deeds be properly understood and adequately evaluated. The Cervantes scholars wrongly assumed that the significance of *Don Quijote* was in what the hero said, or in the way in which he said it. They were unable to see that the only really interesting point was what Cervantes' hero longed to be. Not, of course, because Don Quixote was an incarnation *avant la lettre* of the modern "Faustian spirit," for whom actions were more important than words and deeds. The "Faustian spirit"—as described by Goethe in one of Faust's monologues—is, at bottom, an example of the philosophy of "pure Will," entailing a directionless dynamism. Quixotism, on the other hand, is an example of a will directed toward the performance of the good; an example of an impulse destined to make this good available to all human beings. The philosophy of Quixotism has, therefore, little or nothing to do with the philosophies proposed by either traditionalists or progressives. Traditionalists dream of the false glories of the past; progressives preach the use of "the regenerative decoction, the customhouse poultice, the hydraulic blister plaster." These last solutions—some of which (the least ideological and the most concrete) are still quite vital for Spaniards today—seemed mere abstractions to Unamuno, mere blueprints and programs which amounted to nothing when set beside that supreme reality: the forging of personality—of a "soul of bulk and substance." Don Quixote symbolizes the quest for personality as opposed to the emphasis on fact and ideas. To his fellow men he seems a lunatic, but he is a symbol of "pure spiritual maturity"—an expression that Unamuno, probably on purpose, left undefined. This is why Don Quixote is an enemy of caution; he puts his whole self into every action. But the action he undertakes has a purpose and, basically, it is suffused with prudence. Cervantes frequently uses the term "unreason" ("sinrazón") as a description of quixotic madness; and Unamuno maintained that, far from being a lack of reason, "unreason" was a variety of "superreason." It was a reason proper to ideals and not merely to ideas.

The "Holy Crusade" that Unamuno undertook in order to ransom the tomb of that "Knight of Madness," Don Quixote, was a first step in the search for a "pure spiritual maturity." Accordingly, it was necessary to free Don Quixote from the tomb where the "Knights of Reason"—the rationalists, the worshipers of common sense, the men who acted according to well-defined programs—have him chained—and perhaps embalmed. The "Knights of Reason" pretend to follow the dictates of ideas, but are, in fact, unable to sacrifice their lives for an idea. They are "incapable of marrying a great and pure idea, and begetting children by it"; instead, they "live in concubinage with ideas." They do not understand that ideas must be taken—or rather, embraced—as ideals. On this point Unamuno seemed to be reworking the Socratic attitude that an idea is worthless unless one is willing to commit one's self to it, to live by, and die for it. Being less of a rationalist than Socrates, however, Unamuno did not attempt to define ideas; it was enough for him that he "felt"—them. And he felt them as ideals, for only as ideals could they become the essential ingredients of human life.

The Cervantes scholars, Unamuno thought, failed to grasp the meaning of the Quixotic attitude. To begin with, they paid too much attention to Don Quixote's reasoning, to his knowledge of the Italian language, to his discourse on arms and letters. They treated him as a character in a novel and not as a man of flesh and blood. And if they noticed the Quixotic ideals, they were unable to see that Don Quixote's deeds were always purposeful. As a matter of fact, the deeds had a double purpose, in part ethical: Don Quixote—and also Sancho, his "other half"—constantly strives to become good—"pure good, uncomplicated by theological subtleties, good and nothing but good"; in part, divine: Don Quixote constantly strives to become immortal. The Quixotic defense of ideals is not, therefore, a defense of *just any* ideals, but only those of goodness and eternity.

Don Quixote's striving for immortality manifests itself in a way that at first seems mere self-worship: as the desire for glory and renown. But this egotism is only apparent. It is really the expression of a longing not to die. This is, according to Unamuno, the "innermost core, the core of all the cores of Quixotic madness." Like all human beings who have not been enslaved by things, Don Quixote shows that he can believe (while doubting) in "the impossible." But since man cannot continue to live—as man—without attempting "the impossible," Don Quixote's madness is a sublime expression of sanity, paradoxical as this may seem at first. Don Quixote's madness is thus more sane than the sanity of others, to use the terms employed by Saint Paul in speaking of God. This madness touches common sense, because it is an exaltation of that "personal sense" that Unamuno identifies with the "human sense."

There is little doubt that Unamuno goes too far. There is too much talk of madness in his philosophy of Quixotism. He seems too easily mastered by a desire to *épater le bourgeois*. But, after all, he belonged (as Ortega y Gasset noted) to the same literary generation as Bernard Shaw—a generation that made paradox the norm of expression. Nevertheless, beneath Unamuno's puns and paradoxes lies a sincere desire to remind men of their human condition, to bring into focus the realization that they are mortal and at the same time desire to become immortal. The philosophy of Quixotism is a basic ingredient in Unamuno's philosophy of the "man of flesh and blood." Unamuno wants us to become as real as Don Quixote, because the ultimate reality of man is determined by what each man wants to be.

It is not enough, however, to ransom Don Quixote. We must ransom Sancho too, because, according to Unamuno, his faith is even more admirable than his master's, because it is more beset by doubt. Unamuno declared that Sancho was "an indissoluble half of Don Quixote." The conventional view of the idealism of the master and the realism—one might say, materialism—of the servant, does not observe that as Cervantes' book unfolds Sancho gradually becomes Quixotic. To be sure, he becomes so unconsciously, and never claims to be more than his master's shadow. But by the end of the book he proves that he has completely assimilated Don Quixote's spirit, and that his Quixotism is even more pure than his master's. In the final analysis it is Don Quixote who has corrupted the purity of his own faith through an excessive pride in his self-confidence, whereas Sancho, so full of common sense and so timid in his courage, never once jeopardizes the true Quixotic faith. Sancho's faith is of the right kind; it is not faith in himself, but in his master—who seems to him to be the incarnation of an idea. Don Quixote sees giants where there are only windmills; his mettle and his desire for justice are often simply the result of a feverish imagination. Sancho, on the other hand, sees the windmills as windmills, and yet does not falter in his faith. And finally, Sancho's faith is a truly Unamunian one, for it is nourished by doubt. He does not believe that the barber's basin (*"bacía"*) is Mambrino's helmet (*"yelmo"*), nor does he think that it is only a basin, but a combination of both, a "basin-helmet" (*"baciyelmo"*). And when at the end of his career, Don Quixote betrays his faith, and decides to renounce adventuring, Sancho implores him to return to the highroads of La Mancha in the pursuit of ideal justice. Unamuno is therefore able to conclude that although Don Quixote may die, Sancho never will. He is the true "inheritor of Don Quixote's spirit," and perhaps the very essence of Quixotism.

Unamuno's philosophy of Quixotism was at first a corollary of his philosophy of the Spanish soul, an illustration of it. But although Unamuno was not a systematic thinker in the conventional—or rather, academic—sense of the word, he was extremely consistent, and even repetitious in the development of his favorite themes. Small wonder, then, that his commentaries on the life of Cervantes' hero are interwoven with the themes we have already examined: the problem of the man of flesh and blood, the idea of tragedy, the longing for immortality, and so on. Now, if the name of any philosophical discipline were needed for Unamuno's thoughts on Don Quixote, "ethics" would be the least inappropriate. For Unamuno, Don Quixote is the symbol of a moral ideal, and although Unamuno would certainly resist any attempt to label him, his ethics would be best described as an existential ethics of value. This ethics if not based upon nature, or upon history, and certainly not on a Platonic realm of eternal ideas. It has its roots in the depths of each human being, and yet transcends personality in the sense that any person who behaved as Unamuno proposed must aim at goals that no mortal could ever reach. Thus, in the ethics, as in everything else, conflict is master. Ortega y Gasset's teacher, the neo-Kantian philosopher Hermann Cohen, was not far from the truth when he saw in Don Quixote's deeds and words an instance of Fichte's ethics of infinite effort. Unamuno would have shuddered at the thought that what I have called his ethics resembled Fichte's, or any other philosopher's, for that matter. Nevertheless, they have a common source: both spring from the desire to make personality the dynamic center of a conflicting world. If there is any difference between them, it is that whereas for Fichte the only goal of the human consciousness was that of realizing itself, for Unamuno there were two goals—goodness and immortality. And only in the pursuit of these two goals did man have a chance of becoming himself.

Chapter Five

The Idea of the Word

23 THE POWER OF WORDS

Unamuno occupied a post—that of professor—and exercised a profession—that of philologist; yet neither of these activities was ever the axis of his life; nor where they, on the other hand, mere accidents. The post was, in the vocabulary, at once administrative and "metaphysical," of the Spanish Government, a "destiny" (*destino*): the chair of Greek at the University of Salamanca—and later, in addition, another of the history of the Spanish language. Unamuno felt that the profession he exercised entailed a "mission": to educate people—and not only students—in the use and misuse of words. Together the two chairs provided Unamuno with what he needed most: a rostrum. Not just a chair at the university, and not simply a speaker's platform or pulpit; but rather, an eminence from which to make his powerful and resounding voice heard, the voice that was never silent because its owner never felt that he had said all he should say. I have used the terms "destiny" and "mission"; I might add that Unamuno considered his teaching the consequence of a "call," an "existential" as well as, if not more than, an ethical call.

If Unamuno was, as the French critic Jean Cassou has characterized him, "the professor who above all professed a violent dislike of professors," he was also the professor par excellence, for he made all Spain his classroom. There had been professors of this kind before in Spain (Francisco Giner de los Ríos, for one); but none performed this activity more intensely and passionately than Unamuno. Furthermore, Unamuno distinguished himself from all other "professors on a national scale" in that he expressed the wish not only to educate his countrymen, but also, and above all, to stir their souls. Toward this end he often angered them, but he sincerely believed that this was the only way to awaken them, that is, to renew them.

The instrument of this stirring, this awakening and renewal of souls was the word—the spoken and written word. In these words—words of exhortation, of injunction, of indignation—each man could discover what he unknowingly and even intentionally concealed from himself. The "word" was, as it has always been in crucial times, the instrument of revelation—of "personal revelation." For even when Unamuno's words were aimed at a group, a mass, or a community, they had no public or social character, but always a personal one. Through speeches, monologues, and dialogues Unamuno sought to incite souls and transfigure minds. From the very first Essays (Ensayos), Unamuno championed the cry of "Inward!" against, and instead of, that of "Forward!" "Forward!" was a word of command; "Inward!" a call to renovation. "Forward!" is shouted by those who wish to impose their will; "Inward!" is used by those who struggle to induce a change. The cry of "Forward!" orders one to march shoulder to shoulder with others; that of "Inward!" to stroll "soul to soul" with them. Unamuno would allow only the latter, and he often surmised that one banded together with others only after a previous exasperation with solitude.

If to Unamuno being a professor and a philologist meant more than exercising a profession, this was because both activities allowed him to probe deeply what he considered "the mystery of the word." We say "mystery" because just when we are about to seize its nature, the word eludes us. The "word" cannot be analyzed, Unamuno felt, into meanings or sounds because it is a living, palpitating entity that, like the soul—and for analogous reasons—partakes of matter when most completely immersed in the spirit, and is composed of soul when it seems most nearly reduced to matter—sound waves or splotches of ink. The "word" was, for Unamuno

> blood of the spirit
> and voice that does not diminish
> for all that it fills both worlds.

In view of this, we are almost led to conclude that, in the fashion of that Supreme One described by mystics and Neoplatonists, the word—or the Word—flows forever and spreads without diminishing. Unlike that One, however, the word in Unamuno's sense has body and bulk since it is capable, not only of expressing the truth, but also—and more importantly—of living it. Words are experienced just as joy and sorrow are experienced; words seduce us, exasperate us, move and paralyze us. Words push against the flesh of our souls; we can destroy or convert, lose or save ourselves with words.

For Unamuno, the task of the philologist—the "true" philologist—was not merely that of chasing words in order to pluck out their meaning, structure, or relationships; it was to enter into them in order to live—or die—with them. If Unamuno combated and despised the professional philologists, the "exhumers" of words or traditions, it was because he wished to be a philologist by vocation, that is, a philosopher. For him, a philosopher was a man capable of raising the myriad possibilities of human speech to their highest power, capable of unearthing and developing the secular metaphors of his own language to the greatest possible extent. This was what Plato had done: expressed the philosophical possibilities of the Greek language. Here it would seem that Unamuno shared the doctrine of many contemporary thinkers, that the central problem of all philosophy is language itself. Shall we call Unamuno, the apparent "existentialist," an "analytical philosopher," obsessed with philosophy as "the analysis of language"? Only if we overlook that Unamuno's equation of philosophy and philology had little or nothing to do with the linguistic investigations of contemporary logicians and semanticians, and could only remotely be connected with the philosophical caprices of the grammarians. Neither one nor the other would admit that the word can be "the flesh of concepts," or, if they did, they would immediately apologize for indulging in metaphor or, what would be worse for them, in passion. Unamuno, however, would not give ground: words were like other realities, and in particular like human beings; they lived in a constant state of war, of tension, of conflict. To begin with, they battle with the concepts from which they are inseparable. Words cannot live without concepts, but concepts kill words. The concept is the death that awaits the word, but the word cannot live without the agony with which the presence of the concept provides it. The name, "the flesh of concepts," gives words a richer existence, but at the same time stains them with "the taint of original sin."

24   WORDS AND FACTS

Through words—living, or rather agonizing words—we know, and consequently, according to the biblical connotation, we beget. Thus words constitute the foundation of that truly decisive act: the creative—or poetic—act. This act has many forms, and literature is but one of them. Strictly speaking, the authentic, creative word transcends all "literature"—which is always something consummated and, therefore, dead. For if living words cannot be reduced to concepts, neither can they be compared to signs. Concepts and signs are only manifestations of the voice, that viva voce that makes itself heard primarily in the dialogue. A dialogue with others or—and for Unamuno it is the same thing—a dialogue with one's self: a monodialogue and, as he said, an autodialogue, in the course of which, he who carries on a dialogue with himself becomes two, three—an entire community. An autodialogue, or monodialogue, is more vivifying than a monologue, or than even a dialogue;

for instead of using concepts—which, as a rule, are dogmatic—we then use the live voices of words—which are always "agonizing" and polemical. Polemical and not only dialectical, for the dialectic is, formally, a closed and preordained system of concepts, whereas the polemic is an open, unpredictable discourse. Words are alive only when we do not know what direction they are going to take.

Being "a man of contradictions"—another way of saying "a man of flesh and blood"—means being precisely one of those who, although apparently engaged in a monologue, actually carries on a dialogue, that is, one of those persons who eschews all dogma and all catechism. Living, creative words must express themselves incessantly in dialogue—or rather in autodialogue—since otherwise they would become a dead artifact, comparable to a dogma that admits of no doubt or to a faith that never falters. All this explains, by the way, why Unamuno fought so strenuously against all forms of scientism. Scientism is, in fact, the dead letter of science just as mere literature is the dead letter of poetry. True, living, creative science has little, if anything, to do with scientism. Such a science admits of self-doubt and can thereby constantly purge itself of its own poisons. In the same way, true, living, creative literature is never a purely literary affair; it erases its own conventional contours and is thus able to renew itself over and over again. Scientism and mere literature do nothing but catalogue the universe; science and poetry re-present it and, to a great extent, in so doing, create it. Now although Unamuno was a good deal less "antiscientific" than is generally supposed, he tended to allot an ever greater degree of preeminence to that creative activity par excellence, which he identified with poetry. Real poetry reveals itself by means of the living word; for this reason, in opposition to the Faustian principle that in the beginning was the Action, Unamuno maintained that in the beginning was the Word. The Word was the "true fact" that he upheld against those half-facts, and half-truths, concepts and signs. The pseudofacts hailed by scientism and by literary realism, which one of Unamuno's characters, Fulgencio, in *Love and Pedagogy (Amor y pedagogía)*, called "dilapidated common sense," would immediately fade away when confronted with the real facts, the real words. If facts are creative, it is only because words beget them; that is, give them meaning. The true—*verum*—is, therefore, not the fact itself—*factum*—nor even the good—*bonum*—but the spoken—*dictum*. *Verum* and *dictum* are the only "transcendentals" between which a conversion—an ontological conversion—is possible.

25 WORDS AND LITERATURE

No wonder Unamuno preferred to see his "literary output" as a poetic and creative endeavor that *had* to use signs and concepts. We may even assume that Unamuno wrote books and articles in such staggering numbers, only because it was physically impossible to speak in person with each one of his fellow humans. If it had proved feasible to sustain a dialogue, viva voce, with each and all at the same time, perhaps Unamuno, in this respect a faithful image of the *homo hispanicus,* would not have written a single line. Literary writing is, to a certain extent, "falsification," in the minds of many Spaniards; doomed by its very nature to be for the most part impersonal, such writing soon becomes conventional and artificial. And what is true of the written word is true of all other forms of communication whose vital source has dried up. The contemporary tendency to reproduce the word by means of the tape recorder would have been a diabolical one to Unamuno, for nothing would have been more distasteful to him than to kill the supreme form of communication: live talk.

Whenever Unamuno's "literature" is an object of criticism, it must always be kept in mind that a poetic *élan* breathes within it, that the written word is meant to be only a shadow of the creative voice. As Rubén Darío noted, Unamuno was first and foremost a poet; and a poet is quite unlike, perhaps even the opposite of, an *homme de lettres.* To be sure, true poetry can wear any guise. Poetry is also, and sometimes superlatively so, novel, essay, legend, and even philosophical treatise. It is significant that, when he spoke of the possible expressions of a feeling—and not just a conception—of the universe, Unamuno should declare that such a feeling "is better mirrored in a poem, in prose or in verse, in a legend, in a novel, than in a philosophical system or in a realistic novel." "And among the great novels (or epic poems, it is all the same)," he added, "along with the *Iliad* and the *Odyssey,* the *Divine Comedy* and *Don Quixote,* and *Paradise Lost* and *Faust,* I count the *Ethics* of Spinoza, Kant's *Critique of Pure Reason,* Hegel's *Logic,* the *Histories* of Thucydides and Tacitus, and of other great historian-poets, and, of course, the *Gospels* of the life of Christ." Such pronouncements would be baffling, if not meaningless, had Unamuno not previously stretched the meaning of "poetry" and enunciated the identification between creative and poetic elements. For unlike the philosophical *system* and the *realistic* novel, the poem creates the things themselves as it expresses them, because instead of merely going around them or simply sketching their outlines, it aspires to penetrate their "souls." Poetry is the soul of things. This soul is unearthed, and also enacted, by the poet; the poet gives things their souls and at the same time shapes his own soul through them. Thus poetry is a kind of fusion of man and things, an objectification of man as well as a subjectification of reality.

Unamuno's entire "literary opus," and for that matter any "literary opus" that is something more than "pure (damned) literature," is, therefore, poetry, whether cast in verse form or in prose, novel or essay, speech or drama. Unamuno never admitted that literature—as poetry—could be classified and pigeonholed in literary "genres"; such "genres" were to him as abstract and bloodless as the categories of Hegel's system were to Bradley. Unamuno's opposition to a classification of literature by literary "genres" gives us a clue to why he invented names in order to describe some "genres" that had only one instance to prove their existence. He used such names as 'Nivola' (instead of 'novela'), 'opopeya' (instead of 'epopeya'), 'trigedia' (instead of 'tragedia'). But if he indulged in such fancies it was not because he wanted to add new literary "genres" to the established ones; it was rather because he wished to render absurd the doctrine of literary "genres." Since there are no literary "genres," we can easily admit an infinite number of them—at least one for each poetic work worthy of the name. In the end Unamuno wanted to dissolve all "genres," all classifications, to fuse all "genres" together in the deathless fountain of poetry. For Unamuno the only "literary form" was the poem, and the numerous, perhaps infinite, forms that the poem adopts. Thus we may conjecture that he might even have been willing to compose a "logic," as long as it remained in contact with this primordial fountain—"poetry," the only possible form for him of verbal creation.

26 WORDS AND LIFE

Must we assume, then, that among the diverse forms of expression adopted by Unamuno there is no appreciable difference? That would be a rendering *ad pedem litterae* of what must be understood "according to the spirit" in which it was intended. In accord with the latter, we may say that in Unamuno's "single poem" there are very different "accents" and that the specific quality of each of these lends its character to what we habitually call "poetry," "tragedy," "novel," "speech," "tale," "newspaper article," and "essay." Each of these "genres" possesses its own originality, but this was constituted, as Unamuno had already pointed out with respect to thought, by the accent and the tone rather than determined by the contents or the form. The Unamunian dissolution of the usual literary "genres" no longer seems to be an irritating paradox; it is the affirmation and confirmation of a creative will by which, as Victor Goti remarks in *Mist* (*Niebla*) (Unamuno's 'nivola'), a thing receives a new name, and is thereby given whatever laws the inventor pleases. Unless we forget this admonition we will again fall victim to that "realism" that is, as Unamuno declared, "a purely external, shadowy, cortical, and anecdotal thing," something that "refers to literary art and not to poetic or creative art." We feel, however, that Unamuno's struggle against realism leaves what might be called "poetic realism" unscathed; with it an authentic reality, an intimate reality and not a written or merely literary one, is created. "A poet," Unamuno wrote in the most celebrated of his poetic credos, "does not draw his creatures—living creatures—according to the methods of realism. The characters created by the realists are usually clothed manikins who move when their strings are pulled, and who carry within them a phonograph that repeats the phrases their puppeteer has collected in the streets and town squares and has jotted down in his book." True reality is foreign to ordinary realism; only authentic or poetic realism can capture it. The realistic writer copies—or rather, pretends to copy—reality and, in so doing, falsifies it. The authentically realistic poet refuses to reproduce, merely, what is, but only because he is aware that "being" is merely a part of reality. As we have seen, anything real is made not only of being, but also of the will to be.

In the next chapter I shall give a more elaborate account of Unamuno's conception of "authentic realism." Here it will suffice to note that the creative will (or urge) of which he spoke so often seems to be an image of chaos and disorder. As a consequence, Unamuno's battle against convention may easily lead to confusion. I suspect, however, that he was aware of this danger, for he implied that to lack a plan was not necessarily to succumb to whim and caprice. The plan of a literary work can be compared to the plan of a human life. Such a plan is progressively conceived as the work is produced. Many rules and directions are laid down in the course of the creative process. As Unamuno wrote, "a plan is not made for life, but rather life traces its plan by being lived." Now, just as with human life, the plan of a literary work consists in not having one, but in being itself its own plan. A plan is not a blueprint, a design, or a scheme; it is at most a project of which we are aware only when it is carried out. If any previously established plan can be detected, in life or in literature, it is only the plan of never reaching an end.

To leave everything unfinished, whether a literary work or life itself, was one of Unamuno's constant aims. Small wonder that his works impress us as being a kind of continuous creation, a sort of "interminable poem." Unamuno often expressed a feeling of distaste, and even horror, at anything that was too "finished," too "perfect," at anything that could not be continued. At one with some Greek philosophers, he thought that "to be finished" and "to be perfect" were basically the same thing; but contrary to these philosophers he dismissed the idea of perfection as being contrary to all sincerity and authenticity. He showed a definite dislike for any form of writing in which there were beautifully autonomous units, as if nothing could be added to them or subtracted from them. He rejected that "mere perfection" of verse and prose whose hallmark is completeness. He constantly hailed those writings that were full of "loose ends," that could be taken up again at any moment, to which one could always return. And so Unamuno's works give the impression that they might be continued indefinitely. There are everywhere "loose ends" offered to the reader as an incitement to dialogue, to polemic, to controversy. Unamuno's writings have always a "dramatic form." And this is not surprising, since they are not intended to be writings at all. They are meant to be the sounds of a human voice.

In the essentially unfinished character of Unamuno's works we encounter once again that impulse to overturn, to pour out, to overflow, of which I have spoken on several occasions, and which so faithfully represents Unamuno's temperament, his aims. Such an impulse is present even when, as in poetic forms fixed by tradition—like the sonnet—all would seem to end with the final verse. But if the last line of any of Unamuno's sonnets is a formal conclusion, it is also a new beginning; the poet has ceased to move his pen, but he keeps his spirit—and the spirit of his readers—mobile. Thus in the majority of cases—as in *Teresa*, in *The Christ of Velázquez* (*El Cristo de Velázquez*), in considerable portions of the *Book of Songs* (*Cancionero*)— Unamuno unequivocally adopts those poetic forms that are least encumbered by formal exigencies and abound with "loose ends" that can be resumed at any time—and developed indefinitely. Not that Unamuno avoids rhythm; on the contrary, he finds it everywhere, even in Kant's *Critiques!* But this rhythm is the rhythm of life. It is not difficult to find hendecasyllables in the *Tragic Sense of Life*. But they are not intended as poetic ornament; they are meant to be songs. Perhaps, after all, Unamuno's writings are songs of a sort, sung by a soul made of living words.

Unamuno was not a spectator, like Ortega y Gasset, nor a preceptor, like Eugenio d'Ors, but as Ernst Robert Curtius has written, an "exciter": *excitator* and not *praeceptor* or *spectator Hispaniae.* In all his writings, he set himself the task of performing—without ever finishing—what he considered the fundamental mission of the "human word": to excite, to disturb, to stir up souls, that he might better entreat them to awaken from their momentary dream and immerse themselves in a more substantial and lasting dream—that of the eternal. To excite, was to shake souls and not simply or not only to "agitate" them (as demagogues usually do). This is, of course, another way of saying: to change, to transform, and ultimately, to transfigure souls. Furthermore, he felt that he must excite them individually, since "nothing has any use or value except what springs from the concrete life itself," and is directed toward the concrete life. The "loose ends" that we find in the works of Unamuno are tossed overboard for the salvation—human salvation—of his fellow men and also, equally, in order to see if man can also live in hope, even when rocked by despair. "They say that to define and to separate is Hellenic; my way is to make indefinite and to confuse." But here to confuse means to drown everything in the original fountainhead of creation and of poetry, to dissolve everything in order to begin a new life and a new dream, cleansed anew and purified. Only in this way can what one *is* coincide with what one *wants to be*. We may conclude that only in this way can utopia embrace reality.

Chapter Six

The Idea of Fiction

27 THE "PERSONAL" NOVEL

"To be a man of flesh and blood, that is, one of those we call fictitious, which is the same thing . . .": here we have one of the most patent of all Unamunian paradoxes. It was formulated by him as an answer to the question: What is the "intimate" (the "true," the "eternal," the "creative," the "poetic") reality of an individual? We may be tempted to dismiss the paradox with the excuse that it was only meant to provoke the rationalists' wrath. But if we followed our rational drive, our understanding of Unamuno's worldview would be seriously impaired. The equating of fiction—or, more exactly, a certain type of fiction—with reality, plays a fundamental role in Unamuno's thought. After all, the paradox in question is closely related to the Unamunian doctrine of the dream and of the relation between God and creation—or the author and his characters. It was observed (chapter two) that this relation was similar to the one that existed between the dreamer and the dreamed. But since this idea of a "fictitious entity" is more clearly presented in his theory and practice of the novel than anywhere else, we shall turn now to an analysis of the meaning of the Unamunian novel—of the novels Unamuno wrote and of the comments he made on them.

Novels are written for various reasons: because one is a born novelist—just as one is a born poet or mathematician; because one wishes to make a name for oneself as a writer at a time when the novel has become the most widely read of all the literary genres; in order to eke out a living; in order to articulate one or more theses on the nature of man or on the condition of society; because man (or certain men) enjoy inventing characters and relating adventures; or for a combination of all these reasons. But why did Unamuno write novels? We must exclude the first reason, for Unamuno was not "a born novelist" in the way that Flaubert, Pérez Galdós, Dickens, or Dostoevski were, or in the way that Mauriac, Faulkner, Cela, or Graham Greene are. The second reason cannot be entirely dismissed, since it is operative in Unamuno—at least in the sense of contributing to the expansion of his personality. Yet it cannot be the determining factor, since a similar "expansion" of his own personality was achieved more successfully in his journalism than in his novel writing. The third reason has some importance if we rely on certain declarations of the author himself—for example, those found in some of his letters. But it does not explain why he adopted his rather peculiar novelistic technique. The fourth reason presents a delicate problem, since it is feasible to extract several "theses" from Unamuno's novels. It is not difficult, however, to see that Unamuno's novels are not *romans à thèse* in the strict sense in which some of Zola's purported to be; or as those of Feodor Gladkov or Silone have been. The fifth reason is more basic than it at first appears, because the production of novels would be impossible without some sort of creative drive and the psychological satisfaction that it provides for the novelist. This last reason, however, is too general to clarify the most specific traits in Unamuno's novelistic production, so that it must be taken only with reservation.

Are we then to conclude that, at bottom, Unamuno wrote his novels for no reason, or that only a combination of all the aforementioned reasons will adequately answer our question? That would be either too easy or too trivial. Therefore, let us look for specifically "Unamunian" reasons that will not exclude any of the others, but may prove to be more substantial than all of them combined.

Two of these "deeper" reasons present themselves to any careful reader of Unamuno's novels. On the one hand, as Julián Marías has pointed out, Unamuno seems to wish to make of the novel a means of access to human reality. This is tantamount to making of the novel a kind of epistemological tool for the understanding of this reality. On the other hand, Unamuno seemed to presuppose that reality cannot be defined as "what it is," nor fiction defined as "what it is not." To him fiction and reality were two aspects of a single entity that could only be understood from the "creational" point of view—from the "dream as creation" point of view.

Both reasons are important, but we feel that the latter is more basic or, at least, more "Unamunian" than the former. Let us examine them both.

Marías' thesis has obviously been influenced by what I may call "Ortega y Gasset's epistemology of human reality." According to it, human life is not definable, nor even describable, as a "thing," or a "substance" of any sort. It is best described as a kind of novel (or perhaps drama). One of its fundamental ingredients is, as some existentialists would put it, "self-projection," the fact that man always "anticipates" what he is going to become. It follows that fictional lives, far from being nonentities, are entities of a rather peculiar kind since description of what they "are" is likely to cast some light on human beings that really exist. Thus we can say that the novel—the "personal" or "existential" novel, as Unamuno foreshadowed and anticipated it—possesses a methodological value. Although the description of fictitious entities cannot be conceptualized without the help of a previous "metaphysics of human reality," it nevertheless proves to be extremely useful as a first step toward the development of an "existential analytic" of human existence.

The above thesis seems to fit a number of characteristic traits in Unamuno's novels, as well as a number of Unamuno's own confessions of his aims as a novelist. There is no doubt that the characters in Unamuno's novels are not simply "human natures," always ready to respond in the same basic ways to natural, social, or human environment. The physical appearance, the dress, the actual gestures, the physical background or even the plot are not the important elements of novels. They ought not to be the important part, Unamuno contended, in any novel worth the name. What mattered in a novel was exactly the same thing that mattered in "reality": the fact, namely, that it dealt with "real beings"—or, as Unamuno often wrote, with "tragic agonizers" (meaning, of course, "fighters"). These characters are, or should be, true subjects who do so, just as we and our "actual" fellow humans do, "by a cry, by a sudden action, by a revealing phrase." Only in this way are we given their "intimate reality," which can no longer be ontologically distinguished from that of a "real being" since it has been agreed that the so-called "real beings" as well as those we suppose fictional, possess the same type of "reality."

28 TYPES OF THE NOVEL

There are many passages in Unamuno's novels that support this view of the world of human "fiction." Furthermore, he was himself very generous with explanations of this point. He claimed that a true novelist ought to avoid all false "realism." He emphasized that the characters he depicted—or more exactly, in whose innards he poked about—were truly intimate because of what they revealed of themselves. With the "soul of their soul" laid bare, Unamuno held, they were indistinguishable from truly existing beings. If we feel, however, that Unamuno's *modus explanandi* is obscure, or unnecessarily paradoxical, we may turn to his *modus operandi*. It will make his ideas on the subject, if not acceptable, at least clear.

Let us consider briefly four of his novels: *Mist* (*Niebla;* 1914), *Abel Sánchez* (1917), *Three Exemplary Novels and a Prologue* (*Tres novelas ejemplares y un prólogo;* 1920), and *Aunt Tula* (*La tía Tula;* 1921). All "circumstances" in them are reduced to a minimum—if not simply eliminated. Sensations and emotions, predominant in "classical" novels, become "reactions," strictly personal in tone. Unamuno does not write, for example, "Augusto breathed a sigh of relief," but "Augusto felt calm—entranced." Even when apparently most trivial, Unamuno's dialogue does not create "atmosphere" or "background." It is not a way of describing the "environment." It is a way of shouting, cursing, repenting, and complaining—of laying oneself bare. As a consequence, the characters are not of the flesh but they do have, as Unamuno pointed out, skeletons—"personal skeletons," of course. In this manner, all exteriority—circumstances, environment, even plot itself—is done away with; the "intimate realities," which shine through the merely schematic descriptions, are creative to the extent that they are progressively compounded in the narrative process. "Reality" and "fiction" are inextricably mixed and the question of what allows us to distinguish between them becomes meaningless. The "depths of the soul," the "throbbing innards," the "chill in the bones," the "naked passions" are terms used by Unamuno not only to describe what his characters feel, but also, and above all, to erase the traces of any dividing line between the "material" and the "spiritual," between "flesh" and "soul."

The reader acquainted with Unamuno's novels will have noticed that I have not mentioned either his first or his last: *Peace in War* (*Paz en la guerra;* 1897) or *Saint Emmanuel the Good, Martyr* (*San Manuel Bueno, mártir;* 1933). Is this because they do not follow the same procedure, or—with the author's pardon—the same "pattern"? To a certain extent, yes. Unamuno has said of the first that it belonged to the "oviparous" species—the species of novels cultivated by writers who "make a plan in order to hatch a nucleus." Of the other novels, except the last one, he has said that they belong to the "viviparous" species—the species cultivated by writers who abstain from all carefully drawn plans and allow the novel to make its own plan as it is written. Now, although Unamuno's last novel represents to a considerable degree the culmination of his work along the lines of the "personal novel" and of the "viviparous" method, it also represents the beginning of a new way of writing novels. This way is neither straightforwardly "viviparous" nor elaborately "oviparous," neither exclusively "personal" nor purely "environmental." I suspect that the changes that Unamuno's *Saint Emmanuel the Good, Martyr* reveals are not confined to his method of writing novels, but apply also to the new direction of his philosophical enquiries. In *Peace in War,* Unamuno had proclaimed that we live—or must live—at peace within war. In the "intermediate" novels we are often told that there is a perpetual struggle between peace and war, a struggle that explains the sustained tension between characters, and of each of them with himself. It would seem that in *Saint Emmanuel* men are invited to live at war within peace. A most interesting change in thought, or at least in mood. Therefore, if the idea of the tragic sense of life, so characteristic of

Unamuno's thought, has not entirely disappeared in that novel, it would seem to have changed direction. From what the tormented yet calm protagonist of *Saint Emmanuel* does and thinks, we may conclude that although to live is still to struggle, one no longer struggles only to remain in the struggle, but in order to plunge into that "lake of the eternal" where Valverde de Lucena—the "submerged town"—lives so peacefully. A year after *Saint Emmanuel* was published, Unamuno made a resounding speech, on the occasion of his installation as "Perpetual Rector" of the University of Salamanca. The contents of this speech resemble, curiously enough, the contents of the short story; they both emphasize peace and restfulness. If Unamuno had been able to develop in the direction indicated, it is quite possible that his philosophical thought would have undergone drastic modifications, and that the present book, and not only the present chapter, would have been quite differently written.

For other reasons, *Peace in War* and *Saint Emmanuel the Good, Martyr* are exceptions to Unamuno's most characteristic approach to the problems of fiction. I have, accordingly, excluded them from our previous analysis. It would be unfair, however, to ignore them entirely. After all, the latter novel represents as much a beginning of what might have developed as a culmination of what was actually performed. As for the former, there are certain readily noticeable modes of expression beneath the obviously "oviparous" structure which belie Unamuno's own description of its nature. There is, for example, in the novel a persistent avoidance of all more or less "realistic" description of characters, even if the "bottom of the [characters'] souls" is not yet quite evident.

This last point deserves further elucidation. If we read *Peace in War* without much care, we find it very similar to many of the so-called (rather loosely so) "realistic nineteenth-century novels." It is quite obviously full of circumstantial description, historical references, many of them exact (as in the arrival of the king and his reception by the peasants). We find details of the past of some characters (for example, of José María de Arana's life). We also find vivid descriptions of events (witness the very "realistic" battle scenes). As if all this were not enough, many of the characters cross paths again and again, thus creating an "atmosphere." But on reflection we discover that the means of conveying all this differs from the "traditional" way in several crucial respects. Two examples will, I hope, suffice.

The first has been pointed out by Marías in his analysis of the novel. It refers to the account of the club members' arrival in the back room of Pedro Antonio's store. Each character has his own characteristic gesture—puffing, rubbing hands together, cleaning spectacles, taking off his coat. Yet these gestures are neither circumstantial nor merely "habitual," but truly "intimate" ones. If the objection is raised that the characters are still conditioned by the strictly personal background—which includes typical psychological traits no less than physical surroundings—the second example may be more convincing. It is a passage—by no means the only one of this type in the novel—in which the very existence of "things" is questioned by the author's peculiar way of describing them. Here Unamuno gives an account of the fear felt by Ignacio "when he hears the first shot." How does Unamuno convey this fear? Simply by writing that "the landscape began to melt before his eyes." This way of writing may today be trite, but in the midst of a still overpowering "realism" it was a novelty. For the landscape is not presented as a thing that surrounds the character, but as something that manifests itself in a rather astonishing manner: by "melting." Other passages in the same novel confirm our point: the landscape that surrounds Pachico is not one way or another, not clearly and unequivocally described by the novelist. It is not composed of one kind of tree or another or traversed by this or that river; it is something that flows from itself, blending with the individual whom it ought, in principle, to serve as mere "circumstance." To sum up: instead of beginning with the "exterior" in order to provide a frame for a character, the exterior is personified, tuned to the rhythm of the character's own existence.

This is, of course, entirely different from those methods that "realistic" authors like Pérez Galdós sometimes employ—for example, at the beginning of his novel *The Spendthrift* (*La de Bringas*). I have written "sometimes," because Pérez Galdós' realism is, to begin with, highly problematical, being often more "Unamunian" than he himself suspected. Furthermore, Unamuno's originality in this respect does not preclude his participation in the tradition of the Spanish novel which runs from *Don Quijote* down through not a few of Pérez Galdós' works. (*Mercy* [*Misericordia*] being a revealing example). A substantial element of this tradition is Unamunian *avant la lettre*. For most Spanish authors the novel is not a mirror carried along a highway, not the reflection of an impressionistic universe, and not even the single recounting of a series of human emotions. For them the novel is rather the description of a universe that is, at bottom, personal in nature. Unamuno continued, then, a certain literary tradition, but did not limit himself to repeating it. He gave it new life, and since he was a philosopher as much as, if not more than, a novelist, he managed finally to make it aware of itself.

29   THE WORLD AS A DIVINE NOVEL

As early as *Peace in War,* therefore, Unamuno's characters are described not as individuals (in the modern sense of the word *individual*) nor as psychological types, but as "little Gods." And this brings us to our second "basic reason" for Unamuno's novel writing—and to the central theme of the present chapter:

his wish to prove in a nondiscursive way that all dividing lines between "fiction" and "reality" must be erased once and for all.

This theme is, as we have pointed out, closely related to the one discussed in an earlier chapter: the essential type of "relation" that exists between an author and the characters he describes—or rather, creates. This relationship, analogous to the one that, according to Unamuno, existed between God and man, can be detailed in terms of the already mentioned dependency of "dreamer" and "the dreamed." This dependency is not a simple one. As a matter of fact, the term 'dependency' is rather inadequate in this connection. Just as the characters in a writer's novels rebel against his efforts to make them puppets of his own fancy, or mere loudspeakers of his opinions, the writer, in his turn, rebels against the possibility that his Author—or "the Dreamer"—may direct him according to His fancy. True enough, a writer may feel at times that he is living at the mercy of God's dream, a dream on the point of becoming a nightmare. Unamuno alluded to this feeling—he was obviously quite troubled by it—on several occasions. The appearance and disappearance of characters (and, for that matter, of all events) often seemed to him to mirror the movements of a "divine chess set," so much so that characters, events, and author seemed like nothing so much as pieces and pawns in a grandiose game. But this impression of Unamuno's vanished at once, for however closely the lives of the characters seem linked to the author's dreams, there was always the possibility that, as Unamuno noted in *Love and Pedagogy,* they could ad-lib. Like actors on a stage, men could often take advantage of the author's negligence to slip in some of their own words among those indicated in the script—this, of course, as a stopgap measure until they had a chance to write their own plays. And if they were caught ad-libbing, there would at least be the possibility of modifying the "text" by the inflection of their own "voices"—by their own "accent."

So if man's reality is, in a way, the contents of somebody else's dream, it is not entirely subject to the Dreamer's whims. What we call "a dream" is, in fact, a struggle between the Dreamer and the dreamed. This accounts for the fact that "to be real" means to be dreamed and at the same time to strive to escape the Dreamer's grasp. The dependency between the Dreamer and the dreamed is, basically, an interdependency, for even when the person dreamed finds the dream in which he lives most oppressive, he is still aware that he is capable of influencing the life, and hence the dreams, of his Dreamer—or his Author, for to dream and to create are two sides of the same coin.

Since the characters created by the novelist are related to the novelist just as the latter is related to God, we may be tempted to conclude that a "dream hierarchy" exists which could replace the "hierarchy of being," one in which man would occupy the middle point between two extremes: God, and the characters in novels. This conclusion, however, would be a rash generalization.

On the one hand, there are times when characters and author seem to play on the same field, both dependent upon God's dreams (God could be described here as the personification of "intrareality" and of "intrahistory" in the Unamunian sense). We might then conceive of God as the Supreme Poet or the Supreme Novelist—and that would be neither more nor less reasonable than imagining Him as the Supreme Watchmaker, the Supreme Geometrician, or the Supreme Calculator. "To dream the world" would be a way (perhaps not more metaphorical than most others) of saying "to make the world," or "to create the world." Human beings and the fictitious entities created by novelists would have the same type of being; they would both be describable only in terms of *who* they are (and not of *what* they are). And since God was also, for Unamuno, "each man's dream," there would be no way of telling who dreams whom precisely because everyone would be dreaming everyone else. On the other hand, all these realities are mixed together, and hence resist organization into any hierarchy on account of a presupposition that Unamuno believed to be plain fact: the impossibility of distinguishing between contemplation and action, between telling (or narrating) and doing—and, in general, as we have seen in other instances, between any opposing terms. Thus it would be incorrect to distinguish between an author and the characters he creates. The entire book— Unamuno would prefer to say "the entire cry"— entitled *How a Novel Is Made* (*Cómo se hace una novela*) repeats this point again and again. In this book we see how the character of a novel lives obsessed by the character in another novel. Their deaths should coincide, and for this reason whenever the former reads about what is happening to the latter he lives in a constant state of agony. The lives of the two characters are inextricably intertwined. Should we say that they are both real or that they are both fictitious? Physically speaking, of course, they are fictitious. But as persons, one is as real as is the other. And both are as real, or as fictitious, as their common dreamer, the novelist who created them and was constantly shaped, and therefore created, by them in the process. No true novel can be dismissed as "mere literature." In point of fact, there is no such thing as "mere literature." When a novel can be included in such a category, it is because it is not a novel or, for that matter, an author's book but a mere collection of meaningless words. To be sure, Unamuno could not prove, and did not attempt to prove, that "true literature is life and true life literature." But such an apothegm becomes clearer when we try to understand that unless a character is a puppet—and hence no character at all—he is, in a way, as real as his author. The so-called real persons cannot be distinguished, except by their lack of personality, from the so-called fictitious ones. Both live at the heart of that "mist" to which Unamuno insistently refers—and which may be understood as a further manifestation of that common realm in which all things live, at war and ever seeking peace. As a consequence, the Unamunian theory and practice of the novel appears as a fundamental aspect of his philosophy of tragedy—that tragedy made up of the dialectic of hope and despair.

It would be easy to argue that Unamuno's insistence on the lack of distinction between fiction and reality was merely the expression of a desire to confuse things, or at best to invert all relationships—between God and Nature, Nature and man, man and God, man and his creations, and so on. From a strictly conceptual point of view such an argument would be perfect. It would, however, miss the point, for Unamuno does not here pretend to explain reality, but to make it "coherent." To bring it closer to our experience as authors and readers of novels. From this point of view we can say that the characters in novels are the author's "dreams," while admitting that these characters "should speak for themselves," and be "spontaneous." These two assertions are not too difficult to reconcile provided we admit that the relative autonomy of these characters does not prevent their being ruled by the laws of a common world: the world of "reality-fiction." If the characters were simply fictitious, their independence of the author would be illusory; the author would always lead them by the hand. If they were merely real, on the other hand, their dependence on the author would be abolished; they would become so completely detached from him that they would no longer be characters, but "things."

This hybrid concept of "reality-fiction" offers a further advantage in that it allows us a new glimpse of the most persistent of all Unamunian themes: "the man of flesh and blood." It should by now be clear that this expression does not denote merely a biological entity *nor* a spiritual entity. These entities can be conceptualized by means of such categories as "the real," "the imaginary," and others of a similar kind. Men of flesh and blood, as people, cannot be so conceptualized. They do not belong to a definite order of being; they do not reveal themselves by being this or that, but by making, talking, suffering, enjoying and, of course, "agonizing." Now, these are the properties that belong both to "real people" and to characters in a story. If we still insist on using the verb 'to be' when speaking of them, it would be better to use it as a part of the expression 'the-will-to-be.' In the final analysis, it is the will-to-*be* as fully as possible—to be a person—that makes this "reality-fiction" the most authentic expression of the only truly human—and perhaps, divine—resource: ceaseless creativity, which is possibly another name for the Unamunian concept of "intrareality."

I have just written "human—and perhaps, divine." By forcing meanings—and interpretations—I might have written "human-divine." Has not Unamuno asked himself if the "intimate and supreme I" that he longed to be might not be God Himself? Has he not made it clear that whoever says "novelistic creation" is saying "theological and philosophical creation"? Has he not spoken of the consciousness of "my" body as if it were a "wave in the sea"? The reality of the world as God's dream is, apparently, a novel. But this novel is anchored in the ceaseless novelizing of mankind. A pawn in a divine game, mankind is ultimately, according to Unamuno, the substance of God's dream.

Chapter Seven

The Idea of Reality

30 THE MEANINGS OF 'IS REAL'

Some philosophers have given the predicate 'is real' an explicit meaning; indeed, a substantial portion of their work is devoted to a clarification of the meaning of such a predicate. It was relatively easy for these philosophers to arrive at their conception or idea of reality. Thus, we can describe, or at least discuss, what 'is real' meant to Plato, Aristotle, Hume, or Kant. Other philosophers, however, have never given the question "What does 'is real' mean?" (or, in a more ontological vocabulary: "What is Reality?") an explicit answer. And yet they have nevertheless underwritten a conception or idea of reality; it is just that they have never expressed this idea in terms of analysis or definition. It was very difficult (although not impossible) for such philosophers to know what they felt, philosophically speaking, Reality was.

Unamuno belongs to this latter group. He was, in fact, one of its most typical members, for he never attempted to enlighten his readers as to the meaning (or meanings) he gave the predicate 'is real.' This is, by the way, one of the reasons why he has often been denied the status of philosopher. But this and all other reasons like it, in the main, are quite inconclusive, unless we have a very definite and rather narrow idea of what 'to be a philosopher' means. We may, of course, subscribe to a limited idea, but then neither Kierkegaard nor Nietzsche could be treated as philosophers. If, as I believe, Kierkegaard and Nietzsche were philosophers, then Unamuno was also one. This is why we may submit his apparently nonphilosophical ideas and arguments to a philosophical clarification.

Unamuno fought unceasingly against all abstractions, even while proclaiming the need of paying heed to "realities." As I have said, however, he never made clear what he meant by 'reality.' Philosophers may claim that he even did just the opposite: confused the issue by pointing out that the supreme reality of his—"the man of flesh and blood"—was also a kind of fiction created by a dreamer, at the same time announcing that he considered the fictitious characters in novels to be also, in a very important sense, "real." It would seem, then, that the meaning of the predicate 'is real' in Unamuno's thought was either hopelessly ambiguous or unnecessarily unfathomable. There is apparently no rational approach to the problem, so that the only thing to do is to repeat or reformulate some of Unamuno's contradictions and paradoxes.

On a closer inspection of his writings we find that although Unamuno never attempted to define the meaning of the predicate 'is real,' he was always intent upon representing (by means of descriptions and intuitions) the form and substance of "true realities." Furthermore, he refused to admit that any of the metaphysical entities hailed by some philosophers—matter, mind, ideas, values, and so forth—were in any fundamental sense "real." With the help of these descriptions and intuitions we can reconstruct to some degree Unamuno's idea of reality.

31 WHAT REALITY IS NOT

I will begin by recapitulating Unamuno's reactions to some of the traditional metaphysical entities that philosophers have misused by always presenting them in the guise of absolutes.

Since Unamuno insisted so earnestly on the idea that all beings have "souls" and "innards"—although these are "corporeal souls and innards"—we may suppose that he thought appearances concealed the "true realities," and that the latter were like absolute beings hidden in the core of phenomena. But this supposition would prove to be incorrect. Unamuno never defended a substantialist philosophy as against a phenomenalistic one, nor did he ever pit the latter against the former. For Unamuno there is no thing-in-itself, no metaphysically absolute nature beyond or beneath sensible things. There is nothing that corresponds to Ideas, Substances, or Forms. Things-in-themselves are for him far too abstract and too remote when compared with the "concrete realities" with which we come in contact and to which we cling—such realities as "men of flesh and blood," "*this* character in a novel," "*this* landscape," "*this* star in the sky." To a certain extent, if any 'ism' fits Unamuno at all, it is "radical empiricism." For, whenever Unamuno seems about to accept some metaphysical entity—e.g., the Schopenhauerian Will—it is only in order to strike an immediate blow against all that is abstract in it. Philosophers have often sought "what is most real," but they have always ended by depriving it of reality *simpliciter.* It is most probable that Unamuno would have subscribed to Goethe's well-known verses:

Natur hat weder Kern noch Schale
Alles ist sie mit einemale

("Nature has neither shell nor kernel, it is everything at once"), provided the German poet was ready to include in Nature things he had originally not meant to include.

Nor is reason—or, if one prefers, Reason—real. The world is not crystal-clear, not logical. It is not transparent, but resistant and opaque. When Hegel said that the rational was real and the real rational, he was not speaking, Unamuno surmised, as a philosopher, and much less as a "man of flesh and blood"; he spoke as a bureaucrat. To be sure, reason must not be discarded; Unamuno said more than once that "the reprisals of reason" were absolutely necessary because they bring us into abrupt contact with doubt, and without doubt we cannot stumble upon reality. But reason-in-itself is far from being a real entity: it is one of the extremes between which "we move and are." Nor can the irrational-in-itself be real, for analogous reasons, because to say that the world is, at bottom, irrational, or is "*the* Irrational," is to seek comfort and shun tragedy, that is to say, life. "The Rational" and "the Irrational" are, therefore, nothing more than the metaphorical hypostases invented by philosophers in order to exorcise their spleen—or in order to assuage their desperation.

32   WHAT REALITY IS LIKE

To the above negations others might be added, but those already noted will suffice for our purpose. We can now turn to more positive statements about the basic characteristics of reality. Needless to say, we shall not find "propositions" about the nature of reality in Unamuno's works. On the other hand, we can find numerous descriptions of "what is truly real." These descriptions are patent because of Unamuno's preference for certain terms that he systematically used whenever he meant to convey the impression that he was face to face with true realities. A "linguistic approach" to our problem—in a rather broad sense of the term 'linguistic'—is inescapable; I will therefore attempt to reconstruct Unamuno's idea of reality on the basis of an examination of his language.

Above all, the innermost is real for Unamuno. Words such as 'innards,' 'intimate,' 'pithy,' 'bones,' 'marrow,' 'mesentery,' 'hidden,' 'chasm,' 'abyss,' 'bottom,' 'depth,' 'unfathomable,' 'substantial,' 'soul,' and the like play a fundamental role in Unamuno's thought. These are not, however, terms that purport to designate constitutionally "hidden" realities, and even less "things-in-themselves," since they always refer to what has a decidedly visible, tangible, and palpable aspect. The identification of the real with something "metaphysical," or with something "within," "beneath," or "beyond" appearances is one thing;

the constant "going inward" of the real so often emphasized by Unamuno is another. The innermost is not hidden, nor is it merely on the surface. Strictly speaking, it cannot be said to fall into any of the categories currently used by many philosophers—being as opposed to appearance, reality to its manifestations, noumena to phenomena, and so forth since it possesses a peculiar status: that of manifesting itself *according* to the degree of its intimacy. Not by constituting the foundation of the apparent, nor by being what is apparent, but by becoming apparent *as* foundation. Or, to put it another way: the innermost is the "within" of things to the degree that it is deprived of a "without." For this reason it has two constant characteristics. On the one hand, it is something that moves with a movement similar to that of living— its throbbing, trembling, and pulsating can be perceived. This is why the innards of which Unamuno spoke are always "palpitating innards." On the other hand, it is something that never slackens, that flows ceaselessly: the innermost is inexhaustible. This is why it can be thought of as the analogue of certain physical processes—jet, source, spring, fountain—which frequently, and not by chance, provide the subject matter of poetic description. Like the *physis* of the pre-Socratics, the innermost flows perennially from its own reservoir. Thus we may conclude that the real is always the intrareal—just as history was, as we have seen, intrahistory—if we always keep in mind that there is no strict opposition between an "intra" and an "extra," nor even less, a reduction of one to the other. For once the battle has subsided for lack of combatants. If the innermost struggles, as does everything, with itself, it does not do so in the sense that its being opposes its becoming, or vice versa: the opposition takes the same form as that in which our intimacy—all open and palpitating—fights with itself. Thus what we call "the true reality" is not matter or spirit, flesh or soul, because it can be, and usually is, both. Intramatter is just as real as intraspirit. Only "matter as such" and "spirit as such" are not real; they are mere abstractions lacking in movement, in flowing and overflowing force, devoid of incessantly palpitating intimacy.

The "serious" is real and with it, above all, the dense (*lo denso*). It is easy to see to what extent everything that is swift, lucid, voluble, playful, insinuating, suggestive, allusive, and ironical is alien to the cosmos of Unamuno. But this does not mean that his is a dull universe drowned in circumspection and composure; on the contrary, it continually erupts with shouts, imprecations, and even altercations. Nonetheless, all this is somehow contained within the tightly packed, firm silence of which we said the needlework pattern of Unamuno's life consisted. This seriousness manifests itself in two basic ways. On the one hand, as something possessing a tightly woven, tough texture, hard, if not impossible, to break. The real, to the degree that it is serious, is something vigorous; hard—frequently coarse and unpleasant—and consequently just the opposite of anything that is smooth, fine, polished, pretty, flexible, graceful. On the other hand, the real shows itself as something possessing corporeality or, as Unamuno so often said, bulk; the tangible is real and, above all, the palpable is real. The models for these characterizations of the real are evidently certain physical objects—I would almost say, macrophysical ones. But they are also certain sensations whose grossness is not always to be confused with roughness. Although predominantly "physical," the traits of the real that we have mentioned are not the exclusive attributes of matter; ideals too, if they truly are ideals instead of dissolving abstractions, possess, according to Unamuno, this seriousness and density that make them firm and bulky, almost corporeal. Like the innermost, the serious and bulky are to be found at the bottom of all that is material *and* all that is spiritual inasmuch as they have a consistency, that is, a density.

The abrupt is real, if it is understood not as one of the many possible synonyms for what is harsh and uneven, but as denoting a mode of being characterized by discontinuity. Here the abrupt is, then, a "leap." To a certain extent it may be understood by analogy with the Kierkegaardian notion "the leap." Like that notion, the Unamunian intuition of a leap is equally opposed to any principle of continuity or to a mediation that would reconcile opposites. In philosophical terms, it is equally opposed to Leibnizianism and Hegelianism. The real does not stretch out in a continuous line. Nor does it constitute a logico-metaphysical system that is dependent upon a foreseeable Becoming explained by means of some "dialectical method." What I have suggested here as "explanation" is rather a "decision"—and one that presupposes absurdity and paradox. And yet, the "real" man—the "authentic" man—is not the one who hides behind his social cover, his everyday gestures and conventional words, but he who reveals himself abruptly in all his contradictory being. And reality itself, for Unamuno, is not a more or less rough stratum beneath a smooth surface, but at one and the same time the polished *and* the rough. It will be seen that here again there is for Unamuno no kernel beneath the shell, but a kernel and a shell viewed in cross section from the moment of their birth to the moment of their death.

What Unamuno sometimes called "the contradictory," and what is more properly labeled "the constant conflict of opposites," is also real. The real exists in a state of combat—at war with an opposite and at war with itself. Here we have one of the pillars—not to say the axis—of this book. Let us only recall that for Unamuno war was so fundamental that, not content with declaring it ever-present, he concluded that it makes war on itself and, furthermore, that it fights continually with its antagonist, peace, giving no quarter. Peace is to be found in the heart of war and vice versa: without war there is no possible peace. The struggle between opposites and of each opposite with itself is not, therefore, the result of a logical contradiction; it is the very core of the tragic dynamism of life. The motor of this interminable movement is a conflict whose ontological nature must always be kept in mind: it derives from the eagerness of each being to remain itself while striving to become what other beings are, and hence, longing to cease being what it is. The formal pattern of this struggle is the opposition between the limited and the unlimited. This opposition is apparent everywhere, but it is most obvious in the struggles that Unamuno has most often described: those between fictitious characters and their creators, between what one intends to be and what one is, between man and God.

That which lasts—or, if one prefers, that which is everlasting—is also real. Not, of course, the intemporal and abstractly eternal, but the permanently concrete. This last can be understood in two ways. First, as something whose permanence is being continuously produced or created; true permanence is, Unamuno believes, the result of effort, of an act of will, of a *conatus*, to such an extent that there is no fundamental difference between being and wishing to be. Second, as something whose duration is constantly threatened by annihilation; just as war is the guarantee of peace, death—the imminence of death— is the guarantee of life. To last forever is not to go on existing, to continue to be; it is the unceasing conquest of its own being. This explains why for Unamuno to live was primarily "to agonize," that is, to fight against death.

And finally, whatever feels or, as Unamuno has written, "whatever suffers, has pity and yearns," is real. This has led him to identify reality with consciousness and even to maintain that "the only substantial reality is consciousness." By this time it should no longer be necessary to warn the reader against the tendency to interpret such a phrase in any idealistic sense. Unamuno is not an idealist or a realist for the simple reason that for him suffering, pitying, and relishing constitute ways of being real that affect both the consciousness *and* things. The mode of being of things cannot be deduced, even by analogy, from that of the consciousness: "to feel" is, strictly speaking, "to react"—and to react strongly, with vigor and vehemence. The universe *qua* "sensitive beings" is, therefore, a universe *qua* active being which changes, transforms itself, struggles to be, and even "despairs" of ever being what it wishes to be. Just as the attributes of bulk and palpableness may be imputed to ideas, so that of consciousness may be applied to things, if, of course, we avoid the error of supposing that we are only projecting our consciousness upon them. Therefore, true reality is never passivity. What has been called "consciousness" is, in ultimate terms, a means—however insufficient and equivocal—of recognizing that only what refuses to cease to be really is.

Unamuno

NOTES

A preliminary note

There are two reasons why I have not indicated the places in Unamuno's writings to which the reader might turn for the material quoted or referred to in the text. First, because I have tried to "absorb" Unamuno's ideas and present them only after they were sufficiently "digested." Second, and most important, because any reference to Unamunian texts would be incomplete unless it were tiresomely detailed. Unamuno presented his central ideas frequently and in the most varied places. He drew attention to this tendency of his to repeat his themes and ideas in an article that appeared in the review *Caras y Caretas* of Buenos Aires on September 23, 1923. There he remarked that "the greatest writers have spent their lives reiterating a few points, always the same ones; polishing and re-polishing them, seeking the most perfect, the definitive expression of them." It is hardly necessary to add that this idea about reiteration was, in its turn, reiterated by Unamuno on several occasions.

Although I have taken into account almost all of Unamuno's vast production, at the beginning of each of the notes for the seven chapters I have indicated various of his works in which the material discussed in that chapter appears in particular concentration. In the remaining part of these chapter notes I have done no more than point out certain secondary sources that treat in full detail the various points debated in the text of the chapter.

I have also clarified briefly some terms or problems with which the English reader may not be familiar. But I have not offered additional information about Spanish authors mentioned in the text—for example, the members of the Generation of 1898 and the generation immediately preceding it—because what I might have added there would not have been directly important to an understanding of this book. The reader may easily avail himself of sources (encyclopedias and histories of literature) which will supply the required information. The same applies to other than Spanish authors mentioned occasionally. In most instances these names—Schopenhauer or Kierkegaard—are well enough known. For the rest no more need be known of an author for the purposes of this book than what is adduced in the text. The translations of passages from Unamuno's works have been done directly from the original.

100   THREE SPANISH PHILOSOPHERS

Note to chapter one

In the third section of the bibliography I have included only those works that are of interest for the understanding and interpretation of Unamuno's philosophical thought, or his literary style whenever this is intimately linked with the expression of that thought. Some of these works contain biographical data. For more detailed information about Unamuno's life the reader is referred to Luis S. Granjel's *Retrato de Unamuno* (Madrid, 1957) and to A. Sánchez-Barbudo's *Estudios sobre Unamuno y Machado* (Madrid, 1959), pages 13–198. Additional bibliography by the editor: M. Rudd, *The Lone Heretic: A Biography of Miguel de Unamuno* (Austin, 1963); E. Salcedo, *Vida de Don Miguel* (Salamanca, 1970); M. Villamor, *Unamuno, su vida y obra* (Madrid, 1970); P. Cerezo Galán, *Las máscaras de lo trágico: filosofía y tragedia en M. de Unamuno* (Madrid: Trotta, 1996); J. Marías, *Miguel de Unamuno* (Madrid: Espasa Calpe, 1997).

From among the multitude of studies on the Spanish Generation of 1898 I particularly recommend Pedro Laín Entralgo's *La generación del noventa y ocho* (Madrid, 1945) and the anthology, *The Generation of 1898 and After* (New York–Toronto, 1960) prepared by Beatrice P. Patt and Martin Nozick. This latter work contains brief introductory notes in English which head the various Spanish texts by Angel Ganivet, Ramón María del Valle-Inclán, Pío Baroja, Azorín, Antonio Machado, and others. Additional bibliography by the editor: Ricardo Gullón, *La invención del 98 y otros ensayos* (Madrid, 1969); H. R. Ramsden, *The 1898 Movement in Spain* (Manchester, 1974); Donald L. Shaw, *The Generation of 1898 in Spain* (New York, 1975); Carlos Blanco Aguinaga, *Juventud del 98* (Barcelona, 1978); Pilar Navarro Ranninger (ed.), *La literatura española en torno al 1900: modernismo y "98"* (Madrid, 1994); José Luis Bernal Muñoz, *La generación del 1898: ¿invención o realidad?* (Valencia, 1996).

The term *Krausistas* designates a group of philosophers, notably Julián Sanz del Río (1814–1869), who were influenced by the German idealist Karl Christian Friedrich Krause (1781–1832) and various of his disciples. Spanish Krausism, however, was much more than a simple adaptation of a foreign philosophical system, with a complexity and an autonomous growth of its own. The reader may consult Pierre Jobit's *Les éducateurs de l'Espagne moderne*, 2 vols. (I. *Les krausistes*; II. *Lettres inédites de J. Sanz del Río*) (Paris, 1936) and Juan López-Morillas' *El krausismo español* (México, 1956). Additional bibliography by the editor: Juan José Gil Cremades, *El reformismo español. Krausismo, escuela histórica, neotomismo* (Barcelona, 1969); Elías Díaz, *La filosofía social del krausismo español* (Madrid, 1973); Fernando Martín Buezas, *El krausismo español desde dentro: Sanz del Río autobiografiada intimidad* (Madrid, 1978); Juan López-Morillas, *The Krausist Movement and Ideological Change in Spain, 1854–1874* (Cambridge, 1981); Ricardo Baroja, *Gente del 98* (Madrid, 1989).

Francisco Ayala's idea about Unamuno may be found in the article "La perspectiva hispánica," included in his book *Razón del mundo* (Buenos Aires, 1944), pages 117–164.

Unamuno's "religious crisis," placed in or about the year 1897, has been studied in detail by A. Sánchez-Barbudo in various works: see, among them, op. cit., especially pages 43–79; "La formación del pensamiento de Unamuno: una experiencia decisiva, la crisis de 1897," Hispanic Review, XVIII (1950), 218–243, included in his book *Estudios sobre Galdós, Unamuno y Machado*, 2d. ed. (Madrid, 1968, particularly pp. 67–290).

"Silence" in the life of Unamuno, and his aspiration to "plunge into the eternal" (*zambullirse en lo eterno*) which he expressed in his work on numerous occasions, are a proof that together with the conflictive mode of our author there is also a contemplative one. I have alluded to this latter mode in the present book, particularly in chapter six. The contemplative mode in Unamuno's life and work has been carefully studied by Carlos Blanco Aguinaga in *El Unamuno contemplativo* (Mexico, 1959).

Note to chapter two

The basic works for this chapter are *Del sentimiento trágico de la vida, Ensayos V, Mi religión y otros ensayos, Rosario de sonetos líricos, Rimas de dentro,* and *Niebla*. The first of these is the most important, but, as I have mentioned above, Unamuno constantly returned to the same ideas from various angles, so that there are few of his writings that do not contain some reference to one of his most central themes: the reality of the man of flesh and blood, and the relation of this man to the world and to God. Then, too, the theme of the perpetual tension between opposites is not just an idea with Unamuno, but also a form of expression. This is why all of Unamuno's work is pertinent in this respect.

With regard to the much-debated question of the relation between Unamuno and Kierkegaard, it should be noted that very likely the first discovered the writings of the second only after he had developed ideas of his own similar to those of Kierkegaard. At the same time it is also likely that the reading of Kierkegaard helped Unamuno reaffirm and develop these ideas. The problem has been dealt with by P. Mesnard and R. Ricard, and above all by F. Meyer, in those works by these authors mentioned in the third section of the bibliography. Additional bibliography by the editor: A. Regalado García, *El siervo y el señor. La dialéctica agónica de Miguel de Unamuno* (Madrid, 1968); J. A. Collado, *Kierkegaard y Unamuno* (Madrid, 1970); and also the articles by D. D. Palmer and R. Webber mentioned in the bibliography.

A thorough examination of the influences exercised upon Unamuno throughout a lifetime of reading would demand a separate book. He was a voracious reader who easily assimilated all that he read, and retained most of it for a long time, thanks to a prodigious memory. Furthermore, his reading was tremendously varied. Unamuno read whatever came his way, and this was no small amount; he read classical and modern authors, poets and philosophers, historians and scientists. And he read not only books, but countless articles and essays in reviews and newspapers. Of the philosophers, Unamuno read the greater part of those most influential in his day and ken with a passionate interest—Kant, Hegel, Schopenhauer, Spencer, and also William James and others. He read materialists and spiritualists, realists and idealists. But once the influence of this reading has been established, the most important point to remember is that "absorption" best characterizes the method of Unamuno's reading. Even when he attacked them, he made those writers that he read "his" and, at times, even more securely "his" the harsher and more severe the attack. That Unamuno so often mentioned his reading in what he wrote, even the most recent of it—in many of his essays he would speak of books he was currently reading—should not lead us to the conclusion that there was a simple cause-and-effect relationship between these current readings and his own ideas of the moment. There was rather what might best be called a "resonance" between them—a concept as fertile as it is hard to define.

Note to chapter three

For the fullest understanding of this chapter, besides *Del sentimiento trágico de la vida* and *La agonía del cristianismo*—and the latter is a basic source for Unamuno's ideas on Christianity and history—all of those works must be kept in mind wherein the desire for an "eternity one is constantly striving for" is expressed, which appears in both of Unamuno's modes: that of perpetual tension or conflict and that of perpetual contemplation—and quite possibly in the dialogue between the two. In this respect, see *Paz en la guerra* and *San Manuel Bueno, mártir, Ensayos I, II, V* (and in this volume of essays, particularly the one entitled "¡Plenitud de plenitudes y todo plenitud!"), *Mi religión y otros ensayos, Rosario de sonetos líricos,* and *Vida de Don Quijote y Sancho.* See also *El Cristo de Velázquez* and at least some of the poems in *Romancero del destierro.*

The manner in which Unamuno used—and, consciously or not, falsified—the Spinozian notion of *conatus* has been studied by François Meyer in his book *L'ontologie de Miguel de Unamuno* (Paris, 1955), pages 5 ff.

I have used the expression "The Great Chain of Being" as detailed in the well-known book by A. O. Lovejoy, *The Great Chain of Being* (1936), but in a more limited sense. The Hellenistic, the Christian, and the Hellenic-Christian "doctrinal complexes" have been considerably simplified in my exposition, but there was no need to treat them *in extenso* in order to set down Unamuno's attitude toward them.

The quotation from V. Nabokov is from his novel *Invitation to a Beheading.*

Note to chapter four

For this chapter, the basic texts are *Vida de Don Quijote y Sancho* and the appendix to *Del sentimiento trágico de la vida* entitled "Don Quijote en la tragicomedia europea contemporánea." The reader is also referred to *Ensayos I, II* (in this last see particularly the essay "¡Adentro!"), *VII,* and the collection of essays *De esto y aquello,* volume III. Certain differences between *Ensayos I* and *Vida de Don Quijote Y Sancho* have been omitted because they were not pertinent to the exposition of our thesis. A great number of Unamuno's ideas on Spain appear in the descriptions of landscape in his "travel books." See, for instance, *Por tierras de Portugal y España, Andanzas y visiones españolas,* and the posthumous collection, *Paisajes del alma.* For Unamuno's interest in South American authors, see *De esto y aquello I.*

The bibliography on the so-called "problem of Spain" is without end. Closely connected with the discussions of this problem is the "controversy over Spanish science" to which Unamuno referred on many occasions, particularly in his writings between 1897 and 1905.

For Ortega y Gasset's attitude toward Unamuno on the question of the "europeanization" of Spain, see my book *Ortega y Gasset: An Outline of His Philosophy,* 2d. ed. (New Haven, Connecticut: Yale, 1975), reedited in this volume.

The ideas of Américo Castro to which I have referred in this chapter are to be found throughout that author's writings of the last fifteen years; of primary importance is his *The Structure of Spanish History* (translated by Edmund L. King; Princeton, 1954).

Note to chapter five

I have already referred in the text to various works of Unamuno which are important in this chapter. Here, however, I might also indicate *Ensayos III, IV, V*, and part of *Ensayo VII*, the novels *Amor y Pedagogía* and *Niebla*, the short stories in *Tres novelas ejemplares y un prólogo* (especially the "prólogo"), *Cómo se hace una novela*, and *De esto y aquello II*. Also important are the articles collected by Manuel García Blanco under the title "La raza y la lengua" in volume VI of the *Obras completas*, and the revealing series of articles on style entitled "Alrededor del estilo" in volume IV of the *Obras completas* (and in *De esto y aquello II*). See also Unamuno's "Oración inaugural del Curso académico 1934–35" [29 September 1934], delivered at the University of Salamanca and collected in volume VII of *Obras completas*. Also there are several important allusions to the "word" as "living word" and as "poetry" in *Del sentimiento trágico de la vida*.

Perhaps more than to any other of his concerns, Unamuno returned again and again to the subject of this chapter. Since he felt he was a "voice" whose mission was to awaken, stimulate, and even irritate his readers in order to lead them into themselves, there is not a single one of Unamuno's writings without some bearing, direct or indirect, on the problem of the nature and function of the "word."

The quotation from Jean Cassou is from his preface to the French edition (1925) of *Cómo se hace una novela*: "Comment on fait un roman," Mercure de France, CLXXXVII (1926), 13–19.

The words of Ernst Robert Curtius are from his article on Unamuno in *Die neue Rundschau* (1926), 163–181, reprinted in *Kritische Essays zur europäischen Literatur* (Bern, 1950), pp. 224–246.

Note to chapter six

All of Unamuno's novels and short stories are important as background material for this chapter. The most famous of these have been mentioned in the text; the rest are included in the first section of the bibliography. In order to understand how Unamuno understood and created his fictional works, one should at least read *Paz en la guerra, Niebla, Tres novelas ejemplares y un prólogo*, and *San Manuel Bueno, mártir*.

Many of the problems raised by the "fictional character" and his relation to "reality" are intimately related to the problems posed by the nature of man and his relation to God. Therefore, since the nature of man and his relation to God were treated in chapter two, the reader should consult not only those works mentioned in the present note but also those in the note to chapter two. The two plays, *El otro* and *El hermano Juan o El mundo es teatro*, should also be consulted in connection with the present chapter.

The thesis of Julián Marías is advanced in his book *Miguel de Unamuno* (Madrid, 1943) and in the prologue that he wrote to the edition of Unamuno's *Obras Selectas* (Madrid: Editorial Plenitud, 1950, pp. 11–37).

In this chapter I have dealt with the question of a "contemplative" Unamuno—in no way incompatible with our "conflictive" Unamuno—which Carlos Blanco Aguinaga has subsequently made the subject of a book mentioned in the note to chapter one, *ad finem.*

Note to chapter seven

This chapter is an attempt at descriptive ontology based upon language, that is, upon the author's use of language. It may also be taken as an example of description of "the world of an author"—using the term "world" in a sense that I intend to clarify in a future book on the question. Unamuno's entire work ought to be examined to this end, with primary attention being given to those words and expressions which recur most frequently, and to any other words and expressions which constitute variations on, or shadings of, these.

Miguel De Unamuno

BIOGRAPHICAL NOTE

1864   Born in Bilbao, September 29.
1870   Death of his father.
1875   Studies for Bachillerato degree.
1880   Studies philosophy in the Facultad de Filosofía y Letras, Madrid.
1882   Beginning of his period of atheistic humanism.
1883   Degree in Philosophy.
1884   Completes Ph.D. Thesis. Returns to Bilbao.
1886   Started writing *Filosofía lógica,* an unpublished manuscript.
1888   Competes unsuccessfully for the Chair in the Basque Language, Instituto Vizcaíno.
1891   Marries Concepción Lizárraga. Obtains the Chair in Greek at the University of Salamanca. Resides in Salamanca.
1894   Joins the Socialist Party.
1895   *En torno al casticismo.* (The first four essays.)
1897   *Paz en la guerra.* Gives up membership in the Socialist Party. Religious crisis in Alcalá.
1900   President of the University of Salamanca. Founded the Chair of Comparative Philology.
1902   *Amor y pedagogía.*
1903   *De mi país.* Polemic against Bishop Cámara.
1905   *Vida de Don Quijote y Sancho.* Alfonso XII Great Cross.
1908   Polemic against Ramiro de Maeztu. *Recuerdos de niñez y mocedad.*
1909   Polemic against Ortega y Gasset. First performance of *La Esfinge,* Las Palmas.
1910   *Mi religión y otros ensayos breves.*
1911   *Rosario de sonetos líricos, Una historia de amor, Por tierras de Portugal y España.*
1912   *Contra esto y aquello, Soliloquios y conversaciones.*
1913   *Del sentimiento trágico de la vida.*

1914   *Niebla.* The Minister of Public Instruction and Arts compels him
        to resign from the presidency of the University of Salamanca.
        Strong support of Unamuno throughout the country.
1916   *En torno al casticismo.*
1917   *Abel Sánchez: una historia de pasión.*
1918   First performance of *Fedra*, Ateneo, Madrid.
1920   Prosecuted on occasion of an article against the King. *Tres novelas
        ejemplares y un prólogo, El Cristo de Velázquez.*
1921   Vice-president of the University of Salamanca. Dean of College.
        La tía Tula, Fedra, Soledad, Raquel.
1922   *Andanzas y visiones españolas.*
1923   Confined to the Isle of Fuerteventura (Canary Islands) for
        criticism of the government.
1924   Escapes from Fuerteventura. Chooses voluntary exile in Paris.
        Deprived of his Chair.
1925   Resides in Hendaya. *De Fuerteventura a París, La agonía del
        cristianismo* (French edition).
1927   *Romancero del destierro.*
1930   Returns to Salamanca, Spain. Recovers Chair in History of the
        Spanish Language.
1931   President of the University of Salamanca. Elected Representative
        for Salamanca. *La agonía del cristianismo* (Spanish edition).
1932   *El otro.*
1933   *San Manuel Bueno, mártir ye tres historias más.*
1934   Doctor *honoris causa*, University of Grenoble. His wife dies. He
        retires. He is named Honorary President of the University of
        Salamanca. The University creates a Chair in his honor.
1936   Doctor *honoris causa*, University of Oxford. Message on the Civil
        War. Quarrels with the fascist leader Millán Astray. He is obliged
        to resign from his Honorary Presidency of the University. The
        Chair in his honor is suppressed. Donates his Library to the
        University of Salamanca. Dies in Salamanca, December 31.

UNAMUNO'S WORKS

Only books are listed. Dates refer to the first printing.

"En torno al casticismo," in *La España moderna* (Madrid, 1895); with the
same title, *En torno al casticismo,* in book (Barcelona, 1902); later, reprinted
in *Ensayos, I* (1916).

Paz en la guerra (Madrid, 1897)
De la enseñanza superior en España (Madrid, 1899)
Tres ensayos (Madrid, 1900) [includes "¡Adentro!," "La ideocracia," "La fe,"
    later reprinted in *Ensayos II*]
Amor y pedagogía (Barcelona, 1902; includes the appendix "Apuntes para un
    tratado de cocotología")
Paisajes (Salamanca, 1902)
De mis país. Descripciones, relatos y artículos de costumbres (Madrid, 1903)
*Vida de Don Quijote y Sancho, según Miguel de Cervantes Saavedra, explicada y
    comentada* (Madrid, 1905; 2d enl. ed., Madrid, 1914)
Poesías (Bilbao, 1907)
Recuerdos de ninez mocedad (Madrid, 1908)
Mi religión y otros ensayos (Madrid, 1910)
Rosario de sonetos líricos (Madrid, 1911)
Por tierras de Portugal y Espana (Madrid, 1911)
Soliloquios y conversaciones (Madrid, 1911)
Contra esto y aquello (Madrid, 1912)
El porvenir de Espana (Madrid, 1942) [Unamuno-Ganivet correspondence
    previously published in the newspaper, *El Defensor de Granada, 1897*]
Del sentimiento trágico de la vida en los hombres y en los pueblos (Madrid, 1913)
El espejo de la muerte (Novelas cortas) (Madrid, 1913)
Niebla (Nivola) (Madrid, 1914)
Ensayos, 7 vols., Madrid. Vols. I, II, III, 1916; Vols. IV, V, 1917; Vols. VI, VII,
    1918

Volume I: En torno al casticismo. Cinco ensayos:

La tradición eterna, 1895.
La casta histórica Castilla, 1895.
El espíritu castellano, 1895.
De mística y humanismo, 1895.
Sobre el marasmo actual de España, s.f.

Volume II:

La enseñanza del latín en España, 1894.
La regeneración del teatro español, 1896.
El caballero de la triste figura (ensayo iconológico), 1896.
Acerca de la refoŕma de la ortografía castellana, 1896.
La vida es sueño (Reflexiones sobre la regeneración de España), 1898.

¡Adentro!, 1900.
La ideocracia, 1900.
La fe, 1900.

Volume III:

La dignidad humana, s.f.
La crisis del patriotismo, s.f.
La juventud "intelectual" española, 1896.
Civilización y cultura, s.f.
La reforma del castellano (Prólogo de un libro en prensa), 1911.
Sobre la lengua española, 1901.
La educación, 1902. Prólogo a la obra, del mismo título, de Carlos Octavio
    Bunge.
Maese Pedro (Notas sobre Carlyle), 1902.
Ciudad y campo (De mis impresiones de Madrid), 1902.
La cuestión del vascuence, 1902.

Volume IV:

Contra el purismo, 1903.
Viejos y jóvenes (Prolegómenos), 1902.
El individualismo español (A propósito del libro de Martin A. S. Hume)
    The Spanish People: Their Origin, Growth and Influence, London, 1901),
    1902.
Sobre el fulanismo, 1903.
Religión y patria, 1904.
La selección de los Fulánez, 1903.
La lectura del doctor Montarco, 1904.
Intelectualidad y espiritualidad, 1904.

Volume V:

Almas de jóvenes, 1904.
Sobre la filosofia española (Diálogo), 1904.
¡Plenitud de plenitudes y todo plenitud!, 1904.
El perfecto pescador de caña (Después de leer a Walton), 1904.
A lo que salga, 1904.
Sobre la soberbia, 1904.
Los naturales y los espirituales, 1905.
Sobre la lectura e interpretación del Quijote, 1905.

Volume VI:

¿Ramplonería¡, 1905.
Soledad, 1905.
Sobre la erudición y la crítica, 1905.
Poesía y oratoria, 1905.
La crisis actual del patriotismo español, 1905.
Sobre el rango y el mérito (Divagaciones), 1906.
La patria y el Ejército, 1906.
¿Qué es verdad?, 1906.

Volume VII:

Más sobre la crisis del patriotismo, 1906.
El secreto de la vida, 1906.
Sobre la consecuencia, la sinceridad, 1906.
Algunas consideraciones sobre la literatura hispano-americana (A propósito de un libro peruano), 1906.
Sobre la europeización (Arbitrariedades), 1906.
Sobre la tumba de Costa (A la más clara memoria de un espíritu sincero), 1911.

Abel Sánchez (Una historia de pasión) (Madrid, 1917)
El Cristo de Velázquez, Poema (Madrid, 1920)
Tres novelas ejemplares y un prólogo (Madrid, 1920; includes: "Dos madres," "El marqués de Lumbría," "Nada menos que todo un hombre")
La tía Tula (Madrid, 1921)
Andanzas y visiones españolas (Madrid, 1922)
Rimas de dentro (Valladolid, 1923)
Teresa: rimas de un poeta desconocido (Madrid, 1923)
Fedra. Ensayo dramático (1924)
Todo un hombre (from the novel entitled *Nada menos que todo un hombre,* 1925)
De Fuerteventura a París. Diario íntimo de confinamiento y destierro vertido en sonetos (Paris, 1925)
Cómo se hace una novela (Buenos Aires, 1927. The Spanish text is fuller than the one published in French; translated by Jean Cassou, entitled *Comment on fait un roman,* Mercure de France, CLXXXVII, 1926, 13–39)
Romancero del destierro (Buenos Aires, 1928)
Dos artículos y dos discursos (Madrid, 1930)   ·
La agonía del cristianismo (Madrid, 1931) [French translation by Jean Cassou, *L'agonie du christianisme,* published in Paris, 1925]

El otro. Misterio en tres jornadas y un epílogo (1932)
San Manuel Bueno, mártir y tres historias más (Madrid, 1933)
El hermano Juan o El mundo es teatro (1934)
Discurso leído en la solemne apertura del curso académico 1934–1935 en la
    Universidad de Salamanca (Salamanca, 1934)

Most of the above books have often been reprinted. Unamuno published,
besides, hundreds of articles and essays in Spanish and Spanish-American
newspapers and literary magazines. Among his plays, as well as the three
ones already mentioned, the following may be mentioned: *La Esfinge* (1909),
Fedra (1921), *Soledad* (1921), and *Raquel* (1922); he also translated the *Medea*
by Séneca.

Posthumous Works

La ciudad de Henoc. Comentario 1933 (Mexico, 1941)
Cuenca ibérica (Lenguaje y paisaje) (Mexico, 1943)
Temas argentinos (Buenos Aires, 1943)
La enormidad de España (Mexico, 1944)
Paisajes del alma (Madrid, 1944)
Visiones y comentarios (Buenos Aires, 1949)
De esto y aquello, 4 vols., Buenos Aires (ed. M. García Blanco; I, 1950; II,
    1951; III, 1953; IV, 1954)
Cancionero; diario poético (ed. F. de Onís; Buenos Aires, 1953)
Teatro (Barcelona, 1954)
En el destierro (Recuerdos y esperanzas) (ed. M. García Blanco; Madrid, 1957)
Inquietudes y meditaciones (ed. M. García Blanco; Madrid, 1957)
Cincuenta poesías inéditas (1899–1927) (ed. M. García Blanco; Madrid, 1958)
Mi vida y otros recuerdos personales, 2 vols. (I: 1889–1916; II: 1917–1936) (ed.
    M. García Blanco; Buenos Aires, 1959)
Cuentos, 2 vols. (ed. Eleanor Krane Paucker; 1961)

Most of the above volumes include articles published in book form for the
first time.

Books published in 1998:
Diario íntimo, Madrid: Alfaguara, 1998.
Escritos inéditos sobre Euskadi, Bilbao: Ayuntamiento de Bilbao, 1998.
Mi bochito (foreword by Ángel M. Ortiz Alfan and Manuel García Blanco),
    Bilbao: El Tilo, 1998.
Recuerdos de niñez y mocedad, Madrid: Alianza, 1998.
Alrededor del estilo (introd. and notes by Laureano Robles), Salamanca: Ed.
    Universidad de Salamanca, 1998.

EDITION OF WORKS

Manuel García Blanco (ed.), Madrid, 1959–1964, 16 vols.: I (Paisaje); II (Novela, 1); III (Ensayo, 1); IV (Ensayo, 2); V (De esto y aquello); VI (La raza y la lengua); VII (Prólogos, conferencias, discursos); VIII (Letras de América y otras lecturas); IX (Novela, 2, y monodiálogos); X (Autobiografía y recuerdos personales); XI (Meditaciones y otros escritos); XII (Teatro); XIII (Poesía, 1); XIV (Poesía, 2); XV (Poesía, 3); XVI (Ensayos espirituales y otros escritos); it includes *Del sentimiento trágico de la vida* and *La agonía del cristianismo.*

Obras selectas, Madrid: Plenitud, 1950.
Antología, México: Fondo de Cultura Económica, 1964 [with a foreword by J. L. L. Aranguren].
Obras completas, Madrid: Escelier, 1966, 9 volumes.
Poesía completa, Madrid: Alianza Editorial, 1993, 4 volumes.
Antología poética, (ed. and selection by J. M. Valverde), Madrid: Alianza Editorial, 1998.
Obras selectas, Madrid: Espasa-Calpe, 1998.
The Casa-Museo Unamuno in Salamanca shows a series of nonpublished manuscripts: see P. Cerezo Galán, *Las máscaras de lo trágico,* p. 27.

CORRESPONDENCE

Cartas de Pascoaes e Unamuno, ed. Joaquin de Carvalho and M. García Blanco, 1957.
Epistolario y escritos complementarios Unamuno-Maragall, 1971.
Cartas inéditas de Miguel de Unamuno, ed. Sergio Fernández Larraín, 1972.
Cartas: (1903/1933); Miguel de Unamuno and Luís de Zulueta, 1972.
Cartas íntimas: epistolario entre Miguel de Unamuno y los hermanos Gutiérrez Abascal, ed. Javier González de Durana, 1986.
Epistolario completo Ortega-Unamuno, ed. Laureano Robles, 1987.
Epistolario inédito, ed. Laureano Robles, 2 vols., 1991.
*Bergamín, José. El Epistolario: 1923–1935/*José Bergamín and Miguel de Unamuno, ed. Nigel Dennis, 1993.
Epistolario americano (1890–1936), ed. Laureano Robles, Salamanca: Universidad de Salamanca, 1996.
Correspondencia inédita de Unamuno: Unamuno-Menéndez Pidal, Delfina Molina-Unamuno, San Lorenzo del Escorial: Ed. Escurialenses, 1998.

ENGLISH TRANSLATIONS

Tragic Sense of Life. Transl. J. E. Crawford Flitch; introductory essay by S. de Madariaga. London: Macmillan, 1921. New York: Dover Publications, 1954 [a translation of *Del sentimiento trágico de la vida*].

Essays and Soliloquies. Transl. J. E. Crawford Flitch. New York: A. A. Knopf, 1925 [a translation of *Soliloquios y conversaciones*].

Life of Don Quixote and Sancho according to Miguel de Cervantes Saavedra expounded with comment by Miguel de Unamuno. Transl. Homer P. Earle. New York: A. A. Knopf, 1927 [a translation of *Vida de Don Quijote y Sancho*].

The Agony of Christianity. Transl. Pierre Loving. New York: Payson and Clarke, Ltd., 1928. Another transl. by Kurt F. Reinhardt. New York: Frederick Ungar Publishing Company, 1960 [a translation of *La agonía del cristianismo*].

Mist. A Tragi-comic Novel. Transl. Warren Fite. New York: A. A. Knopf, 1928 [a translation of *Niebla*].

Three Exemplary Novels and a Prologue. Transl. Angel Flores. New York: A. and C. Boni, 1930. Reprinted, with introduction by Angel del Río. New York: Grove Press, Inc., 1956 (contents: *The Marquis of Lumbria, Two mothers* and *Nothing less than a man*) [a translation of *Tres novelas ejemplares y un prólogo*].

Perplexities and Paradoxes. Transl. Stuart Gross. New York: Philosophical Library, 1945 [a translation of *Mi religión y otros ensayos,* with minor alterations].

The Christ of Velazquez. Transl. Eleanor L. Turnbull. Baltimore: Johns Hopkins Press, 1951 [a translation of *El Cristo de Velázquez*].

Poems. Transl. Eleanor L. Turnbull. Foreword by John A. Mackay. Baltimore: Johns Hopkins Press, 1953 [Spanish and English on opposite pages] [a translation of poems from various sources].

Abel Sánchez and Other Stories. Transl. Anthony Kerrigan. Chicago: Henry Regnery Company, 1956 [a translation of *Abel Sánchez* and a few additional stories from various books].

San Manuel Bueno, mártir. Transl. by Francisco de Segovia and Jean Pérez. London: G. G. Harrap, 1957.

Selected Works of Miguel de Unamuno. 7 vols. Translated and annotated by Anthony Kerrigan, Allen Lacy and Martin Nozick. Bollingen Series LXXXV. Princeton: Princeton University Press, 1967–1984.

1st. vol.: *Peace in War* (1983);
2nd. vol.: *The Private World: Selections from the* Diario Intimo *and selected letters 1890–1936* (1984);
3rd. vol.: *Our Lord Don Quixote* (1967);
4th. vol.: *The Agony of Christianity and Essays on Faith* (1974);
5th. vol.: *The Tragic Sense of Life in Men and Nations* (1972);
6th. vol.: *Novela/Nivola* (including *Mist, Abel Sánchez,* and *How a Novel Is Made*);
7th. vol.: *Ficciones* (including *La tía Tula, San Manuel Bueno, Martir,* and other short works).

Miguel de Unamuno's Political Writings, Edited by G. D. Robertson. Lewiston & Lampeter: Edwin Mellen, 1996.

Political Speeches and Journalism (1929–1932). Edited by Stephen G. H. Roberts. Exeter: University of Exeter Press, 1996.

A sizable number of essays, articles, and stories from a great variety of Unamuno's books have been translated and published in English and American journals.

BIBLIOGRAPHIES

Federico de Onís. "Bibliografía de Miguel de Unamuno," *La Torre,* 9 (1961), 601–636.

David William Foster. "Acotaciones y suplemento a la bibliografía de Unamuno," *La Torre,* 48 (October–December 1964), 165–172.

H. Pelayo Fernández. *Bibliografía crítica de Miguel de Unamuno,* 1976.

Varios. "Bibliografía unamuniana de los Cuadernos" in "Miguel de Unamuno: Historia de su Cátedra," *Anthropos, Genealogía científica de la cultura,* n. 3 (1992), pp. 92–147.

Elías Amenaza. *Ficha bio-bibliográfica de Miguel de Unamuno.* Navarra, Acedo: Wilsen Editorial, 1992.

SELECTED BIBLIOGRAPHY ON UNAMUNO

Only works and essays related to the topics discussed in the present book are mentioned.

C. Barja. *Libros y autores contemporáneos*, 1935, pp. 39–47.
Guillermo de Torre. "El rescate de la paradoja" (originally published in 1937) and "Unamuno y Clarín (originally published in 1924), in *La aventura y el orden*, 1943.
J. Kessel. *Die Grundstimmung in Miguel de Unamunos Lebensphilosophie*, 1937.
Julián Marías. *Miguel de Unamuno*, 1943.
Miguel Oromí. *El pensamiento filosófico de Miguel de Unamuno*, 1943.
Juan David García Bacca. *Nueve grandes filósofos contemporáneos y sus temas*, vol. I, 1947 (pp. 95–176).
P. Mesnard and R. Ricard. "Aspects nouveaux d'Unamuno," *La vie intellectuelle*, XIV, 2 (1946), 112–139. Also, F. Meyer "Kierkegaard et Unamuno," *Revue de Littérature comparée*, XXIX (1955), 478–492.
N. González Caminero. *Unamuno. I. Trayectoria de su ideología y de su crisis religiosa*, 1948.
J. L. L. Aranguren. "Sobre el talante religioso de Unamuno," *Arbor* XI (1948), 485–503.
H. Benítez. *El drama religioso de Unamuno*, 1949.
J. López-Morillas. "Unamuno and Pascal. Notes on the Concept of Agony," *Publications of the Modern Language Association*, XLV (1950), 998–1010.
S. Serrano Poncela. *El pensamiento de Unamuno*, 1951.
Carlos Clavería. *Temas de Unamuno*, 1953.
Diego Catalán Menéndez-Pidal. "Aldebarán," *Cuadernos de la Cátedra Miguel de Unamuno*, V (1953).
Manuel García Blanco. *Don Miguel de Unamuno y sus poesías*, 1954.
François Meyer. *L'ontologie de M. de Unamuno*, 1955.
C. Calvetti. *La fenomenologia della credenza in M. de Unamuno*, 1955.
A. Sánchez-Barbudo. *Estudios sobre Unamuno y Machado*, 1959.
Carlos Blanco Aguinaga. *El Unamuno contemplativo*, 1959; 2d. rev. ed., 1975.
Armando F. Zubizarreta. *Tras las huellas de Unamuno*, 1960.

ADDITIONAL BIBLIOGRAPHY

In chronological order; it consists of part of the secondary bibliography on Unamuno from the last edition of Ferrater Mora's *Diccionario de Filosofía*, Barcelona: Ariel, 1994, and includes some additional bibliography.

M. Romera Navarro. *Miguel de Unamuno, novelista, poeta, ensayista*, 1928.

C. González Ruano. *Vida, pensamiento y aventura de Miguel de Unamuno*, 1930.

Arthur Wills. *España y Unamuno*, 1938.

Julián Marías. *La filosofía española actual: Unamuno, Ortega, Morente, Zubiri*, 1948.

Agustín Esclasans. *Miguel de Unamuno*, 1948.

A. Sánchez Barbudo. *Estudios sobre Unamuno y Machado*, 1959 (includes the articles "La formación del pensamiento de Unamuno. Una experiencia decisiva: la crisis de 1897," "El misterio de la personalidad de Unamuno" and "Los últimos años de Unamuno, 'San Manuel Bueno' y el Vicario saboyano de Rousseau").

A. Benito y Durán. *Introducción al estudio del pensamiento filosófico de Unamuno*, 1953.

M. Ramis Alonso. *Don Miguel de Unamuno. Crisis y crítica*, 1953.

Manuel García Blanco. *Don Miguel de Unamuno y sus poesías*, 1954.

René-Maril Albères. *Unamuno*, 1957.

Luis S. Granjel. *Retrato de Unamuno*, 1958.

Bernardo Villarrazo. *Miguel de Unamuno. Glosa de una vida*, 1959.

Armando F. Zubizarreta. *Tras las huellas de Unamuno*, 1960.

F. de Onís, A. Castro, Jean Cassou et al., "Homenaje a Don Miguel de Unamuno," en special issue of *La Torre* (1961), 13–638.

Theo G. Sinnige. *Miguel de Unamuno*, 1962.

Jesús-Antonio Collado. *Kierkegaard y Unamuno: La existencia religiosa*, 1962.

Ezequiel de Olaso. *Los nombres de Unamuno*, 1963.

Iris M. Zavala. *Unamuno y su teatro de conciencia*, 1963.

Millagro Laín. *La palabra en Unamuno*, 1964.

Anón, J. Marías, J. Carballo, M. García Blanco et al., "Homenaje a Unamuno," special issue of *Revista de Occidente*, vol. XIX, Oct., 1964.

Eleanor Krane Paucker. *Los cuentos de Unamuno, clave de su obra*, 1965.

Elías Díaz. *Revisión de Unamuno: Análisis crítico de su pensamiento político*, 1969.

A. Regalado García, *El siervo y el señor. La dialéctica agónica de Miguel de Unamuno*, 1968 [particularly on Unamuno and Kierkegaard].

O. Gómez Molleda. *Unamuno socialista*, 1978.

J.-G. Renart. *El Cristo de Velázquez de Unamuno. Estructura, estilo, sentido*, 1982.

A. Cecilia Lafuente. *Antropología filosófica de Miguel de Unamuno*, 1983.

Julio López. *Unamuno*, 1984.

N. R. Orringer. *Unamuno y los protestantes liberales (1912). Sobre las fuentes de "Del sentimiento trágico de la vida,"* 1985.

116   THREE SPANISH PHILOSOPHERS

Pedro Cerezo Galán. "En torno a Miguel de Unamuno," in L. Geymonat. *Historia del pensamiento filosófico y científico*, vol. XXth century (III), 1985, chapter 7, pp. 464–485.

M. Padilla Novoa. *Unamuno, filósofo de encrucijada*, 1985.

Enrique Rivera. *Unamuno y Dios*, 1985.

Paulino Garagorri. *Introducción a Miguel de Unamuno*, 1986.

F. Abad, P. Cerezo Galán, et al. *Volumen-Homenaje a Miguel de Unamuno*, Casa-Museo Unamuno, 1986.

L. González Egido. *Agonizar en Salamanca*, 1986.

F. Fleche Andrés et al., *Lecturas de Unamuno*, 1987.

Nemesio González Caminero, *Unamuno y Ortega: estudios*, 1987.

D. Gómez Molleda. *Actas del Congreso Internacional: Cincuentenario de Unamuno: Universidad de Salamanca, 10–20 December 1986*, 1989.

A. Sánchez-Barbudo. ed. *Miguel de Unamuno*, 2nd. rev. ed., 1990.

Juan Marichal. *El Intelectual y la política en España: 1898–1936: Unamuno, Ortega, Azaña, Negrín*, 1990.

Iris M. Zavala. *Unamuno y el pensamiento trágico*, 1991.

Luís Jiménez Moreno. *Práctica del saber en filósofos españoles: Gracián, Unamuno, Ortega y Gasset, E. d'Ors, Tierno Galván*, 1991.

Anna M. Fernández. *Teoría de la novela en Unamuno, Ortega y Cortázar*, 1991.

Iris M. Zavala. *Unamuno y el pensamiento dialógico*, 1991.

César Medina. *La existencia y la vida humana*, 1992.

Manuel Blanco. *La voluntad de vivir y sobrevivir en Miguel de Unamuno: el deseo del Infinito imposible*, 1994.

Miguel A. Carazo. *Unamuno desde una perspectiva interdisciplinaria*, 1994.

Jesús García Maestro. *La expresión dialógica en el discurso lírico: la poesía de Miguel de Unamuno*, 1994.

Carlos Rojas. *¡Muera la inteligencia! ¡Viva la muerte!*, 1995.

José Ignacio Tellechea. *El eco de Unamuno*, 1996.

Francisco La Rubia Prado. *Alegorías de la voluntad: pensamiento orgánico, retórica y deconstrucción en la obra de Miguel de Unamuno*, 1996.

Pedro Cerezo Galán. *Las máscaras de lo trágico: filosofía y tragedia en Miguel de Unamuno*, 1996.

Dardo Cúneo. *Sarmiento y Unamuno*, 1997.

Manuel M. Urrutia. *Evolución del pensamiento político de Unamuno*, 1997.

Varios. *Anuario Filosófico*, 31(1), 1998 (special issue on Unamuno).

José M. Fernández Urbine. *Los Vascos del 98: Unamuno, Baroja y Maeztu*, 1998.

Joan Fuster. *Contra Unamuno y los demás*, 1998.

José M. López-Marrón. *Unamuno y su camino a la "individualización,"* 1998.

Alejandro Martínez. *Lenguaje y dialogía*, 1998.

Francisco La Rubia Prado. *Unamuno y la vida como ficción*, 1999.

María de las Nieves Pinillos. *Delfina, la enamorada de Unamuno,* 1999.
Jesús Castañón Rodríguez. *El estudio científico del idioma en Miguel de Unamuno,* 1999.

ADDITIONAL BIBLIOGRAPHY IN ENGLISH

Monographies

Barcia, J. R. and Zeitlin, M. A. eds. *Unamuno: Creator and Creation.* Berkeley: University of California Press, 1964.

Barea, Arturo. *Unamuno.* Cambridge: Bowes and Bowes, 1952.

Baskedis, Demetrius. *Unamuno and the Novel.* "Estudios de Hispanófila," no. 31. Chapel Hill, 1974.

———. *Unamuno and Spanish Literature.* Berkeley: University of California Press, 1967.

———. *Tres nivolas de Unamuno.* Eaglewood Cliff, New York: Prentice Hall, 1971.

Batchelor, R. E. *Unamuno Novelist: A European Perspective.* Oxford: Dolphin, 1972.

Bleiberg, German ed., and E. Inman Fox. *Pensamiento y Letras en la España del siglo XX. Spanish Thought and Letters in Twentieth Century.* Nashville: Vanderbilt University Press, 1966, 610 pages (some studies are in English and some in Spanish).

Butt, J. W. *Miguel de Unamuno: San Manuel Bueno, mártir.* London: Grant & Cutler/Tamesis, 1981.

Choi, Jae-Suck. *Greene and Unamuno: Two Pilgrims to La Mancha.* New York: Lang, 1990.

Donald, L. Shaw. *The Generation of 1898 in Spain.* London: Benn, 1975 (pages 41–74).

Earle, Peter G. *Unamuno and English Literature.* New York: The Hispanic Institute, 1960.

Ellis, Rober Richmond. *The Tragic Pursuit of Being: Unamuno and Sartre.* Tuscaloosa: University of Alabama Press, 1988.

Eoff, Sherman H. *The Modern Spanish Novel.* New York: New York University Press (particularly the chapter "Creative Doubt [Miguel de Unamuno]" pp. 186–212).

Franz, Thomas R. *Parallel but Unequal: The Contemporizing of Paradise Lost in Unamuno's Abel Sánchez.* Valencia: Albatros Hispanofila, 1990.

Hansen, Keith W. *Tragic Lucidity: Discourse of Recuperation in Unamuno and Camus.* New York: P. Lang, 1993.

Huertas-Jourda, José. *The Existentialism of Miguel de Unamuno.* Gainesville: University of Florida Press, 1963.

118   THREE SPANISH PHILOSOPHERS

Ilie, Paul. *Unamuno: An Existencial View of Self and Society.* Madison: University of Wisconsin Press, 1967.

Jurkevich, Gayane. *The Elusive Self: Archetypal Approaches to the Novels of Miguel de Unamuno.* Columbia: University of Missouri Press, 1991.

Lacy, Allen. *Miguel de Unamuno. The Rhetoric of Existence.* La Haya: Ed. Mouton, 1967.

Martínez López, Ramón, ed. *Unamuno Centennial Studies.* Austin: University of Texas, 1966.

Moore, S. H. *Miguel de Unamuno.* London: The Hibbert Journal, 1937.

Nozick, Martin. *Miguel de Unamuno.* New York: Twayne, 1969.

Olson, Paul R. *Unamuno: Niebla.* London: Grant & Cutler/Tamesis, 1984.

Ouimette, Victor. *Reason Aflame: Unamuno and the Heroic Will.* New Haven: Yale University Press, 1974.

Round, Nicholas G. *Unamuno: Abel Sánchez.* London: Grant & Cutler/Tamesis, 1974.

Round, Nicholas G. *Re-reading Unamuno.* Glasgow: University of Glasgow Press, 1989 [papers read to a colloquium held at Glasgow University, 22–24 March, 1986].

Rubia García, J. and Zeitlin, M. A. *Unamuno, Creator and Creation.* Berkeley: University of California Press, 1967.

Rudd, M. *The Lone Heretic: A Biography of Miguel de Unamuno.* Austin: University of Texas Press, 1963.

Serrano, Susana. *The Will as Protagonist: The Role of the Will in the Existentialist Writings of Miguel de Unamuno.* Sevilla: Padilla Libros, 1996.

Stabomvsky, Philip. *Myth and the Limits of Reason.* Amsterdam: Rodopi, 1996.

Turner, David G. *Unamuno's Webs of Fatality.* London: Tamesis, 1974.

Ulmer, Gregory L. *The Legend of Herostratus: Existential Envy in Rousseau and Unamuno.* Gainesville: University of Florida Press, 1977.

Valdés, Mario J. *Death in the Literature of Unamuno.* Urbana: University of Illinois Press, 1966.

Valdés, Mario J., and María Elena de Valdés. *An Unamuno Sourcebook: A Catalogue of Readings and Acquisitions with an Introductory Essay on Unamuno's Dialectical Inquiry.* Toronto: University of Toronto Press, 1973.

Watson, Peggy W. *Intra-historia in Miguel Unamuno's Novels.* Potomac, Md: Scripta Humanistica, 1993.

Wyatt, John. *Commitment to Higher Education: Seven West European Thinkers on the Essence of the University: Max Horkheimer, K. Jaspers, F. R. Leavis, J. H. Newman, José Ortega y Gasset, Paul Tillich, Miguel de Unamuno.* Bristol: Society for Research into Higher Education and Open University Press, 1990.

Wyers, Frances W. *Miguel de Unamuno: The Contrary Self.* London: Tamesis Books, 1976.

Young, Howard Thomas. *The Victorious Expression. A Study of Four Contemporary Spanish Poets.* Madison: University of Wisconsin Press, 1964 (on Unamuno, pp. 1–31).

Articles

Abrams, Fred. "Sartre. Unamuno and the «Hole Theory»," *Romance Notes,* V (1963–1964), pp. 6–11.

Alluntis, Felix. "The Philosophical Mythology of Miguel de Unamuno," *New Scholars,* 29 (1955), pp. 278–317.

Anderson, Reed. "The Narrative Voice in Unamuno's San Manuel Bueno, mártir," *Hispanófila,* n. 50 (1974), pp. 67–76.

Basdekis, D. "Miguel de Unamuno," *Columbia Essays on Modern Writers,* New York: Columbia University Press (1971).

Berkowitz, H. "Unamuno's Relations with Galdós," *Hispanic Review,* vol. 8 (1940).

Berns, G. "Another Look through Unamuno's Niebla, Augusto Pérez Lector," *Romance Notes,* vol. XI (1969–1970).

Blanco Aguinaga, Carlos. "Unamuno's Niebla: Existence and the Game of Fiction," *Modern Language Notes,* LXXXIX (1964), pp. 188–205.

Braun, Lucille. "Ver que me ves: Eyes and Looks in Unamuno's Works," *M.L.N,* 90 (1975), pp. 212–30.

Butt, J. W. "Determinism and the Inadequacies of Unamuno's Radicalism," *Bulletin of Hispanic Studies,* vol. XLVI (1969).

Butt, J. W. "Unamuno's Idea of Intrahistoria: Its Origins and Significance," in *Studies in Modern Spanish Literature and Art.* Presented to Helen F. Grant, edited by Nigel Glendinning, 13–24. London: Tamesis, 1972.

Carey, Douglas M., and Philip G. Williams. "Religious Confession as Perspective and Mediation in Unamuno's San Manuel Bueno, mártir." *M.L.N,* 91 (1976), pp. 292–310.

Dickens, Robert S. "Unamuno on Tragedy: Agony and the Tragic Sense of Life," *Journal of Existentialism,* 8 (1967–1968), pp. 161–177.

Dienstag, Joshua Foa. "The Pessimistic Spirit," *Philosophy and Social Criticism,* 25 (1999), pp. 71–95.

Dobson, A. "Unamuno's Abel Sánchez: An Interpretation," *Modern Language Notes,* vol. 54 (June, 1974), pp. 62–67.

Donoso A., "Philosophy as Autobiography. A Study of the Person of Miguel de Unamuno," *Personalist,* 49 (1968), pp. 183–196.

Durand, F. "Search for Reality in Nada menos que todo un hombre," *Modern Language Notes,* vol. 84 (1969), pp. 239–247.

Earle, P. "Unamuno and History," *Hispanic Review,* vol. XXXII (1964).

Falconieri, John V. "Sources of Unamuno's San Manuel Bueno, mártir," *Romance Notes,* 5 (1963), pp. 18–22.

————. "San Manuel Bueno, mártir, Spiritual Autobiography: A Study in Imagery," *Symposium,* 17 (1964), pp. 128–41.

Ferrater Mora, José. "On Miguel de Unamuno's Idea of Reality," *Philosophy and Phenomenological Research,* 21 (1961), 514–520.

Franz, Thomas. "Parenthood, Authorship and Immortality in Unamuno's Narratives," *Hispania,* 63 (1980), pp. 647–57.

Hughes, Roger. "Education and The Tragic Sense of Life: The Thought of Miguel de Unamuno," *Educational Theory,* 28 (1978), pp. 131–138.

Jurkevich, Gayana. "The Sun-Hero Revisited: Inverted Archtetypes in Unamuno's *Amor y pedagogía*," *MLN,* 102 (1987), pp. 292–306.

————. "Archetypal Motifs of the Double in Unamuno's Abe Sánchez," *Hispania,* 72 (1990), pp. 345–52.

————. "Unamuno's Intrahistoria and Jung's Collective Unconscious: Parallels, Convergences, and Common Sources," *Comparative Literature,* 43 (1991), pp. 43–59.

Ilie, Paul. "Unamuno, Gorky and the Cain Myth: Toward a Theory of Personality," *Hispanic Review,* vol. 29 (1961), pp. 310–323.

Kail, A. "Unamuno and Gide," *Hispania* (California), vol. XLV (1962).

Kinney, Arthur F. "The Multiple Heroes of Abel Sánchez," *Studies in Short Fiction,* 1 (1964), pp. 251–57.

Kirsner, Robert. "The Novel of Unamuno: A Study in Creative Determinism," *Modern Language Journal,* 37 (1953), pp. 128–39.

Livingstone, L. "Unamuno and the Aesthetics of the Novel," *Hispania* (California), Vol. XXVI (1941).

Marías, Julián. "Presence and Absence of Existentialism in Spain," *Philosophy and Phenomenological Research,* 15 (1954), pp. 180–191.

Mermall, Thomas. "Unamuno's Mystical Rhetoric," in *The Analysis of Hispanic Texts,* edited by Isabel Taran et al., pp. 256–64. New York: Bilingual Press, 1976.

————. "The Chiasmus: Unamuno's Master Trope," *PMLA,* 105 (1990), pp. 245–255.

Morales, Carmen. "Unamuno's Concept of Woman," *Fu Jen Studies,* 5 (1971), pp. 91–100.

Muyskens, James L. "Religious-belief as hope," *International Journal for Philosophy of Religion,* 5 (1974), pp. 66–74.

Natella, Jun., A. A. "Saint Theresa and Unamuno's San Manuel Bueno," *Papers on Language and Literature,* vol. V (1969).

Nozick, M. "Unamuno and La Peau de chagrin," *Modern Language Notes,* vol. LXV (1950).

————. "Unamuno Gallophobe," *The Romantic Review* (February, 1963).

Olson, Paul R. "The Novelistic Logos in Unamuno's *Amor y pedagogía*," *MLN,* 82 (1969), pp. 248–268.

———. "Unamuno's Lacquered Boxes: *Cómo se hace una novela* and the Ontology of Writing," *Revista Hispánica Moderna,* 36 (1970–1971), pp. 186–199.

Palmer, D. D. "Unamuno's Don Quixote and Kierkegaard's Abraham," *Revista de Estudios Hispánicos,* vol. III (1969).

Paxton, C. "Unamuno's Indebtedness to Whitman," *Walt Whitman Review,* vol. IX (1963).

Palley, Julian. "Unamuno: The Critique of Progress," *Revista de estudios hispánicos,* 10 (May 1976), pp. 237–260.

Phenix, Philip H. "Unamuno On Love and Pedagogy," *Philosophy of Education,* 24 (1968), pp. 47–59.

Predmore, R. "Flesh and Spirit in the Works of Unamuno," *PMLA,* vol. LXX (1955).

———. "Unamuno and Thoreau," *Comparative Literature Studies,* vol. VI (1969).

———. "*San Manuel Bueno, mártir;* A Jungian Perspective," *Hispanófila,* 22 (1978), pp. 15–29.

Priestley, F. E. L. "Twenty five years of Unamuno Criticism," *University of Toronto Quarterly,* vol. XXXVIII (1969).

Rasmussen, Dennis. "Immortality: Revolt against Being," *Personalist,* 56 (1975), pp. 66–74.

Ribbans, G. "The Development of Unamuno's Novels," *Hispanic Studies in Honour of I. González Llubera,* Dolphin Book Co., Oxford (1959).

Richards, Katherine C. "Unamuno and the 'Other,'" *Kentucky Romance Quarterly,* 23 (1976), pp. 439–449.

Sánchez Barbudo, A. "The Faith of Unamuno: His Unpublished Diary," *Texas Quarterly,* 8 (1965), pp. 46–66.

Sarmiento, E. "Considerations Towards a Revaluation of Unamuno," *Bulletin of Spanish Studies,* vol. 20 (1943), pp. 84–105.

Seator, Lynette. "Women and Men in the Novels of Unamuno," *Kentucky Romance Quarterly,* 27 (1980), pp. 39–55.

Sedwick, Frank. "Unamuno and Womanhood: His Theater," *Hispania,* 43 (1960), pp. 309–313.

Shaw, Donald L. "Concerning Unamuno's *La novela de Don Sandalio,*" *Bulletin of Hispanic Studies,* vol. 54 (1977), pp. 115–123.

Sobosan, Jeffrey G. "Passion and Faith: A Study of Unamuno," *Religious Studies,* 10 (1974), pp. 47–59.

Summerhill, Stephen J. "*San Manuel Bueno, mártir* and the Reader," *Anales de la literatura española contemporánea,* 10 (1985), pp. 61–79.

Valdés, Mario J. "Archetype and Recreation: A Comparative Study of William Blake and Miguel de Unamuno," *University of Toronto Quarterly,* vol. 40 (1970), pp. 59–72.

————. "Metaphysics and the Novel of Unamuno's Last Decade: 1926–1936," *Hispanófila*, n. 44 (1972), pp. 34–44.

Wardropper, B. "Unamuno's Struggle with Words," *Hispanic Review* (July, 1944).

Weber, Frances W. "Unamuno's *Niebla*: From Novel to Dream," *PMLA*, 88 (1973), pp. 209–218.

Webber, Ruth House. "Kierkegaard and the Elaboration of Unamuno's *Niebla*," *Hispanic Review* (Philadelphia), XXXII (1964), pp. 118–134.

Willers, Jack Conrad. "Unamuno Centennial," *Educational Theory*, 15 (1965), pp. 317–320.

Zahareas, Anthony N. "Unamuno's Marxian Slip: Religion as Opium of the People," *Journal of the Midwest Modern Language Association*, 17 (1984), pp. 16–37.

Part II

Ortega y Gasset: An Outline of His Philosophy

EDITOR'S NOTE

Ortega y Gasset: An Outline of his Philosophy was published in 1957; it was not a translation from a Spanish edition but was originally written in English. In 1963 Ferrater published—as he usually did—a revised and amplified version which we reproduce here. In the preface to that second edition, he announced the incorporation into the text of most of the last chapter, whose function, according to him, was to serve "as a summary and appraisal of Ortega's basic philosophical thoughts, with particular attention to the manner in which he developed them during the last years of his life."

Here—as we did with the text on Unamuno—we also have completed the notes and the bibliography of works in English at the end of the text.

Preface

This is a revised and enlarged edition of a book originally published in 1957. Since that date most of Ortega's posthumous works have been published. Furthermore, more of his books have been translated into English. I have taken into account the posthumous works and the new translations not only in the bibliographical footnotes but also in the text.

The description and analysis of Ortega's ideas on philosophy are now included in the final chapter. This chapter, the first section of which is an entirely new addition, is intended to serve as a summary and appraisal of Ortega's basic philosophical thoughts, with particular attention to the manner in which he developed them during the last years of his life.

I wish to thank Milton C. Nahm for the many extremely helpful suggestions he made on the text of the first edition. For suggests and corrections relative to parts of the present text I wish to thank George L. Kline and Mrs. Willard H. Cohn.

José Ferrater Mora

Bryn Mawr College
December 1962

Chapter One

Introduction

A short book on Ortega y Gasset's work and thought is a difficult undertaking if only for one reason: the astonishing range of Ortega's[1] intellectual interests. Ortega is, in the best sense of the word, a versatile writer. True, he has written neither novels nor plays and has almost invariably been loyal to one literary genre: the essay. Within this frame, however, there has been practically no subject upon which he has not touched. Skimming through the 6000-odd pages of his complete works, we find a staggering variety of writings: philosophical studies, articles on literary criticism, political essays and speeches, landscape descriptions, and historical interpretations. If we glance casually through the index of names appended to the collection of his works, we are no less impressed by the author's versatility; Renan and Einstein, Caesar and Husserl, Kant and Goya, Proust and Ibn Khâldun are only some of the many men not only occasionally mentioned or quoted but discussed at some length. Some of the essays are unclassifiable. One, for example, is about the frame of a painting; another is a preface to a still unwritten book. Among the more conventional essays, it is not unusual for the author merely to broach the subject announced; considerable time is spent in preliminary or tangential considerations. As for the topics discussed, they seem to be unbounded. Ortega has written on the fountains in Nürnberg, on the French language, on the Gioconda, on the Russian ballet, on African ethnology and, of course, on history, love and metaphysics. In view of these facts, we may be inclined to believe that Ortega's variety of topics is either a mark of frivolity or an omen of superficiality. But the more carefully we look at the strokes of the brush, the more consistent and organized appears the picture.

This does not mean that Ortega is a system-builder. Nor does he, we hope, pretend to be one. The emphasis that has been placed by both his followers and opponents on his 'system' or on his 'lack of system' is false. Ortega's is certainly no philosophical system in the Hegelian manner. It is true that Ortega himself has made occasional remarks about his 'philosophical system,' but the word 'system,' like the word 'being' according to Aristotle, has an analogical rather than a univocal meaning. Its meaning in Ortega is not, certainly, the 'strong' one—the meaning a system takes on when it is almost completely formalized. But it is not the 'weak' one either—the meaning it takes on when reduced to a style of writing or to a relatively uniform method of approach. It has a somewhat subtler meaning, depending both on cogency of thoughts and recurrence of themes. If Ortega is said therefore, to have a 'system,' it must be added that it is an *open* rather than a *closed* one.

In the present book we shall be primarily concerned with some of the most obvious features of Ortega's 'open system.' We shall, in other words, give a brief and somewhat sketchy account of his philosophy. We assume accordingly that Ortega's work, in spite of its diversity of subjects, its complexity, its 'allusions and elisions,'[2] is chiefly of a philosophical nature, with all its elements organized around a core of philosophical assumptions. Now the word 'philosophy' is as ambiguous as the word 'system.' After all, the term 'system' has a commonly accepted, if vague, connotation—you cannot have a system unless you have a certain 'order'—while the term 'philosophy' seems to possess no universally accepted meaning except the one based upon the fact that the most extraordinary variety of human thoughts are usually recorded in books pretending to be philosophical. The student of philosophy has always been a little distressed to learn that Marcus Aurelius and John Stuart Mill are equally to be considered as philosophers. As his familiarity with the history of philosophy increases, so will his distress, for there was a time when practically all human intellectual endeavours, provided they were formulated at a reasonably reflective level, were regarded as philosophical. When classifying the work of an author as philosophy, we must, therefore, be cautious and provide a minimum of clarification of the meaning carried by such an ambiguous word.

Ortega's philosophy is extremely difficult to classify, because he is one of the very few in modern history who has been aware of the problematic character of philosophical activity. We shall clarify this point later, and, for the time being, just say that Ortega's philosophy should not be presented in a pedantic manner.

The first problem Ortega's philosophy raises is the choice of a suitable method of presentation. A number of methods are available, but none of them seems to be altogether satisfactory. If too much attention is focused upon the unity of Ortega's thought, we incur the risk of losing the flavor of its variety. If we insist too much on the diversity of subjects, sight may be lost of the one continuous stream of thought running through all of them. Ortega himself, however, has provided an answer to our problem. He has said that the only way to approach human reality (and possibly human thought) is the narrative way. Accordingly, the right method of explaining Ortega's philosophy would be the biographical one. Now, 'biographical method' is an expression that must be given a precise meaning. It would be a mistake to interpret it in the usual fashion, as if it consisted of a mere enumeration of facts arranged in chronological sequence. In Ortega's sense of the word, 'biography' is almost a technical term, indicating the peculiar 'systematic' structure of human life and human achievements. From this point of view, the use of a biographical method involves a certain understanding of the whole of that reality to which it is applied. We are here confronted, incidentally, with one of the perplexing vicious circles so frequent in philosophy. In order to understand a system of thought we must describe its various stages, but in order to understand each one of the stages we must have a certain idea, however vague, of the whole system. This method is, in fact, the one we commonly use when attempting to understand the significance of a particular human life: the early stages in a person's life help us to understand the later ones, but it is only its later stages that provide us with a basis for the interpretation of the earlier ones; and although these two modes of explanation are not exactly alike, the first concentrating more on the cause-effect relation and the second more on the whole-part relation, we use them simultaneously. They are indeed not really separate methods but part of the same one. It is the method we shall employ throughout the present book.

This biographical method will allow us to discuss now and then certain typically Ortegean topics that a more formal method would rule out of the picture. Furthermore, the biographical method makes it easier to give an adequate, if brief, account of some of the external circumstances that have prompted Ortega's most significant philosophical and literary creations. We shall, however, limit the application of the method to an outline of some fundamental stages or phases in Ortega's intellectual development.

The first may be taken to extend from 1902 to 1913, the second from 1914 to 1923, the third from 1924 to 1955. It may prove convenient to attach a name to each phase, even if we recognize that such a label is more a mnemonic device than a defining category.

The first phase we shall label *objectivism*. Ortega himself has given occasion for adopting such a label if we remember that in a preface (1916) to his volume *Persons, Works, Things* (*Personas, Obras, Cosas*) he recognized how one-sided his earlier objectivism was and how befitting it would be to emphasize again subjectivism stripped of its nineteenth-century connotations.[3] Although the preface in question was written in 1916, we can easily perceive a change in his book *Meditations on Quixote* (*Meditaciones del Quijote*) (1914) and perhaps even earlier. As a matter of fact, some of the intellectual seeds that will bear fruit much later can be traced as early as 1910, and much that will be recognized as typically Ortegean makes its first appearance in two articles published in 1904 and reprinted only in 1946.[4]

The second phase we shall label *perspectivism.* Some doctrines other than this can, of course, be detected during the period 1914–1923, but the above label provides a convenient designation for the entire phase. A noteworthy difference between the objectivist and the perspectivist stages is that, while the former contains much that will never again recur, the latter is an essential ingredient of the third period. The label arises out of the first essay in *The Spectator (El Espectador),*[5] but the doctrine of the *modi res considerandi* set forth in the *Meditations* may be held as an earlier formulation of it. Perspectivism can be considered from two angles: as a doctrine and as a method. The two combine frequently and the reader is sometimes left in doubt about the rôle that perspectivism plays in the whole system.

The third phase we shall label *ratio-vitalism,* a shorthand description used by Ortega himself.[6] It will prove to be Ortega's main achievement in philosophy. We fix 1924 as a beginning date because in that year Ortega's article 'Neither Vitalism nor Rationalism' ('Ni vitalismo ni racionalismo') was published. But we might also go back to 1923, the date of the publication of a major work containing ratio-vitalistic assumptions: *The Modern Theme (El tema de nuestro tiempo).* Nevertheless, in this book, as if reacting against a widespread contemporary 'idolatry of culture' (the so-called 'culturalism'), Ortega emphasized the theme of life far more than his own doctrine of vital reason would permit. We shall consequently rule this work out of the third period and study it instead as the crowning point of the second. Needless to say, the third period will provide us with most of the themes that have come to be viewed as characteristically Ortegean. It is not only the longest phase in Ortega's life and work but also the most 'systematic' of all. We shall devote to it, therefore, relatively more space than to any of the others, and we shall interpret the first two in the light of the third. Now the presentation of the third period will gain in clarity if we divide it into a number of themes. These will be: (a) the concept of vital reason; (b) the doctrine of man, and (c) the doctrine of society. Thus unity will be achieved without necessarily eschewing diversity.

To strengthen our account of Ortega's philosophy we have devoted a final chapter to a discussion of two basic philosophical problems. Ortega had been stirred by these problems since the very beginnings of his intellectual career, but he tackled them in a rigorous manner only during the third phase of his philosophical development. Since a substantial portion of his posthumous works is devoted to a detailed treatment of these problems, our final chapter can be considered both as a summary of Ortega's general position in metaphysics and as a brief presentation of the substance of the posthumous works.[7]

The present book is intended for a non-Spanish-speaking public. It will accordingly be impossible to avoid mentioning a few facts that Spanish readers are likely to take for granted. As a result, interpretation will often be accompanied by mere information. On the other hand, certain questions intriguing to the Spanish-speaking public cannot be discussed here. We shall pay little attention, for example, to the problem of whether Ortega's claims of having long since foreshadowed many later philosophical developments in contemporary thought can be substantiated or not.[8] Ortega is probably more original than his detractors proclaim and less original than his adherents preach, but in any case the achievements of a philosopher must be measured in terms of truth, cogency, precision, economy of thought, etc., rather than exclusively in terms of originality. We shall also ignore the question of whether ideas *not* playing a central role in Ortega's philosophy are faulty. We can see little purpose in noticing that Ortega's considerations on Debussy's music[9] are contradicted by facts, or in remarking that his interpretation of Quine's statement, 'There must always be undemonstrable mathematical truths,'[10] is a misinterpretation. We are not concerned with errors irrelevant to the central themes; some distorted facts or some questionable reasonings may very well be lodged in an interesting and even sound philosophy. We shall indulge in neither bickering nor applause, but try to keep close to the spirit of a famous apothegm: Neither bewail nor ridicule, but understand.

NOTES

1. Throughout this book we shall use the name 'Ortega' instead of 'Ortega y Gasset,' 'Ortega' being, according to Spanish usage, the philosopher's surname and playing thus the role of the English last name.

2. José Ortega y Gasset, *Obras completas,* Madrid: Revista de Occidente, VI, 344 (1932). The arabic numeral inside parentheses designate the date of first publication, either in periodical or in book form. Quotations will follow the edition of *Obras completas* (Madrid: Revista de Occidente, 1946 ff.), except for a few books not included therein or to be included in forthcoming volumes. If an English translation in book form is available, it will be mentioned in brackets. It should be noted that English titles do not always correspond to Spanish ones and that sometimes, as in the case of the English translation of *España invertebrada* (*Invertebrate Spain*), some other texts have been added to the one providing the title of the book. Information on the contents of some of the English translations, as well as on the contents of *Obras completas,* is appended at the end of this volume. Most of our quotations will be mere references to *some* of the places where Ortega has developed the subjects dealt with in our book. Literal quotations will be restricted to a minimum.

3. I, 419–20 (1916).

4. I, 13–18 (1904); I, 19–27 (1904).

5. II, 15–21 (1916).

6. VI, 196, note (1934) [*Concord and Liberty,* henceforth called *Concord,* p. 164].

7. Occasional reference to some of the posthumous works has also been made in other sections of this book.

8. For readers interested in this problem we have indicated in parentheses the date, or dates, of publication of each of the writings mentioned in footnotes. It should be noted that in some cases the date of publication may be misleading, for some of Ortega's writings were published only many years after they were composed. Outstanding examples of belated publication are: *¿Qué es filosofía?* [*What is Philosophy?*], published in 1958 on the basis of a series of university lectures given as early as 1929; the first chapter of *El hombre y la gente* [*Man and People*], published in 1957 on the basis of the first essay included in *Ensimismamiento y alteración* (1939); and *Prólogo para alemanes,* published in 1958, but written more than twenty years earlier. We may add that "Historia como sistema" was originally published (in English) in 1941, and that *En torno a Galileo* [*Man and Crisis*] is based on a series of lectures given in 1933. Since different parts of *Man and Crisis* have been published at different dates, we have consistently indicated 1933 as 'the original date.'

9. II, 236–46 (1921).

10. V, 528 (1941) [*Concord,* p. 62].

Chapter Two

'Objectivism'

From 1902 to 1913 Ortega published no book, but his name began to be known among Spaniards as the author of a number of noteworthy articles. These articles were occasionally published in literary magazines—*Vida Nueva, La Lectura, Europa,* etc.—and very often in a daily newspaper, *El Imparcial.* The last fact deserves consideration. It has been, of course, quite common for Spanish writers to publish articles in newspapers. Not a few of the best examples of Spanish literature of the nineteenth and twentieth centuries first appeared in daily journals. But Ortega has always shown an extreme predilection for newspapers—at least of a certain type—and has been associated in various ways, and not merely as an occasional contributor, with some of the outstanding Spanish daily journals: *El Imparcial* first, then *El Sol,* and finally *Crisol* and *Luz.* It was said of him that he was born 'on a rotary printing press.' Since 1936 he has often complained of 'not having a paper,' meaning a paper where he could without restraint set up rules of intellectual policy. Ortega has been a newspaperman *par excellence,* in a sense almost forgotten today even in countries where newspapers still play an important cultural and educational role. On the other hand, he has provided newspapers with a type of literature that has been truly exceptional, even taking into consideration the high intellectual standards of some of the Spanish and Spanish-American newspapers.[1] We do not for a moment forget that other Spanish thinkers, such as Unamuno, Maeztu, d'Ors, have given to daily journals half, if not more, of their intellectual production. But Ortega has tried to introduce through the medium of newspapers not only ideological issues or cultural information but also a certain amount of philosophical speculation and clarification. His tendency to inundate the Sunday issues with philosophical literature has been growing steadily since 1920. To give *some* examples: a series of articles on the question 'What is knowledge?' in all likelihood derived from his university lectures, came out in *El Sol's* Sunday feuilleton;[2] an article on 'Leibniz and Metaphysics' was published in *La Nación* in the twenties;[3] his most publicized book, *The Revolt of the Masses* (*La rebelión de las masas*), was delivered for the first time to the public in the form of newspaper articles from 1926 on.[4] We do not wish to give the reader the impression that everything written by Ortega has come out in the same fashion. Essays in literary magazines, articles in learned journals, and also formal books account for a substantial part of his production. But on the whole publication in newspapers has been, as it were, a 'constant' in Ortega's way of communicating his thoughts to the public. Such a fact is not lightly to be dismissed. Two reasons may be adduced to account for it. One is Ortega's personal fondness for this form of literary activity, a fondness helped, if not brought forth, by the attraction he felt for a new subject as soon as another had been broached. The other reason was emphasized by Ortega's faithful disciple, Julián Marías, when he remarked that Ortega *had* to use 'ostentatious' public media of communication.[5] We shall briefly follow Marías' account of Ortega's reason for choosing such media, inasmuch as it will help us understand some of our philosopher's aims, at least during the first period of his intellectual activity.

The substance of Marías' argument, to which we shall add some of our own reflection, runs as follows. When Ortega began writing, Spanish culture was still suffering from nineteenth-century intellectual indigence. The so-called generation of 1898 had already revived Spain's spiritual nerve, but ideas, and in particular philosophical ideas, seemed still to lack either depth or precision. Most of the current literary output was either pure literature—and often very fine literature, indeed—or mere erudition. Exceptions to this rule might, of course, be found, but even these had to breathe in a rather murky ideological atmosphere. The first one to try to clear it was Miguel de Unamuno. But Unamuno, who left nothing to be desired as to seriousness of purpose and breadth of information, cared little for precision. As we have shown elsewhere,[6] his aim as a writer with regard to the public may be summed up in one word: stimulation. Inspiration rather than argument had been his driving power. The fact that we acknowledge today in Unamuno's works and deeds a great deal of what has become an essential ingredient of European contemporary philosophy does not prevent us from admitting that his aims were quite different from Ortega's. The latter aspired to inject into Spanish culture an element it badly needed: thoughtfulness. In an intellectually enlightened atmosphere Ortega might have done what was being done at the same time by other European philosophers: Bergson, Husserl, or Russell. In other words, he might have limited himself to working out a core of philosophical intuitions and delivering them to a restricted public by the usual means: papers read before learned societies, contributions to scholarly journals, lectures in universities. But what if learned societies are few, scholarly journals practically non-existent, universities dominated by routine? Was it not therefore much better to take a roundabout course? Would not a long detour avoid the pitfalls of a shortcut? What has in fact happened is that Ortega's encircling method has been highly responsible for giving form and substance to the Spanish intellectual atmosphere. Thus we can understand his renunciation of specialization and his choice of newspapers as the chief medium of public communication.

There is, however, another reason for Ortega's choice. Ortega is not only a philosopher; he is also, and in large measure, a writer. He belongs to the group of twentieth-century Spanish authors who have offered Spain a new Golden Age in literature. This new Golden Age is dominated by a poetic sensitivity that permeates a good many pages written in the last sixty years. As it has been said, twentieth-century Spanish prose is more 'poetic' than nineteenth-century Spanish poetry.[7] Now the word 'poetic' must be understood here as meaning something other than the vague language of feeling. It designates above all a recognition of a writer's commitment in his use of language. The problem of language, rather than the problem of rhetorical expression—or, in the case of the poets, of technical versification—has been, indeed, predominant with all these writers. Ortega has certainly been no outsider to this revival. No doubt, he has been primarily interested in philosophical thought; but he has also created a new style. This style is not free from mannerism. It is hard to understand why, in the middle of a very able exposition of Max Weber's ideas on the decadence of the Roman Empire, a passage is inserted in which the author, supposedly writing by the seashore, compares the ocean to a huge crossbow and his own heart to an arrow.[8] A few of these mannerisms were unfortunately imitated by some young Spanish essayists, and frequently Ortegean catchwords were substituted for real concepts. Yet there is no point in blaming Ortega for his brilliant style. At a time when intellectual production is marred by dullness, a brilliant style is far more refreshing than harmful. Literary craftsmanship is indeed one of Ortega's outstanding accomplishments. Some of his best pages are his travel descriptions, which he himself regrets are too few.[9] Ortega's literary style is, however, always adapted to the thoughts he tries to convey to the reader. And thoughts are always the background, if not the foreground, of his writings. Even when description predominates over analysis, he seems anxious to take it only as a starting point for reflection.[10] No wonder Ortega has come to the defence of metaphorical expression as a valid tool of philosophical analysis.[11] Even if we think his ideas on this point somewhat far-fetched, we cannot help detecting therein the keen perception that a purebred writer has of the scope and limitations of his own instrument.

Ortega therefore started his career as a thinker by choosing a literary style and certain media of communication that were particularly apt to bring him into the limelight of the Spanish intellectual scene. All the writings we shall discuss in this section bear the mark of his unusual combination of literary skill and philosophical sagacity.

In these formative years the foremost theme is objectivity. In more than one passage Ortega assured the reader, and in particular young Spanish readers, that too much attention has been paid so far to human beings and too little to things or to ideas. We might choose a number of quotations; we shall limit ourselves to a most revealing sentence. It is the one in which Ortega says that he cannot understand how it is possible for men to arouse more interest than ideas, and persons more than things; and he adds that an algebraic theorem or a huge old stone in the Guadarrama Sierra is more meaningful than all the employees in a government office.[12] He accordingly asks his fellow-citizens to get rid of 'the secret leprosy of subjectivity.'[13] It should be noted that a few years later a footnote was added to the above sentence stating that such an opinion is 'sheer blasphemy.' Nevertheless, this stress upon objectivity recurs in different ways and in different tones throughout the articles written during the 1904–1913 period.

There are many reasons for the adoption of the above intellectual policy. An obvious one is Ortega's dislike for the high-pressure personalistic atmosphere pervading Spanish life. The word 'personalistic' can, nevertheless, be understood in two ways: a superficial one, as the deplorable habit of a people wasting time on barren personal discussion, and a deep one, as the living basis of a community that has chosen *person* as the highest value in the universe.[14] We suspect that Ortega placed too much emphasis on the former and too little on the latter. This fact has been recognized, at least implicitly, by Ortega himself, for otherwise he would not have renounced his earlier opinions on this issue. Yet as a reaction against a certain state of affairs, those opinions were by no means groundless. On the other hand, in the very core of his objectivistic claims lies much that later became the link between the first and the second period.

Ortega went abroad to study philosophy. He spent several years in Germany, specially in Leipzig, Berlin, and Marburg. In Marburg he studies under the guidance of Hermann Cohen, the head of one of the two great neo-Kantian schools flourishing in Germany at the beginning of this century. Going abroad, in particular going to Germany, in order to study philosophy was not unusual in Spain. More than half a century before Ortega a great Spaniard, Julián Sanz del Río, went to Germany in search of new ideas. But as the pilgrims and the times were quite dissimilar, the two intellectual pilgrimages yielded quite different results. Sanz del Río imported into Spain a philosophical system that, while having gained but little credit in Europe, had conquered the hearts of a handful of brave and enthusiastic adherents: Krausism, the somewhat involved system of Karl Christian Friedrich Krause, a sincere and pedantic idealist. Sanz del Río very soon gave Krausism a Spanish turn, emphasizing its ethical, personalistic and absolutistic aspects. Ortega, on the contrary, did not import any philosophy. The system he followed for a time was the one then relevant in the most sophisticated German circles. He preached, certainly, an intensive study of Kant, and he declared later that he had lived in a Kantian atmosphere, in a philosophical edifice that was at the same time a prison.[15] But he spread Kantianism, or rather neo-Kantianism, in a rather perfunctory way, more as a method of exact thinking than as a definite set of philosophical statements. The result of Ortega's training, helped if not fostered by his own temperament, was thus the moulding of a critical spirit, allergic to received opinions, to intellectual clumsiness, to obsolete ideas. Again, this was not new in Spain. But Ortega carried to extremes an attitude that he has often summed up by means of one of his favourite phrases: to be abreast of the times.[16] He tried to become the spearhead of a new intellectual movement capable of sweeping away all that was shaky, rotten or dead in Spanish life and culture, but not necessarily all that was traditional. In a significant article, published as early as 1906, Ortega sharply attacked traditionalists, not because of their fondness for tradition but because of their inability to preserve tradition.[17] Traditionalists, he writes, want to carry the present back to the past. They feel accordingly no respect for the past as such. If they loved it, they would certainly not attempt to petrify it. The living past, on the other hand, is rooted in the present and will survive in the future. Therefore, it would be a mistake to interpret Ortega's concern for the present and future as naïve anti-traditionalistic rhetoric. His struggle against the dead past is quite compatible with his insistence upon the crucial role played by history, in exactly the same sense that his insistence upon the preeminence of the living future is quite consistent with his fight against utopia. However, the vigour with which he attempted to change routine intellectual habits was conspicuous. The justification of the past as past occupied only a small part of his thoughts. Practically all of his thinking in this period was focused upon one basic issue: how can Spain be abreast of the times.

From the beginning of his intellectual career Ortega was therefore involved in the time-honored struggle between *hispanizantes* (those who wanted to hispanicize everything and were reluctant to admit foreign habits or ideas) and *europeizantes* (who wanted to inject into Spain what was called, rather vaguely, *European civilization*). This distinction is, of course, misleading, because the words *hispanizante* and *europeizante* have more than one meaning. Granted this ambiguity, however, we can say that Ortega was, and has always remained, an *europeizante.* To be such in Ortega's sense of this term has little to do with the straight importation of foreign habits or of foreign techniques. Unlike a good many Spaniards of his time, Ortega was not dazzled by the

brilliant side of modern industrial revolution and did not for a moment
believe that the mere introduction of Western European techniques would
automatically heal all Spanish ills. He welcomed modern techniques but warned
that they were a by-product of something far more fundamental than technique: science, culture, education. Pure science in particular—including, of
course, philosophy—he considered the root of European civilization.[18] Therefore, in order to change Spain into a European country, it was necessary to
turn away from all superficial cures based upon imitation. Let us not, he
wrote, call simply for railways, industry or trade, and still less for European
costumes. Let us rather strive for a way of civilization that, while being
positively Spanish, can become at the same time fundamentally European.[19]
The so-called 'Spanish problem' is thus a problem of discipline. Spaniards
must no longer live in a state of abulia or torpidity. They must above all give
up 'adamism,' the fatal mistake of starting everything afresh without intellectual seriousness, continuity of purpose or cooperation. In fact, only on the
basis of intellectual discipline will Spain become a 'European possibility.'[20]
But in doing so, Spain will cease to be a passive reservoir of foreign thoughts
and habits and will become instead a powerful source of European renovation. As he said later, in another context, the first thing to do in a national
community is 'not to imitate.'[21]

    This attitude clashed, of course, rather violently with the opinions of the
out and out *hispanizantes*. Among the latter we may provisionally include
Unamuno, although the word *hispanizante* is quite inadequate to typify
Unamuno's attitude. Unamuno was not a hispanicist in the usual sense of the
term. He shared with Ortega a horror of the conventional shallow Spanish
traditionalism. Unamuno's hispanicism and anti-Europeanism were therefore
of a more subtle character than he himself indulged in believing when launching
such slogans as 'Let them [the Europeans] invent' or 'Europe is a shibboleth.'
His notion of the 'eternal tradition' was clearly indicative of his abhorrence
of the dead past. In order to divulge his views on the subject, however,
Unamuno used a method that was closer to paradox than to reasoning. He
declared, among other things, that if it was impossible for the same nation
to bring forth both Descartes and Saint John of the Cross, he would rather
retain the latter. This must be understood, of course, in the light of Unamuno's
deep sense of 'personalism,' and is in tune with his later proclamation that
Saint Theresa's deeds are at least as worthy as any European institution or any
Critique of Pure Reason. Now Ortega could not accept, and in his objectivistic
period not even endure, such irritating paradoxes. The point is worth mentioning, because it gives a clear picture of what Ortega stood for before
watering down his own enthusiastic Europeanism. His opinions on the issue
in question appeared most clearly in an article on 'Unamuno and Europe,'[22]
in which he emphatically declared that Unamuno—whom he praised in other

respects and to whom he paid moving homage thirty years later[23]—was an obscurantist who introduced nothing but confusion. He even called him an *energúmeno,* a 'violent person.' In Ortega's opinion, it was sheer confusion to prefer Saint John of the Cross to Descartes; not because the Spanish saint and poet was an unimportant figure, but because without Descartes—who was, according to Ortega, the key figure in all modern European philosophy—we would remain in the dark and become incapable of understanding anything, including the 'brown sackcloth' of Juan de Yepes, the worldly name of the great mystic. The confusion was all the more unfortunate in that Unamuno was often hailed by Ortega as a very powerful mind and, indeed, as a mentor of the Spanish intelligentsia. Unamuno was, according to Ortega, one of the last bastions of Spanish hopes.[24] All this conceded, however, Ortega deemed it proper to substitute his 'brand-new' thoughtful Europeanism for Unamuno's paradoxical and harsh 'Africanism.'

Against overemphasis on ideals—of all sorts—Ortega was thus insistent upon ideas—but not of all sorts. The point deserves further elucidation, for it marks the transition from objectivism to perspectivism. The link between these two phases lies in Ortega's shifting the emphasis from ideas at large to certain kinds of ideas. At the beginning of his philosophical and literary career Ortega was in fact so haunted by the need of intellectual discipline that he seemed prone to accept all ideas provided they had a modern European tinge. He even seemed to be willing to shirk many issues for the sake of a much needed virtue: clarity.[25] His arguments in favor of precision,[26] both in thought and in volition, his fondness for 'system,'[27] at least as a program for the future, his strong dislike for the blending of literature and science, no matter how literary-minded he was himself—all this aimed at a revival of Spanish spiritual life based upon a great wealth of ideas. No wonder he was called a rationalist and even accused of intellectualism. Now intellectualism would be a very inadequate label for a philosopher who amidst his struggle for clear ideas never forgot that ideas, however abstract, must not be divorced from life. We shall see later that the relation between life and ideas is a central issue in Ortega's philosophy, one of his favourite tenets being that while ideas cannot be separated from life, life cannot exist without ideas. It may be pointed out that, *in nuce,* this position can already be detected in those early pages in which Ortega dismisses certain ideas in favour of certain others. As early as 1911[28] he claimed that if discipline—intellectual, moral and aesthetic discipline—is still what Spain needs most of all, such a discipline has a very definite purpose: to bring us back to 'the vital.'[29] We need, to be sure, ideas, but only 'essential' ideas.[30] We must, in other words, abandon idealism,[31] which is a by-product of the tendency to substitute abstract notions for real, or living, thoughts. These opinions are all the more surprising because they were held at a time when Ortega still appeared to many to be advocating a sort of philosophical rationalism. They are, however, a mere sample of an attitude that, while having due regard for reason, never allowed rationalism to lead the way. This is, incidentally, one of the reasons why Ortega, who had little reverence for German political rigidity and harshness—he was in favor of the Allies during World War I—felt more at ease with German 'vital culture' than with the polished civilization of the French. Germany, he claimed, had more to teach in the way of ideas, even if France had better things to offer by way of manners[32] and England more to give by way of political ability.[33] Very soon Ortega began to display a profound mistruct of any encroachments of pure reason upon life. He even appeared sometimes to go so far in this new direction that many people again mistook his position and interpreted it as plain 'vitalism.' He was then compelled to declare that both reason and life are one-sided, and that a new stand has to be taken by those who want to prevent either one from being eliminated by the other. Now the link between objectivism and perspectivism is to be found in this shift from the rational to the vital, or rather in this effort to restore life and reality in their own right. The method Ortega advocated most frequently in order to achieve that purpose is the perspectivistic method. In the light of it we shall try to account for Ortega's main tenets during the next, very active, phase of his intellectual development.

NOTES

1. Ortega has also contributed to some fine newspapers in Spanish America, principally *La Nación* of Buenos Aires.

2. See *El Sol,* February-March, 1931.

3. III, 431–34 (1926).

4. IV, 141–278 (1930) [*The Revolt of the Masses,* henceforth called *Revolt, passim*].

5. J. Marías, *Ortega y la idea de la razón vital,* Santander-Madrid: Colección 'El Viento Sur,' 1948, pp. 13–14. By the same author, *Ortega,* vol. I *Circunstancia y vocación,* Madrid: Revista de Occidente, 1960, pp. 113 ff. Cf. VI, 353 (1932). For an opinion on books as 'falsifications,' III, 447 (1927).

6. José Ferrater Mora, *Unamuno. A Philosophy of Tragedy.* Philip Silver, trans. Berkeley and Los Angeles: University of California Press, 1962, p. 96.

7. See Pedro Salinas, *Literatura española siglo XX,* México: Séneca, 1941, pp. 59–82; 2nd enlarged edition, México: Robredo, 1949, pp. 34–44.

8. II, 544 (1926).

9. IV, 386 (1932).

10. Outstanding examples are: II, 249–68 (1915) [fragmentary translation in *Invertebrate Spain,* pp. 103–15], where the description of a journey from Madrid to Asturias serves as a starting point for an interpretation of Castile; II, 413–50 (1925) [*Op. cit.,* pp. 116–42], where along the thread of a trip through Castile he develops

his ideas on liberalism and democracy; II, 553–60 (1915) [*Invertebrate Spain*, pp. 202–12], where a description of the Monastery of El Escorial is used as a frame for an essay on the idea of 'pure effort,' with a comparison between Cervantes' *Don Quixote* and Fichte's philosophy.

11. II, 387–400 (1924).

12. I, 443 (1909).

13. I, 447 (1909). Also I, 87 (1908).

14. A brilliant interpretation of this deep meaning of personalism can be found in Américo Castro's *The Structure of Spanish History*, Princeton: Princeton University Press, 1953, a translation of the second much revised and practically rewritten edition of his work *España en su historia*, Buenos Aires: Losada, 1948 [2nd ed.: *La realidad histórica de España*, México; Porrúa, 1956; 3rd ed., *ibid.*, 2 vols., 1962–63].

15. IV, 25 (1924).

16. IV, 156 (1930) [*Revolt*, p. 31]. The English translator writes: 'at the height of times.'

17. I, 425–9 (1906). Also II, 43 (1911) and I, 363–5 (1914) [*Meditations on Quixote*, henceforth called *Meditations*, pp. 100–03].

18. I, 102 (1908).

19. I, 107 (1908).

20. I, 138 (1910).

21. *Rectificación de la República*, Madrid: Revista de Occidente, 1931.

22. I, 128–32 (1909).

23. V, 264–5 (1937).

24. I, 118 (1908).

25. A restatement of this opinion is in VI, 351 (1932). See also *La redención de las provincias y la decencia nacional*, Madrid: Revista de Occidente, 1931.

26. I, 113 (1908).

27. I, 114 (1908).

28. I, 551 (1911).

29. I, 551 (1911).

30. I, 209 (1911).

31. 'Idealism' is used here and henceforward as a technical term, denoting a certain modern philosophical tendency, typified, among others, by Kant and in part by Descartes and Leibniz.

32. I, 209 (1911).

33. On English political ability see especially III, 450 (1927); IV, 293 (1937); and V, 261–3 (1937).

Chapter Three

'Perspectivism'

Between 1914 and 1923 Ortega published a number of important books. They may be roughly classified in two groups. The first includes books of selected articles, essays, notes, meditations, etc., most of them previously printed in journals or newspapers. The second includes books dealing with, or at least centering upon, a single topic. To the first group belong the three first volumes of the eight-volume series entitled *The Spectator* (*El Espectador*, I, 1916; II, 1917; III, 1921).[1] To the second group belong three major works: *Meditations on Quixote*, hereinafter called *Meditations* (*Meditaciones del Quijote*, 1914), *Invertebrate Spain* (*España invertebrada*, 1921) and the book translated into English as *The Modern Theme* (*El tema de nuestro tiempo*, 1923). To these volumes a number of articles, which came out in book form only much later, should be added. On the whole this makes an impressive number of pages, swarming with questions, analyses, insights, flashes of wit and literary inventiveness. It appears by no means easy to detect in them traces of a systematic philosophy.

Fortunately, we possess some sort of a philosophical program at the very threshold of the *Meditations*. This book opens with a declaration of war upon any attempt to make the world of the philosopher a cloistered universe. Following a tendency that had been fostered by the German philosopher Georg Simmel and had increased through the years in some sections of European philosophy, Ortega claimed that no reality, however humble, and no question, however unusual, can be put aside by a truly alert philosopher. Not all realities and questions lie, of course, on the same level. At issue with the positivists' flat universe, Ortega has often asserted that hierarchy permeates reality.[2] But this does not preclude the fact that each reality has a depth of its own and that the philosopher's task is to penetrate its surface in order to peer into its hidden nature. Thus the method to be adopted stands out in sharp contrast to the favourite approach of traditional academic philosophy. Instead of dismissing our nearby realities as unworthy of notice, we must try rather to discover their meaning. As Ortega himself writes, we must raise each reality to the plenitude of its significance. This point deserves some attention. Since the advent of phenomenology and existentialism, we have fallen into the habit of reading philosophical works encumbered with analyses of realities that only thirty years ago would have been barred in academic circles as irrelevant if not impertinent. We have been taught again and again that no reality, however unacademic, can escape the cutting edge of philosophical clarification. This situation has given cause for concern, and in some quarters the complaint has been heard that at this rate philosophy will soon dissolve into a hunting for minutiae. But such complaints become pointless as soon as we discover that in many instances the elaborate analysis of unacademic themes has led to the core of the deepest philosophical questions. This open-door policy in philosophy was preached by Ortega at the beginning of his career and has since been consistently carried on by him against wind and tide. The variety of his intellectual interests appears thus in a new light. It is not a result of intellectual instability, or at least, not solely, but also a consequence of a philosophical attitude.

Ortega has given this attitude expression in different ways. One seems to be particularly adequate for our purpose. We may call it the theory of circumstances. At the beginning of his *Meditations* Ortega claimed that man communicates with the universe by means of his circumstances.[3] He may try, and he has often tried, to do away with them, but no fruitful result has ever ensured from this attempt. Some people may prefer to look at the world *sub specie aeternitatis.* It is far more rewarding to look at it *sub specie circumstantiarum,* or, circumstances being after all temporal, *sub specie instantis.* In fact, no other method is available if we aim at a real, living universe instead of contenting ourselves with a spectral and dead one. Circumstances are not only the momentous realities and problems of the world we live in but also the seemingly humble things and questions that surround us at every moment of our existence. Therefore, it would be wrong, and even unfair, to dismiss them lightly. Circumstances are, at it were, the umbilical cord that ties us to the rest of the universe. We must accept them as starting points and perhaps as landmarks of our philosophical inquiry. Circumstances, however, are more than our surrounding universe. They are also an essential element of our lives. Thus Ortega was soon led to formulate a sentence that later proved to be a corner-stone of his philosophy: 'I am myself and my circumstances.'[4] The phrase may sound trivial. In fact, it is not more trivial than most philosophical sentences are when we persist in taking them only at their face value. In Ortega's formula a self is identified with himself *and* his circumstances, and therefore the thesis is maintained—against idealist philosophers—that a self can never be postulated as an ontologically independent being. Far from being a trivial tautology, this phrase appears rather as an involved double assumption according to which I cannot conceive of myself without conceiving at the same time of my own circumstances and, conversely, I cannot conceive of any circumstances without conceiving of myself as their dynamic centre. Man is, in Ortega's conception, a 'circumstantial being'; whatever he does, he must do in view of his circumstances.[5] We shall ponder later over this question, which will prove to be decisive in our more formal presentation of Ortega's philosophical anthropology. At the present stage it will suffice to keep in mind that Ortega conceives of human circumstances as the natural and whole medium of every human being, as the thing we must unhesitatingly accept unless we resign ourselves to turn our real being into a pure abstraction. This is certainly in tune with some other contemporary philosophers who stand for an 'open world' against the 'closed universe' postulated by idealist thinkers. It must be remembered, however, that Ortega does not simply advocate a 'philosophy of the open world' but insists upon the *fact* that whatever your philosophy may be you cannot avoid living in such a world. As Kant began his *Critique of Pure Reason* by considering the *factum* of physical science, Ortega begins his philosophy by considering the *factum* of human life existing among circumstances.

Circumstances are thus a crude fact. They are not, however, an opaque reality. Contrary to all irrationalist tendencies, Ortega stresses again and again the need for rational clarity. True, such a need has always been acknowledged by most philosophers. The very existence of philosophy evinces a taste for rationality that is at the same time a perpetual quest for clarity. But Ortega's notion of clarity differs in some respects from the traditional one. Clarity is not something superimposed on life as if it were external to it. Neither is it life itself, but rather 'the plenitude of life.'[6] Hence the conception of reason as a 'vital function'[7] that Ortega worked out later in detail and that appears already in the *Meditations,* coupled with the assertion that the usual state of war between reason and life must be looked at with suspicion. Now in order to attain such a plenitude two elements are needed: one is the *concept;* the other is the *perspective.*

Let us start with Ortega's notion of concepts. He has defined them in various ways. Concepts are not intended, for example, to serve as substitutes for the living impressions of reality.[8] In so far as we aim at the concrete reality of things, we cannot help living under the spur of our impressions. They are, as it were, the basic layer of our existence, the main body of our spontaneous life. To dismiss impressions as sources of error, as is done too often by idealists and rationalists, is only a subterfuge. Against mistrust of impressions and, in general, of vital spontaneity, Ortega proclaims the necessity of developing and even

of cultivating them. To act otherwise is a fatal error or, still worse, sheer hypoc-
risy. Hence his insistence upon the need for attending to a great many segments
of life usually disregarded by philosophers. In this respect Ortega fully agrees
with Nietzsche's demand—and with Simmel's recommendation—to unfold the
wings of life to the utmost. Science and justice, art and religion are not the sole
realities worthy of man's thought and sacrifice. It would be highly desirable
some day in the pantheon of illustrious men to have not only a genius in
physics like Newton and a genius in philosophy like Kant but a 'Newton of
pleasures' and a 'Kant of ambitions.'[9] Pleasures and ambitions must therefore be
given their full scope. Contrary to Nietzsche though, Ortega does not believe
that the layer of spontaneity, out of which impressions arise, is self-sufficient.
It seems to be unbounded; actually, it has many limitations: among others, the
fact that pure spontaneity, deprived of cultivation, is a blind and senseless force.
In order to give it meaning, it is necessary to introduce concepts. In a statement
reminiscent of a celebrated sentence of Kant, Ortega seems to imply that
impressions without concepts are blind and concepts without impressions are
shallow. Unlike Kant, however, he couples impressions and concepts as if they
were two sides of the same reality. Here lies, incidentally, a source of difficulties
for Ortega's philosophy: the same difficulties that have perennially baffled
philosophers as soon as they have attempted to correlate sense impressions and
ideas. Ortega does not overlook these difficulties, but he thinks he has found
a clue to the solution by watering down both impressions and concepts, the
former being in his opinion more than sense impressions and the latter being
less than formal schemata. We will not take him to task for this solution,
inasmuch as our purpose is to understand rather than to blame. We shall simply
point out that Ortega wavers between a definition of concepts as 'ideal schemata' and their characterization as pragmatic tools for grasping reality. At all
events, he seems to be quite convinced that without concepts we should be at
a loss amidst the whirlwind of impressions. Hence the importance attached to
the process of conceptualization—an importance that is enhanced rather than
lessened by the fact that, contrary to Hegel's opinion, concepts for him are not
the metaphysical substance of reality. They are organs of perception in exactly
the same sense that the eyes are organs of sight. But 'perception' must be
understood here as 'perception of depth'[10] or perception of the order and connection of realities. Perceptions take us from the level of spontaneous life to the
level of reflective life. Spontaneous life, however, is never laid aside; it is always
the beginning and the end of our inquiry. We do not know whether Ortega
would agree with the definition 'Concepts are good conductors of impressions,'
but we think it not too inaccurate a statement of his views on the subject.

Concepts are thus closer to life than most people would admit. They are
also very close to that other notion often referred to as 'perspective.'

We can trace its origins as far back as 1910, when Ortega emphatically declared that there are as many entities as there are points of view.[11] This doctrine was at the time allied to two other theories: one affirming that beings are reduced to values and another affirming that no entity can be said to exist unless related to other entities, so that what we call a thing is nothing but a bundle of relations. The former theory is substantially Platonic; the latter fundamentally Leibnizian. Ortega dropped both theories a few years later. In return, the 'doctrine of the point of view' was reasserted and developed on several occasions. Three of them will be mentioned here.

The first one was in the *Meditations.*[12] Contrary to traditional opinions that reality consists in matter or spirit or any other of the usual metaphysical constructions set up by philosophers, Ortega boldly puts forward the proposal that the basic layer of reality is a perspective. Now while in the former stage perspectivism was dependent upon an abstract ontology of a relationistic type, in the present phase it is based in a large measure upon a will to concreteness which permeates the philosopher's *Meditations* from start to finish. No wonder therefore that we find on the same pages an attack on the conception of wholes as abstractions of parts and even a definition of the hammer as the abstraction of the sum of its strokes. Nevertheless, the theory of perspective is still wrapped in the doctrine of circumstances and lacks the chiselling its author gave it later. Only in 1916, in an article entitled 'Truth and Perspective,' included in the first volume of *The Spectator,* the doctrine of perspective is presented stripped of distracting incidental remarks. Ortega begins by raising the question of the old-established opposition between scepticism and dogmatism. Scepticism asserts that inasmuch as reality is split up into individual perspectives universal truths are unattainable. Dogmatism, and in particular rationalistic dogmatism, asserts that inasmuch as there are universal truths no individual perspective is ever possible. Now Ortega takes it as a *fact* that individual perspective is the only way of seizing reality and, therefore, of formulating universal truths. He is not unaware, of course, that such a perspectivism is an old time-honored view in the history of philosophy. He quotes in this connection Leibniz, Nietzsche, and Vaihinger; he might have quoted, too—to mention only a few—Teichmüller, Simmel, or Russell. But he declares that his predecessors, while having similar aims, started from different assumptions. This seems quite clear as far as Nietzsche or Vaihinger is concerned. It appears less clear with regard to Leibniz. There is, however, in our opinion, a fundamental difference between Leibniz's perspectivism and Ortega's. While Leibniz's doctrine was couched in a monadological realism, Ortega's doctrine is embedded rather in a pluralistic realism. Thus Ortega proclaims the fact that strict coincidence of two views of reality would yield a pure abstraction, unless it were the outcome of a hallucination. Two views on the same reality cannot be strictly coincident, but at most complementary. This does not mean that complementary views are easy to obtain even if, following Ortega's recommendations, the individual tries to avoid distortion by faithfully reproducing his own perspective.[13] Confronted with Ortega's optimism on this issue, the reader may retort by simply pointing out the strenuous and unsuccessful attempts made by contemporary philosophers to solve the problem of the so-called intersubjectivity of particular statements. He may recall that schools of philosophy differing as widely among themselves as Husserlian phenomenologists and logical positivists have been compelled to slice off extensive fragments of their theories because of their failure to avoid solipsism after upholding a certain type of perspectivism. To such objections it is probable that Ortega would remain unyielding. He would certainly argue that his own brand of perspectivism is free from these drawbacks, precisely because he had previously got rid of subjectivistic or idealistic assumptions. He would, in short, claim that perspective is never a merely 'subjective' affair but an element or constituent of reality itself. Had Ortega used in this connection a more technical vocabulary, he might have stated that the term 'perspectivistic' is both an ontological and a psychological predicate. Perspectives, in other words, are the concrete sides of reality as perceived by concrete beings.

Ortega's theory of perspectives received both a confirmation and a clarification in 1923 in his *The Modern Theme*. As his first written attempt to present his arguments in a cogent way, this new exposition of perspectivism is particularly noteworthy. Perspectivism is now no longer an incidental remark or a mere project to be carried out when time permits. It is the cornerstone of a philosophical discipline: theory of knowledge. Leaning upon certain results of contemporary biology and psychology, Ortega assumes as a matter of fact that the reality denoted by the term 'subject' is, so to speak, an epistemological 'medium.' This medium of knowledge is, however, neither purely active nor entirely passive; namely it is neither a distorting nor a transparent vehicle of outside impressions. It may be compared to a selective screen, indefatigably engaged in sifting out what philosophers call 'the given.' Hence the possibility of considering each knowing subject as a private and yet faithful mirror of reality, barring of course conscious and deliberate distortion. That Ortega's analysis in this respect is couched in biological language is a fact that some commentators on his thought have not failed to notice and even to censure. Such comments seem to be all the more plausible as Ortega has often shown a predilection for biological science, in particular of the von Uexküll-Driesch brand. He has even seemed prone to consider 'life' from the point of view of biological impulse, thus sharing the well-known biologistic tendencies of such philosophers as Nietzsche or Simmel, not to speak of the numerous attempts at reducing knowledge to a process guided by biological utility. These interpretations have, in short, denounced Ortega's philosophy as biologically oriented. This, of course would not be in the least vexatious for a positivistic-minded philosopher, one who would dismiss as meaningless talk not only Heidegger's contempt for a merely 'ontical' view of life but also Dilthey's conception of life as a historical reality. Ortega, however, is not a positivistic-minded philosopher and consequently he has been rather touchy on this issue. Various reasons may be adduced in his defence. Let us mention three of them.

The first of these is based upon Ortega's idea that statements *in modo obliquo* cannot be avoided by a philosopher. Among such statements we may count, on the one hand, comparisons, and on the other hand, metaphors. It might then very well be the case that Ortega's biological language was either comparative or metaphorical. The second one is derived from the need of meeting the requirements of polemics. Faced with the question of how to lay sufficient stress on life against the encroachments of pure reason, the philosopher might have imagined that biological language would give more cogency to his arguments than the usual ontological or epistemological vocabulary. As the third reason, we may again point out that since perspectives belong both to the subject and to the object they cannot be reduced to a mere biological sifting of impressions. We do not know which reason Ortega would prefer. It is beyond doubt, however, that he would not accept a biological interpretation of knowledge, however difficult it proves to lay down a theory of knowledge free from biological commitments without purging it at the same time of a biological terminology. He would argue that, after all, he had soon coupled the notion of the 'vital' with historical perspective, to such an extent that the word 'life' in a sentence like 'Each life is a point of view directed upon the universe'[14] denotes not only, or exclusively, a human individual but also a national community or a historical period. Here we have, be it said in passing, a theme that will grow bigger in Ortega's thought: historicism. This we shall discuss in our next section; for the time being let us conclude by saying that in Ortega's opinion perspectivistic truth, although partial, is none the less absolute. It fails only to be complete. But completeness, in the nonformal sense of this word, can only be attained if we are willing to sacrifice a real point of view to a fictitious one.[15]

Reality, as given to concrete human life and not as perceived by an abstract being, located nowhere, is thus one of the main tenets of Ortega's philosophy, at least during the period we are now discussing. He seems to be eager above all to show that the complaints of both rationalists and supernaturalists against the transient character of life and reality are nothing but phraseology and insincerity.[16] Reality and life are not supposed to stay for ever: their value and gracefulness are enhanced rather than diminished by their ever-changing nature. They are, in short, temporal, and only those who prefer to substitute shallow abstractions for them will attempt to deny what is not a theory but the most simple and evident of all facts. The passages in which Ortega keeps insisting upon the fact that reality and life are *both* valuable and perishable—or rather valuable because perishable—are too numerous to be quoted here.[17] Let us simply sum up his views on the subject by stating that he tries again and again to lay stress on mutability as opposed to fixity, on playful behavior as opposed to reverence for utopia. The pleasures of life are ephemeral. So much the better; they are thus authentic. Spontaneity ruins conventions. No matter; it will give rise to new and better ones. Play seems to lack dignity. It is because we forget that pure science, art, and philosophy are products of purely disinterested behavior. The philosopher must therefore foster all that is living and real, namely all that is authentic. Echoing Nietzsche, Bergson, and Simmel, Ortega seems now to overpraise the values of life and, in particular, of human life.

It would be too hasty, nevertheless, to reach such a conclusion. True, we often miss in Ortega's writings of this period, in spite of the undeniable plasticity and incisiveness of his style, the sharp-cut outlines that should be the rule among philosophers. As we have already pointed out, he makes so much of life at a bare biological level that we often find it difficult not to take his statements in this respect at their face value. A case in point is his flat assertion that 'pure biology must be given preference to ethics when judging the values of vitality.'[18] Another case in point is his contention that culture consists in certain biological activities 'neither more nor less biological than digestion or locomotion.'[19] All this seems to be perfectly clear. But a number of passages may also be quoted that suggest a far less biologistic and, for that matter, vitalistic orientation. They show that life must not be understood in the classical sense of a substance, that is to say, as something existing by itself and being conceived only by itself. Life is not subsistent. It is not independent. In a quite significant passage Ortega writes that his fondness for the spontaneity and authenticity of life has nothing to do with Rousseauistic primitivism. Attention must be paid to the spontaneous and primitive life of the spirit 'in order to secure and enrich culture and civilization.'[20] So-called spontaneous life would be of little value if it consisted in pure savagery or rusticity. Quite the contrary: the value of life must be measured by its capacity to create the values of culture. A reason for this is that life—and in particular human life—is always 'life with,' with something or with somebody. Life exists in an 'environment,' a word that has, of course, biological connotations but also sociological and even ontological ones. In another passage the philosopher writes that the biological notion of life is only a segment of a much broader concept and therefore cannot be reduced to its somatic meaning.[21] We are thus left in doubt about a concept that plays a fundamental role in Ortega's philosophy. Fortunately enough, such a doubt does not last. Vitalism, to be sure, remains as one important side of Ortega's thought, but as *one* side only. That this is the case we can see quite clearly in the more systematic presentation of Ortega's views contained in the book to which we have been referring, but which needs closer scrutiny: *The Modern Theme.*

The title itself, later considered by Ortega as being 'too solemn,'[22] suggests to the reader the main aims of the author. Roughly speaking, the point is this. Modern philosophers, at least since the time of Descartes, have shown a strong propensity to rely almost entirely upon abstract universal truths. This propensity has been given a name: rationalism. According to it, man is supposed to be primarily a rational animal whose task consists in unearthing flawless, rational principles capable of working to perfection not only in the fields of philosophy and science but also in the fields of ethics and politics. This assumption leads to some momentous consequences: the mistrust of human spontaneity, the propensity to utopian thought and, last but not least, the growing tendency to superimpose culture on life and pure reason on spontaneous behavior. The reader may judge that this picture is oversimplified. As a matter of fact, it is. It may be reasonably doubted that the modern age, even if considered only in the works of the scientists and philosophers, is explicable solely in terms of rationalism. Ortega is not unaware of this difficulty. Accordingly he brings in another modern position, one running counter to the above. This position consists chiefly in the denial of universal truths and in the assertion of the mutability of life. It too has been given a name: relativism. Many modern empiricists and sceptics may be counted among its followers. Now as we have seen, neither rationalism nor relativism is in a position to cope with the difficulties raised by the coexistence of individual with historical perspective and the undeniable yearning for universal truth. The theme of our time amounts thus to the effort to settle the dispute between rationalism and relativism. This statement is in tune with former views held by Ortega, who in 1916 had already declared that he felt no longer compelled to bear the label of 'modern man,' because he wanted to be a 'twentieth century man.'[23] By this he implied that 'the modern theme' was already exhausted and the twentieth century marked the beginning of a new age facing new problems and striving for new solutions in philosophy, in science, in art, and in politics.[24] Thus the book is not merely written in opposition to the theme of the 'modern age' but in an effort to overcome it.

Against the alternative of pure reason *or* pure vitality a new doctrine is set forth according to which reason emerges from life while at the same time life cannot subsist without reason. Ortega takes this stand especially in relation to the much discussed clash between life and culture. He engages, of course, in a bitter struggle against all rationalistic tendencies to overpopulate the world with abstract principles. He asserts that principles must not be deprived of their vital basis otherwise they would become, as Bradley wrote of Hegel's metaphysics, 'a bloodless ballet of categories.' He emphatically proclaims that overemphasis on 'culture,' 'spiritual life,' and the like is most of the time the result of an ostrich-like, indeed a pharisaical attitude. We must therefore adopt a radically sincere attitude toward the requirements of life. We must acknowledge that at least in its first stage the emergence of human culture and hence of values and principles is, to use Toynbee's terminology, a response to the challenge of human life by its physical and historical environment. Cultural values have, in short, their immediate origin in the *vital* needs of the human individual. Once this is conceded, however, another no less undeniable fact must be admitted. Cultural values as vital functions are ultimately subjective facts. But these facts obey objective laws. Pure vital functions, as, for instance, the biological ones, are so to speak immanent in the biological organism. Cultural functions, on the other hand, are transcendent or, as Ortega puts it, 'transvital.' It will be said perhaps that such an idea is anything but novel, yet there is a sense in which Ortega's conceptions may be said to differ from those of his predecessors. It is a fact that, contrary to many, the Spanish philosopher would never agree to the theory that there is a break of continuity between pure vital functions and objective laws governing cultural values. Hence his assertion that *all* cultural values are *also* subject to the laws of life.[25] The word 'life' has therefore a very broad meaning, certainly not only a biological meaning. As a matter of fact, it has a double meaning: a biological and a spiritual one.[26] These two meanings appear often as mutually exclusive. Moral values are sometimes incompatible with the pleasures of life. The recognition of aesthetic values is not always accompanied by delight. But on neither side are we permitted to conclude that each time the biological side exercises its rights spiritual claims must be withdrawn and vice versa. Although extreme separate poles, they belong to the same world and they often counterbalance each other. In other words, men willing to lend their ears to the 'modern theme' must not be caught in the trap either of primeval vitality or of sophisticated civilization.

True enough, Ortega insists at this stage more upon life and its values—sincerity, impetuosity, pleasure—than upon culture and its values—truth, goodness, beauty. He does this because he believes that modern civilization has overemphasized the latter. As a matter of fact, such overemphasis is not limited to the modern epoch but has been a striking characteristic of the whole of Western civilization. The predominance of life still prevailed in the beginnings of Greek culture and civilization; but Western man from the time of Socrates has tried to enforce the laws of reason. Vital spontaneity has been curbed to such an extent that at the end of this long historical process it has been assumed that reason, namely pure reason, was the real substance of the universe.[27] Instead of viewing reason as 'a tiny island afloat on the sea of primeval vitality,'[28] philosophers considered it the sea itself. They made a mistake, but it was, so to speak, a necessary mistake. If they had not tried to oust life from the realm of reason, life would never have crossed the boundaries of pure biological spontaneity. But they obviously went too far in that direction, and with the ousting of life came the ousting of reality. Pure reason finally conquered a whole kingdom, but it proved to be a kingdom without subjects. In view of this, a rediscovery of the potentialities of life remains imperative. But this rediscovery must not be a simple counterclockwise movement. Pure reason or thinking *more geometrico* is 'an acquisition we can never forgo.'[29] What remains to be done is to put it back in its place. Therefore, neither Rousseauistic primitivism nor romantic irrationalism can be accepted as healthy corrective measures. Thus the problem is how to pass a fair judgment on life. But before pronouncing sentence on the place of life in the whole of reality it is necessary to liberate it from its subservience to pure reason. In other words, we must recognize that 'reason is merely a form and function of life.'[30] Only then will a new type, *vital reason,* emerge.

With this new concept we are in a position to keep our former promise: to describe the third phase of Ortega's intellectual career by means of a formal presentation of his philosophy.

NOTES

1. Although *Persons, Works, Things* was published in 1916 and belongs apparently to the first group, all of the essays and articles it contains were written and published in periodicals before 1914.

2. I, 319, 321–2 (1914) [*Meditations,* pp. 45, 67–69].

3. I, 319 (1914) [*Meditations,* p. 45].

4. I, 322 (1914) [*Meditations,* p. 45; the English translators write: 'I am myself plus my circumstances'].

5. There is clearer restatement of this opinion in VI, 348 (1932).

6. I, 358 (1914) [*Meditations,* p. 99].

7. I, 353 (1914) [*Meditations,* p. 93].

8. I, 352 (1914) [*Meditations,* p. 92].

9. I, 320 (1914) [*Meditations,* p. 43].

10. I, 320 (1914) [*Meditations,* p. 62].

11. I, 475 (1910).

12. I, 321 (1914) [*Meditations,* pp. 67–8].

13. II, 18–20 (1916).

14. III, 200 (1923) [*The Modern Theme,* from now on cited as *Theme,* p. 91].

15. III, 199 (1923) [*Theme,* p. 89].

16. On sincerity see II, 481–90 (probably 1924) and IV, 513–6 (1924).

17. See, for instance: II, 232–3 (1919); II, 283, 290–1, 293, 302 (1920); III, 141–242 (1923) [*Theme, passim*].

18. II, 293 (1920).

19. III, 166–7 (1923) [*Theme*, p. 41].

20. II, 283 (1920). See also III, 179 (1923) [*Theme*, p. 60].

21. III, 164, note (1923) [not included in *Theme*, p. 38]; III, 189 (1923) [*Theme*, p. 74]. A *mise au point* in VI, 348 (1932) and in part in III, 270–80 (1924).

22. IV, 404 (1932).

23. III, 22–4 (1916). This incidentally makes the English translation of Ortega's title *El tema de nuestro tiempo* as *The Modern Theme* somewhat misleading. An exact rendering would be *The Theme of Our Time*.

24. See VI, 304 (1922); 306 (1922) and 312 (1923).

25. III, 169 (1923) [*Theme*, pp. 45–6].

26. It should be noted that the meaning of the word 'spiritual' in Spanish does not strictly coincide with its meaning in English. In Ortega's works 'spiritual' is usually a designation for the realm of values as well as for objective scientific laws.

27. III, 176–7 (1923) [*Theme*, pp. 55–6]. Also III, 540–3 (1927).

28. III, 177 (1923) [*Theme*, p. 57].

29. III, 178 (1923) [*Theme*, p. 58].

30. *loc. cit.*

Chapter Four

'Ratio-Vitalism'

1 THE CONCEPT OF VITAL REASON

Although outlined in *The Modern Theme*, the concept of vital reason was badly in need of further clarification. As we have seen, Ortega's emphasis on life had led some critics to interpret his philosophy as a purely vitalistic, indeed biologistic philosophy. It has also been pointed out that such an interpretation, although it may be justified by the philosopher's tendency to use biological language, does not accord with some of his most notable statements. A year after the publication of *The Modern Theme* Ortega issued an article in his *Revista de Occidente* in which he expressed his opinion on that delicate subject. The article, characteristically entitled 'Neither Vitalism nor Rationalism,'[1] made it perfectly plain that both philosophical tendencies were, in the author's opinion, entirely outmoded. Rationalism was to be rejected because it confused the use of reason with its abuse. As for vitalism, the very ambiguity of its meaning made it hardly acceptable to a philosopher. To begin with, two brands of vitalism can be singled out for distinction: biological vitalism and philosophical vitalism. The former is the name of a specific scientific theory and is, accordingly, of little help for the present purpose. The latter is the name of a method of knowledge and must be carefully scrutinized.

Now the expression 'philosophical vitalism' is again highly ambiguous. On the one hand, it claims to be a doctrine (defended among others, by pragmatists and empirio-criticists) according to which reason is a biological process governed by biological laws: the struggle for life, the law of economy, the principle of least action. On the other hand, it purports to be a theory (chiefly worked out by Bergsonians) according to which reason is epistemologically helpless and must give way to intuitive insight which only 'life' is capable of affording. In this last sense, vitalism is a method of 'knowledge' sharply opposed to the rational method. Finally, it claims to be a philosophy asserting that knowledge is, and must necessarily be, of a rational character, except for the fact that as life remains the central philosophical issue, reason must try above all to probe its significance. Only this third brand of philosophical vitalism is accepted by Ortega as a fair description of his own philosophical position.

It will be seen that the very meaning of the term 'vitalism' has been considerably watered down. This is, incidentally, one of the reasons why other less controversial and more descriptive labels are preferable, such as the doctrine of vital reason, the doctrine of historical reason, the doctrine of living reason[2] and, of course, ratio-vitalism. Nevertheless, all have a common aim: to show that if philosophy is 'philosophy of life,' this expression cannot be understood in exactly the sense given to it by some other philosophers: Simmel, Spengler, Bergson, or Dilthey. True, Ortega does not consider his own philosophizing as strictly running counter to the Bergsonian and still less to the Diltheyan. But he has often implied that his 'philosophy of vital reason' lies on a more advanced level both in time and in philosophical acuteness than the plain 'philosophy of life' of his predecessors. The mistrust of reason pervading all of them is no longer held by Ortega as a necessary condition for acknowledging the central place of life in a philosophical system. In his opinion, such a mistrust is due to the fact that the term 'reason' was invariably identified by these philosophers with the expressions 'pure reason,' 'abstract reason' and 'physical reason' (we may add 'mathematical reason' and 'physicomathematical reason'). The failure of pure reason to understand life was, of course, a sound warning that such reason was in need of strong criticism.[3] But the collapse of pure reason is not the collapse of *all* reason. It would therefore be a mistake to suppose that the failure of traditional rationalism leaves the way clear for mere irrationalism. As a matter of fact, irrationalism, so unfortunately welcomed in certain contemporary philosophical circles, is no less dangerous—and is far more helpless—then rationalism. Once more, then, rationalism and irrationalism are the result of a blindness to two equally significant sides of reality. Rationalism in particular has been guilty of sterilizing reason 'by amputating or devitalizing its decisive dimension,'[4] by forgetting that reason 'is every such act of the intellect as brings us into contact with reality.'[5] Thus a new type of reason emerges, but, it must be noted, this type of reason is not a new *theory* about reason but the plain recognition of the *fact* that, whatever man thinks of reason, it is always rooted in his life.

Vital reason appears therefore to Ortega as a reality—a simple, unassailable, self-evident reality. As a matter of fact, the expression 'vital reason' is tantamount to the expression 'life *as* reason.' For it is assumed that life—which we shall henceforth understand as human life—is not an entity *endowed with* reason but rather an entity that *necessarily uses* reason even when it seems to behave unreasonably. No matter how thoughtlessly a man acts, in some way or other he will always account for what he does. The way he does it is quite immaterial. He may repent of behaving as he does, or he may claim that man is a strange sort of animal, loving the good and yet bowing down to evil. At any rate, life cannot exist without tirelessly accounting for itself. Now since to live is, as Ortega would put it, to contend with the world,[6] human life must also account for the world that surrounds it. Let us add, however, that this process of 'accounting for' is not exclusively of an intellectual nature. Intellectual explanations of oneself and of the world are, indeed, latecomers in the process of human living. Ortega keeps repeating that life is impossible without knowledge, because knowledge is, above all, *knowledge of how to act*—a rather clumsy translation of Ortega's definition: *saber es saber a qué atenerse.*[7] In other words, man can live as he pleases, but he cannot live without doing his utmost to dispel the mist of doubts ever surrounding him. In fact, reason was, as it were, invented by man in order to counteract his tendency to cast doubts on everything, and in particular on himself.[8] Reason becomes thus the only possibility offered to man in order to help him carry on his own existence on the slippery ground of his life. Man is *not* therefore a rational animal, if this definition is understood in the sense that being an animal is the *genus proximum* and being rational the *differentia specifica.* But he is a rational animal if this definition is understood in the sense that reason emerges from human life. Descartes' principle *Cogito ergo sum* ('I think, therefore I am') must be replaced by a more basic principle: *Cogito quia vivo* ('I think, because I live').[9]

Although, as has been observed, vital reason is a reality, it is also a method.[10] Unfortunately, this method cannot be based upon a set of simple rules. As an outcome of life itself, vital reason as a method must follow the windings and meanderings of life. In a very radical sense of the word 'empirical,' the method of vital reason is an empirical method. Now 'empirical' does not necessarily mean 'chaotic.' Idealist philosophers have assumed that the world is a chaos of impressions upon which a certain order is imposed by means of the so-called categories. To Ortega this is a completely gratuitous supposition. Experience shows rather that as soon as we bring life back to the center of philosophical inquiry, the world reveals itself as a well-ordered, a 'systematic' reality. Vital reason is thus no luxury for us. It is our guiding principle in our search for the 'system' of being. Faced with the problem of our own life, we cannot fail to throw upon it the light of understanding. The fact that most of the time such an understanding is vague or distorted or gathered from the beliefs treasured up by society is not an argument against its absolute necessity. Man's search for security is precisely one of the most powerful reasons for acknowledging the insecurity of his living. And as the best tool man has ever produced to cope with such a feeling of insecurity is reason, it will be now less hard to accept, and less difficult to understand, Ortega's repeated assertion that reason must always be conceived as something functional in human existence.[11] Again, thought is not something that man possesses and accordingly uses,[12] but something that he painstakingly brings to existence because he needs it.[13]

Stumbling through his own life and through the world into which he has been thrown, man is compelled to brood over his own situation, that is, to think about his circumstances. But to think about circumstances is really to think *in view of* circumstances. Therefore, the attempt to discover what we are and what are our surroundings is not a task exclusively incumbent upon the 'intellectual'—the philosopher, the scientist, the artist; it is a burden we shoulder for the mere fact of living.[14] Man *needs* to know himself and his circumstances. He needs, accordingly, an idea or an 'interpretation' of the world. This is the primary sense of the expression 'Man must have his own convictions.' For what is called 'a man without convictions' is a non-existent entity.[15] These convictions may be of a negative character. A given individual may be, for example, a sceptic. It is none the less true that negative convictions are still convictions. Ortega has clarified this important point in many of his writings. One of them, however, is particularly enlightening for our purpose. It is the essay entitled 'Ideas and Beliefs' ('Ideas y creencias') which purported to be the first chapter of a systematic book on historical reason—and hence, as we shall see later, vital reason.[16] A brief description of its content will help us to understand the meaning of vital reason both as a method and as a reality.

In the first place, it is necessary to introduce a distinction. Hitherto we have referred indiscriminately to 'reason,' to 'ideas,' to 'convictions,' but the term 'idea' may be understood at least in two senses. On the one hand, ideas are thoughts which *occur* to us or to somebody else and which we can examine, adopt or even parrot. These thoughts have a varying degree of truth. They may be ordinary thoughts or very rigorous scientific statements. In both cases, thoughts arise from within a human life existing before them. On the other hand, ideas are interpretations of the world and of ourselves which do not arise from within our existence but are, so to speak, an essential part of this existence. If the former ideas may be called, after all, *ideas,* we need another name for the latter ones. Ortega calls them *beliefs.* Contrary to ideas *simpliciter,* we do not arrive at beliefs by specific acts of thinking. As a matter of fact, we do not *arrive* at them at all. They are already in us, making up the substance of our life. In us? In fact, inasmuch as we coexist with our beliefs we can also be said *to be* in them. Consequently, beliefs are not ideas that we hold but rather ideas that we are. So deep-rooted are beliefs that we confuse them with reality and we find it difficult to disentangle our beliefs about reality from reality itself.

Thus the difference between ideas and beliefs is tantamount to the difference between thoughts which we produce, examine, discuss, disseminate, accept, deny or formulate, and thoughts which we do not formulate, discuss, deny or accept. As Ortega says, we really *do* nothing with beliefs; we *are* simply *in* them. It will be easily seen that the distinction between ideas and beliefs is not of a psychological nature and has little to do with degrees of psychological certainty. Evidence, for instance, does not make up a belief. It is rather the result of mental acceptance and, as such, can only be predicated of ideas. The point of view of psychology, although highly respectable, is insufficient for tackling this problem. Another less specialized point of view must be taken, 'the point of view of life.' In short, a thought is called an idea *or* a belief according to the rôle it plays in human existence. The contrast between ideas and beliefs boils down, therefore, to the contrast between thinking about a thing and taking it for granted. 'To be in a belief' is, in fact, the same thing as to take an idea for granted. Here lies, be it said in passing, the reason why it would be a gross misunderstanding simply to identify beliefs with religious beliefs. Religious beliefs, it is true, often do deserve this name, but this is not necessarily so, because we frequently call religious beliefs what are in many cases nothing but plain ideas. On the other hand, many simple and elementary assumptions may be called beliefs. We believe, for instance, when deciding to go out into the street, that there is a street, even if the thought of the existence of a street has not entered our minds and seems to play no role in our decision. We believe that there is a certain regularity in natural phenomena in exactly the same sense as certain people have formerly believed that there was no regularity in natural phenomena. Examples could be multiplied. All of them, however, would converge on the same characteristics of a latent, nonformulated and sometimes even nonformulable thought we take continually for granted and which sustains, impels and directs our behaviour. No wonder beliefs form the foundation of our life and take the place of reality. Reality is not discovered by us. Nor is it proven by us. It is simply something we come up against. This means that to a certain extent we dominate our ideas, but are, in return, dominated by our beliefs. However important ideas may prove to be for us, they cannot take root in our life unless they cease to be ideas and become beliefs. This is why it is hard to accept the usual intellectualist interpretation of ideas. Intellectualists are incapable of understanding that ideas are external to us, that we can take or leave them at random. They are even incapable of understanding that on some occasions the reality upon which they place the highest value—reason—*may* become an authentic belief and accordingly escape criticism and examination. But perhaps the most striking difference between ideas and beliefs is that which Ortega has pointed out at the very beginning of his essay on this subject: while we can set so high a value on ideas that we are willing to fight and even to die *for* them, it is utterly impossible to live *on* them.

The reader may find that, no matter how plausible all this may seem, Ortega's arguments are not flawless. A moment ago we suggested that man is unceasingly casting doubts upon his own life or, in other words, that man's existence is deeply problematic. Furthermore, we shall discover that this is by no means an incidental remark, but a central issue in Ortega's philosophy of human existence. How are these assertions to be reconciled with the above scheme? Ortega is not unaware of this difficulty. And in order to avoid confusion he makes it plain that doubt is not something opposed to belief but is rather 'a kind of belief.' Two considerations may help to understand this paradoxical opinion. First, beliefs are never without gaps—and 'enormous gaps,' indeed. Second, doubts—in the very radical sense of this word—are simply upheld by us and, accordingly, are not ideas. Doubts belong, in short, to the same stratum of life as beliefs: the former make up our reality in a sense not altogether different from the latter. And this means, of course, that we *are in* doubts in exactly the same sense as we *are in* beliefs. The sole difference between them is that while beliefs are 'stable things' doubts are 'unstable things.' Doubts are, properly speaking, 'what is unstable' in human existence. But, of course, we live simultaneously with both of them, so that our existence would be as little thinkable without doubts as it is without beliefs.

The fact that we are *also* in doubts or even, as Ortega writes, 'in a sea of doubts,' does not preclude, however, the fact that we accept this situation as a normal state of affairs. As a matter of fact, we are unceasingly doing our utmost to rise above the doubt undermining our existence. Now in order to free ourselves of doubts we have but one choice: to think about them or, what comes to the same thing, to bring forth ideas. Ideas are supposed to fill the gaps that open here and there in the beliefs that make up human life. This seems at the outset to be scarcely plausible if we scrutinize our experience, for experience teaches us that actions rather than ideas cut the Gordian knot of our doubts. But plausibility increases if we pay attention to the fact that, according to Ortega, no clear-cut line is to be drawn between action and contemplation. Action, he writes, is certainly governed by contemplation, but at the same time contemplation—adumbration of ideas—is in itself a project for action.[17] Ideas may thus be considered as our sole possibility of keeping afloat on the sea of doubts. And it is not in the least uncommon to replace our former beliefs, shaken to the roots, by new ideas—which have a tendency to become beliefs. This can be experienced in our personal life. But there is a field in which the substitutions referred to are revealed with the utmost clarity: human history. Many of Ortega's examples are drawn from historical experience. To Ortega's reader this will not come as a surprise. Our philosopher has always been a true lover of history. Some of his finest essays are devoted to historical problems. He has, besides, often claimed that one of the outstanding characteristics of contemporary Western society is the full development of a feeling that had already been foreshadowed in the eighteenth century: the feeling that man is not an immutable creature living in a historical setting but an entity whose reality is decisively shaped by his own history. We shall call this feeling 'historical sense.' Since 1924, Ortega has made many remarks on this issue.[18] He has even been led to acknowledge that history is not only the subject-matter of a science but the ultimate condition of human existence. We shall later examine Ortega's assertion that man has no nature but has instead history. At present we shall limit ourselves to pointing out that the interplay between beliefs and ideas on the one hand and between beliefs and doubts on the other hand is confirmed by the events of history. The theory of historical crises and the detailed analysis of some of these crises[19] has made it clear that human life starts from beliefs, that is to say, from convictions which lie deep in the historical environment. As these convictions are shaken every now and then, they must be replaced by others— including the conviction that no convictions are at present available. The most adequate tool for the understanding of this problem is the method of historical reason. Now, before bringing this matter to an issue, we cannot help but venture a few remarks on a question which appears to be purely verbal, but which has given Ortega's commentators some trouble: that of the relationship between historical reason and vital reason.

First of all, if man is a historical being it seems inescapable that vital reason is identical with historical reason. Ortega's occasional hesitations in the use of these expressions have led some interpreters to assert that he jumped from the first to the second as a consequence of the deep impression made upon him by Wilhelm Dilthey's philosophy.[20] In some respects this does seem to be the case. Nevertheless, there is no denying the fact that Ortega has been eager to include historical reason in vital reason by emphasizing at the same time their homonymity and their synonymity. Let us assume for a moment that it would have been more plausible to substitute 'historical epoch' for 'human life' and 'historical reason' for 'vital reason.' But the fact that human life is basically a historical entity can be interpreted in two ways. First, we can do it in an all-our manner. In this case, Ortega's philosophy of vital reason would emerge as a sample of pure historicism. Yet there is also a moderate way of interpreting it. Then the philosophy of vital reason may provide the metaphysical basis for all philosophies, including historicism. In other words, if the first interpretation of the doctrine is accepted, then vital reason will be at the mercy of the waves of history. If, on the other hand, the second interpretation is preferred, then the statement that man is a historical being will have to be diluted and lose many of its implications. Two solutions may be offered in order to overcome these difficulties. One is Julián

Marías' contention that Ortega's notion of historical reason, unlike Dilthey's, is to be understood as an operation *of* life and history rather than as life and history themselves.[21] Another is Ortega's assumption that what we call the doctrine of vital reason is not, properly speaking, a doctrine, but the consequence of a plain fact: the fact that human life—which again is historical in character—is an entity that cannot escape using reason at large if it aspires to penetrate its own structure and significance. We cannot unfortunately elucidate this momentous question here. The analysis of human existence that follows will perhaps help the reader to make up his mind on this thorny subject.

2   THE DOCTRINE OF MAN

The doctrine of human life is a central issue—or rather *the* central issue—in Ortega's philosophy. Let us hasten to assure the reader that no idealism and, of course, no anthropocentrism is involved in this position. Human life is certainly not the sole reality in the universe. It can hardly be said to be the most important reality. But it is, as Ortega puts it, the *basic* reality, since all the other realities appear within it.[22]

The relationship between human life—namely, *each* human life—and the other realities must not be misunderstood. It would be a deplorable error to suppose that human life is a 'thing' within the frame of which other 'things' exist. Not being a thing, human life cannot be defined the way things usually are—by saying, for instance, that it has a certain nature, or that it is a substance or a law governing apparently unrelated phenomena. Human life—an expression synonymous with 'life,' 'our life,' 'human reality,' 'man,' etc.—is not reducible to our body, although, as we shall presently see, it cannot keep itself in existence without a body. To think otherwise is to contradict what has been said earlier about vital reason. In other words, it is tantamount to imagining that pure reason or 'physical reason' (e.g., 'scientific reason') sheds on human life that same vivid light it casts upon natural phenomena. Realism and naturalism, useful though they are in particular fields of knowledge like physics or biology, must be laid aside when the reality we face is the 'basic reality.' Shall we say then that our life is a soul, or a spirit, or a mind, or a consciousness? Idealists have, in fact, made this proposal. But idealism, or the philosophy of mind, is as useless for our purpose as realism, or the philosophy of things, or as naturalism, or the philosophy of matter. They are all the wrong type of philosophy or, to be more exact, the wrong type of ontology. After all, soul, mind, spirit, consciousness, thought and the like are to a certain extent things, as Descartes made clear in calling matter *res extensa* and thought *res cogitans*. In spite of the efforts of idealist philosophers to describe the reality of the ego without falling into the traps set by pure naturalism, they have always patterned their theories on the assumptions of traditional ontology. The same old mistakes made by realists have again and again crept into their analyses of human existence, thus making it impossible to seize hold of its paradoxical structure.

Human life is, therefore, neither body nor mind, neither a thing like matter nor a thing like spirit. What is it then? Some philosophers, anxious to solve the riddle of the mind-body problem, have reached the conclusion that human life is a 'neutral' entity, which can be called mind *or* body, depending upon the viewpoint taken upon it. It would seem at first that there is no wide difference between this opinion and Ortega's. If that were the case, Ortega's philosophy of human life would be quite close to a 'neutralism' of Mach's or Russell's type. Confronted with this issue, he would, however, emphatically deny such 'neutralistic' leanings. He would at most admit that his doctrine of man coincides with that of the neutralists in what they deny, but not in what they assert. For neutralism uses also willy-nilly the same concepts of traditional ontology. Like idealists or realists, neutralists assume that the reality of human life follows the pattern of the ontology of 'things.' But again human life is not a thing. It is not even a 'being.' It has no fixed status; it has no nature. Life *happens* to each one of us. It is a pure 'happening' or, as Ortega puts it, a gerundive, a *faciendum,* and not a participle, a *factum.* Instead of being something ready-made, we have to make it unceasingly. Life, in short, is a 'being' that makes itself, or rather 'something' consisting in making itself. In consequence of it, the concept of becoming, which some philosophers have propounded as a substitute for the concept of being, is only a trifle more adequate than the latter for the description of human experience. True, Ortega's philosophy draws nearer to a 'metaphysics of becoming' than to any other type of philosophy. After all, he has written that 'the time has come for the seed sown by Heraclitus to bring forth its mighty harvest' and he has agreed that Bergson, 'the least Eleatic of thinkers,' was right in many points.[23] But Heraclitus' philosophy of becoming was a mere hint, and Bergson's conception of *l'être en se faisant* is marred by an irrationalistic metaphysics for which Ortega feels but little sympathy. Fichte was, in fact, closer to grasping the true being of life than any other philosopher and was even on the point of discovering its basic structure. But his persistent intellectualism compelled him to think in 'Eleatic fashion.' A new ontology is, therefore, needed—an ontology equally distrustful of intellectualism and irrationalism, and capable of getting rid of the Eleatic remains still dragged along by the so-called dynamic philosophies of becoming.

How is such an ontology to be created? The answer has already been given: by the method of vital reason. When pure rationalism has collapsed in its attempt to understand human life, and when irrationalism has dissolved into an affected pathos, life as reason comes to the rescue. It shows that practically everything that has been said about human life is nothing but a more or less gratuitous theory superimposed upon life. But human life, again, is no theory: it is a plain fact. Before proceeding to theorize *about* human life, it will be wiser to give an account of it. Theory will thus emerge as a result of our description instead of being an *a priori* mental framework having only a very remote bearing on our 'basic reality.'

What does vital reason discover in its description of human life? To begin with, we have already indicated the negative features. Human life is, properly speaking, neither mind nor body. Mind and body are realities we have to live and contend with, in exactly the same sense as we have to live and contend with out physical and social environment. We find ourselves in a world which has been chosen by us. We live in constant intercourse with our circumstances. We are not a 'thing' but *the* person *who* lives a *particular* and *concrete* life with things and among things. There is no abstract and generic living. Ortega's old principle, 'I am myself and my own circumstances,' therefore plays a fundamental role in the descriptive ontology of human life. Against realists, Ortega claims, as we have seen, that our life is the basic reality and the point of departure for any sound philosophical system. Against idealists, he holds that life can only be understood as an entity fully immersed in the world. Ortega's statements in this respect are abundant. Life exists as 'a perpetual migration of the vital Ego in the direction of the Not-self.'[24] To live is 'to hold a dialogue with the environment,'[25] namely, to deal with the world, to turn to it, to act on it.[26] To live is to be outside oneself,[27] to contend with something,[28] with the world and with oneself. In short, to live is always *to live with*. For that reason, human life is not a 'subjective event.' It is the most objective of all realities. Now, among the realities we live and contend with, we must count our physiological mechanisms and our psychological dispositions. Helped by them *or* hindered by them, we must make our life and be faithful to our innermost *ego*, to our 'call,' to our 'vocation.'[29] This 'vocation' is strictly individual. Not all human destinies have the same degree of concreteness, but all personal 'vocations' are untransferable. What psychologists call 'character' is, in fact, only one among the many factors determining the course of our existence. It would be a gross mistake to suppose, therefore, that our life is solely determined by the external environment or by our character. Schlegel's belief that our talents correspond to our tastes is a grave misunderstanding. For if it is sometimes true that our tastes and our talents happily harmonize, it is unfortunately not unusual for them to clash violently. Let us suppose that you have a gift for mathematics. But what if you are irresistibly called to become a lyric poet? Let us imagine that we are endowed with the talents of a merchant. But what if we secretly crave to become scholars? The above examples are, however, not entirely to the point. Being a merchant of a lyric poet is, after all, a way of life set up by society and, as such, cannot be compared to the 'call' that forms the very basis of our personal 'destiny.' The examples are to the point though, in so far as they show that tastes and talents do not always go together and that the ensuring struggle between a man's personal destiny and his psychological character often accounts for the frequent feeling of frustration so characteristic of human existence. They are effective also in so far as they show that the world is not for us a collection of 'things' but rather a complex of 'situations.' Things—and ideas—are nothing but difficulties or facilities for existing.[30] We can even say that as books are made up of pages, human existence is made up of situations.[31] Thus man finds himself with a body, with a mind, with a psychological character, exactly as he finds himself, with capital left by his parents, with a country where he was born, with a historical tradition.[32] As we have to live with our liver, be it healthy or diseased, we have to live with our intelligence, be it bright or dull. However much we may complain about the weakness of our memory, we have to live with it and carry on our life *by means* of it. The life of a man is not, therefore, the operating of the mechanisms with which Providence has graced him. We must constantly ask in *whose* service these mechanisms operate. The question, in short, is not what I am but *who* I am.

Confronted with *all* these circumstances, man is forced to make his own life and to make it, whenever possible, in an authentic fashion.[33] This is, incidentally, the main reason why what we do in our life is *not* immaterial. In his essay on Goethe, Ortega has pointed out that Goethe's celebrated sentence, 'My actions are merely symbolic,' was but a way of concealing from himself the *decisive* character of his behaviour. As a matter of fact, our actions are not symbolic; they are real. We cannot, therefore act 'no matter how.' Human life has nothing to do with 'No matter,' 'Never mind,' or 'It is all one to me.' Neither can we act as we please. We have to act as we must act; we have to do what we have to do. It is unfortunate, of course, that upon reaching this deep stratum of our existence the only statements we seem capable of uttering are either tinged with morality or marred by triviality. 'To act as we must act' seems to be a moral rule—a kind of categorical imperative still more formal and far less normative than the Kantian one. It is nothing of the kind. It simply states that we must bow to our purely individual call, *even if it runs counter to the conventional rules of morality.*[34] It is possible, of course, to offer resistance to our destiny. But our life will be then less authentic and, to a certain extent, less real. 'To do what we have to do' seems to be a tautology. It is rather a way of enlightening us about the fact that our concrete actions, if they are to be real and not merely symbolic, must spring from the sources of our authentic, and often hidden, *ego,* and must not be diverted by any conventional rule, by any of the many temptations leading to the falsification of our existence. For human life can easily falsify itself and thus become less real. Nature does not admit of degrees of reality, but human existence does. Therefore, 'what man does can be more or less authentic and hence more or less real.'[35] This does not mean, of course, that to be unauthentic and to be nonexistent are exactly the same thing. It means that human life possesses sometimes the 'defective mode' of reality which we call inauthenticity.

Every reader will agree that the above descriptions raise a number of questions. How do we know about our authentic *ego?* Would an authentic life be possible without a certain amount of falsification and hence frustration? Why are moral rules of the so-called conventional kind to be so drastically discarded? The elucidation of any one of these questions would certainly fill an entire volume. Here it will be sufficient to say that whatever objections are raised, they will have to meet Ortega's assumptions on a common ground. This ground is not ethical but metaphysical—perhaps we should say, onto-logical. Only from a metaphysical point of view will the above assertions become meaningful. The same viewpoint must be taken when interpreting such Ortegean apothegm as 'Life is a problem,' 'Life is a task,' 'Life is a preoccupation with itself,' 'Life is a shipwreck,' and 'Life is a vital program.'

'Life is a problem' is not a trivial, matter-of-fact statement. It does not simply mean that we are often beset by problems. After all, a number of people seem to get along surprisingly well with their troubles. It means that life *itself* is a trouble, a problem, or, to use Ortega's vocabulary, that human life is made up of the problem of itself.[36] Human life is accordingly a most serious business, certainly far more serious than art, science or philosophy. The so-called great problems amount to little when compared to the startling problem of our own life. Now life is a problem because it is a task, a prob-lematic task. Again, we are not faced here with the tasks and toils of life but with *the* task and toil that human life itself *is.* Making use of a very suggestive Spanish term, Ortega defines life as a *quehacer*—what *has* to be done.[37] But *what* has to be done? In principle, only this: our *own* life. Is this not an overwhelming, almost unbearable toil? To begin with, we cannot make our own lives as we make other things—houses, symphonies or philosophical systems. These things we make according to a delicate mixture of rules and inspirations. But there are no rules for the making of our lives. The sole rule we can lay down is: perpetual discovery of our being. We can thus say that our life is a *causa sui,* a cause of itself. But even this proves to be an under-statement. In fact, human life has not only to cause itself; it has also to determine the self it is going to cause. We have always to decide what we are going to do with our lives. Not for a single moment is our activity of decision allowed to rest.[38] Here lies the reason why freedom is not something we are endowed with but something we really *are.* We are free beings in a most radical sense, because we feel ourselves *fatally* compelled to exercises our freedom. Man is free by compulsion,[39] for even when he forsakes his liberty he has to decide it beforehand. We must therefore commit ourselves perpetually, not because there is a moral rule stating that we have to, or because we happen to think that commitment is a nobler attitude than noncommitment, but because we cannot escape this inexorable condition of our existence. Freedom is so absolute in human life that we can even choose not to be 'ourselves,' namely, not to be faithful to that innermost self of ours which we have given above the name of personal destiny. Our freedom, however, will not decrease owing to the fact that our life becomes inauthentic, because freedom is precisely the absolute possibility of reaching or not reaching the inner 'call' sustaining our lives.

No wonder therefore that human life is always a preoccupation with itself. We are constantly worried by the diverse possibilities among which we have to choose. It is true that society helps us to decide in a great number of cases; otherwise, our life would become an unbearable burden. It is true also that circumstances, *in view of* which and *by means of* which we carry out our lives, are a most welcome guide in the course of our decisions. It is true, finally, that however 'plastic' our existence is, it is an irreversible process, so that the past—personal and collective past—shapes our present and imposes more and more limitations on our future behavior.[40] But ultimate decisions are always a purely personal affair. Inasmuch as solitude—'existential' and not merely 'physical' solitude—is an outstanding feature of human life, only decisions made in complete solitude will really be authentic.[41] Moreover, such decisions must always be made 'from the future.' Human life is also, therefore, a 'vital design,' a 'vital program'[42]—expressions which, to a certain extent, are synonymous with 'call,' 'vocation,' and 'destiny.' Again, to this design we may or we may not respond. For that very reason life exists in a constant state of uneasiness and insecurity. It has been said, incidentally, that this last statement conflicts with some other typically Ortegean opinions. Some critics, for example, have argued that you cannot define life as uneasiness if you have previously stated that sportive activity is the most serious and important part of life,[43] or if you have asserted that it is necessary, whenever possible, to get rid of dullness and austerity and to steer a course for joy.[44] To such criticisms Ortega would probably retort that uneasiness is not incompatible with joyful vitality and that his definition of life as insecurity is old enough for him to wave aside any objections.[45] At all events, Ortega's metaphysics of human life implies insecurity as one of its outstanding features. The opinion that life is in itself a problem, the comparison of life with a shipwreck, are quite common in Ortega's works.[46] But insecurity is *not* everything in human existence. Together with man's perennial state of uneasiness, we must take into account his perpetual craving for security. What we usually call 'culture' is at bottom nothing but a lifeboat which we launch and to which we cling in order to prevent us from sinking into the abyss of insecurity. Culture keeps us afloat.[47] This is, be it said in passing, one of the reasons why culture must *also* be authentic. We must prevent it from overloading itself with adipose tissue. We must do our utmost in order to reduce it to pure nerve and pure muscle. Otherwise we shall fall into a sin often exposed by Ortega: the bigotry of culture.[48] Culture is, in short, a possibility for liberation *or* for oppression. Whether it goes the one way or the other depends, of course, on its vitality, namely, on its authenticity.[49] Like human life, culture has to narrow itself down to the essential and throw off all that is nonessential.

Life is, therefore, task, problem, preoccupation, insecurity. It is also a drama.[50] For that very reason Ortega says that the primary and radical meaning of life is a biographical and not a biological one. We understand the meaning of life when we proceed to give a narrative of it, that is to say, when we try to describe the series of events and situations it has come up against and the vital design underlying them. Many reasons have been adduced to endorse the dramatic character of human existence. We shall add now another: the obvious fact that man is an ephemeral and transient being.[51] Man is always in a hurry. Life itself is haste and urgency. Pressed by time,[52] man cannot cast about for excuses. He has to dash along in order to make the right decisions at the right time. He cannot wait. His life is precisely the opposite of the Greek calends.[53] He cannot form projects only to be carried out in an indeterminate future. He must strive urgently, hurriedly, for the main aim of his life: the 'liberation *toward* himself.'[54] He cannot simply let events do away with the estrangement that constantly threatens his existence with inauthenticity and falsification. Only after his liberation will he be able to discover what is perhaps the ultimate conclusion in his search for the basic reality: that it is useless to search for a transcendent reality, because what we call 'the transcendent' is life itself: man's own inalienable life.[55] Life is thus, as it were, *the* reality. This does not mean, again, that human life is the sole reality in the universe or even that it is a purely independent, incommunicable reality. After all, we have already emphasized that to live is 'to live with'— with the world, with other people, with society. But after due consideration we find that when man loses the beliefs that had nourished his existence, the only reality still left to him is his life, 'his disillusioned life.'[56] We seem thus driven to despair. But, in fact, only when we are ready to glance coldly and lucidly at this uncanny nature of our existence shall we become capable of holding our own ground and starting afresh our perpetual search after new forms and ways of living.

3   THE DOCTRINE OF SOCIETY

Among the realities man lives with, society is a conspicuous one. Without prejudice to the individual's rights, there is no objection to saying that man is a social being. The analysis of society is accordingly a question of first importance.

From the beginning of his career, Ortega has acknowledged the exceptionally significant role played by social problems. Thoughts on the nature of society at large and on concrete societies, past or present, are frequent in his works. As a matter of fact, some of his most popular writings, like *Invertebrate Spain* and *The Revolt of the Masses,* are to a large extent analyses of social facts and problems. We do not therefore lay undue stress on this question by tackling it immediately after the problem of the 'basic reality.'

Some of Ortega's views on social topics are well known. In particular, his 'dissection of the mass-man,' as contained in *The Revolt of the Masses,* has become a matter-of-course basis for many discussions on the problem of contemporary society as 'mass society.' Indeed, the treatment of contemporary society as 'mass society' has become a trite subject, and, as a consequence, the very notion of 'mass society' has been abandoned, or is accepted only with qualifications. It should be noted, however, that Ortega began speaking of the 'power' and of the 'revolt' of the 'masses' as early as 1927, at a time when very few thinkers were concerned with the question. In this respect Ortega can be considered an intellectual pioneer, if not a prophet. Nevertheless, his treatment of contemporary society as 'mass society' was not, or not merely, sociological. Ortega was interested in a particular type of man rather than a given type of society. He sharply indicated the then emerging 'mass man' as a rebel with no other cause than his own feelings of self-satisfaction. Even if we grant the assumption that all men are born equal, such an assumption will not suffice to give everyone the right to mingle in all matters. But the 'mass man' thinks that he has all the privileges without any of the responsibilities. He ignores, or feigns to ignore, that some men are superior to others and that there is such a thing as nobility. Now 'nobility' does not mean membership in a given social class; in Ortega's opinion, nobility is a human rather than a social characteristic. Indeed, 'nobility' is a predicate definable by the demands it makes on us rather than by the concessions or favors we may enjoy. The 'mass man' can be found on *all* levels of society, and within all possible psychological types. There is little doubt that Ortega was somewhat aristocratic-minded in so far as he tended to look for 'superior men' in the upper levels of society. But his theory of the 'mass man' should not in principle lead to a doctrine asserting that an aristocracy, even an intellectual aristocracy, has in itself any superior qualities. Aristocrats can be, and often are, mass-minded. Therefore, although the indictment of 'the revolt of the masses' seems to favor some sort of social hierarchy it does not affirm that such a hierarchy must be based on inheritance, on wealth, or even on intellectual ability. Ultimately speaking, the hierarchy hailed by Ortega is founded upon the sense of social responsibility and upon the eventual recognition by each individual of his own place in society. What exactly this place is, or should be, in any particular instance, is unfortunately a question that Ortega never bothered to elucidate in any great detail.

Notwithstanding his emphasis on the 'moral' (in a wide and flexible sense of 'moral') rather than the sociological aspects of the 'revolt of the masses,' Ortega also analyzed the meaning of such a revolt as a sociologist and as a philosopher of history. From this viewpoint, he was considerably less critical of the 'revolt' than a superficial reader would expect. After all, Ortega did not want to set the clock back. The emergence of the 'mass man' may morally speaking be a deplorable affair. Historically speaking, however, it must be acknowledged that the rule of the masses 'presents a favorable aspect, inasmuch as it signifies an all-round rise in the historical level, and reveals that average existence today moves on a higher plane than that of yesterday.'[57]

Ortega's analyses of social facts and problems, as well as his scrutiny of the nature and development of diverse societies, in particular the old Roman society and the modern European one, are based on the assumption that society is a constantly changing reality which, like the individual, has no fixed nature but only a history. Society, like man, is, according to Ortega, an entity impervious to pure, abstract reason. Its being can be disclosed only by means of vital, that is, narrative and historical, reason. Yet, the examination of particular societies leads us sooner or later to an understanding of 'society as such.' To be sure, there is no such thing as 'society as such.' On the other hand, it is legitimate to raise the question 'What is society?' if we are constantly aware that we are dealing here with 'occasional concepts,' namely, concepts having only 'a formal identity that serves precisely to guarantee the constitutive nonidentity of the matter signified.'[58]

In his general theory of society Ortega lays down a set of fundamental notions. The first we have already pointed out: just as man exists in a physical world, so he also exists in a social world. Society is thus an 'element' where man 'moves and is.' The physical and the social world have something in common: they bring pressure to bear on our lives. The fact that social pressures are for the most part invisible does not mean that they do not exist; they exist in so far as they act. For social pressures are not exerted by things; they are exerted by usages, customs, rules, etc.[59] Usages are here particularly important, for without them we could not understand the nature of any society. It must be pointed out that usages are not reducible to customs. Nor are customs reducible to 'habits.' For one thing, a usage is not necessarily an action performed with a given frequency. Breathing is performed very frequently, indeed, and yet it is not a usage. The Roman *ludi saeculares* were held only once every century, and yet they were usages. It is true that most usages exert an action through their frequency. But even then it would be more reasonable to say that something is a usage not because it is frequent but rather 'we do it frequently because it is usage.'[60]

Usages can be 'weak' (as with birthday parties) or 'strong' (as with so-called 'public opinion').[61] In either case they are so obvious that we do not even think of their existence, and still less of their pressure. In fact, we begin thinking of a usage only when we begin to feel it overwhelming us. We realize the existence of a 'pressure' when it is exerted in a direct, almost physical way. An example of this kind of pressure is the one exerted by the State through its institutions. But the State, says Ortega, is only *one* of the pressures of society, although it is the strongest one. The State is 'the superlative of society.'[62] Now, social pressure is not always unwelcome. It would be preposterous to think of society as Kant's dove 'thought' of the surrounding air: that without it we could enjoy much better our freedom of movement. Society does, in fact, a great deal to keep us afloat amidst our constant worries. It is a complex system of reciprocal actions between masses and minorities[63]—and, therefore, of reciprocal helps. Thus we cannot dispense with society lest we want to do everything by ourselves—and 'everything' would at the end mean practically nothing. A considerable fragment of our individual being is accordingly made up of social realities, namely, of social usages and customs.[64] At the same time that they stifle and oppress us, they 'support' us. This is obvious even in the case of the strongest of all social pressures: the State. The State is not everything in society; it is only a part of society.[65] To deify it, as Hegel did, is a 'senseless mysticism.'[66] But even the State is inescapable. Our only hope lies in the possibility of living in an epoch when the State envelops the social body as elastically as the skin covers the organic body.[67] Such happens when the history of society is 'in the ascendant,' when people can shape the State after their vital preferences instead of adapting themselves to the iron mould of the State. In other words, when the State functions like a skin (to use Ortega's image), we have 'life in freedom'; when it functions like an orthopedic apparatus, we have 'life as adaptation.' The State thus plays a dual role. This also happens with society. The concept 'society' proves, therefore, to be an 'occasional concept' with its meaning depending upon particular societies in particular epochs, although preserving always a certain degree of identity.

Society is thus both beneficial and harmful. It is like the air we breathe and also like a stumbling block we encounter. This seems to wave aside all possible objections and dispense with further analysis. Unfortunately, the problem is somewhat more complex. To begin with, we find Ortega's description of the simultaneously beneficial and harmful character of society somewhat puzzling. On the one hand, society is necessary for us to the degree that we cannot conceive of ourselves except as welded to it. And this is not, of course, because we start with an *a priori* definition of man as a 'social being' or because we discover in our everyday life and in historical records an overwhelming empirical confirmation of the sociability of the human person. In Ortega's opinion, reasons accounting for the social structure of human beings are of a deeper nature. They are based upon the fact that a belief 'is unlikely to occur as belief of individuals or particular groups.' Not being an idea or an opinion, a belief 'will normally be of a collective nature.'[68] Now, in spite of watering down this statement by means of the word 'normally,' we cannot fail to be impressed by Ortega's insistence on the weight of social ties if we remember the deep significance of the word 'belief' in his vocabulary. Must we therefore conclude that the social element is the most powerful of all elements in the human being? We are prone to give an affirmative answer when we consider Ortega's treatment of the problem of social concord. In his opinion, society cannot subsist for long when dissent, instead of being an outcome of the strength and vitality of the body politic, affects the basic layers of common belief. When there is no consent in certain ultimate matters, and in particular when there is no agreement as to who shall rule, society dissolves and fundamental concord is replaced by fundamental dissent. It appears, in short, that Ortega ties up belief with social belief, leaving the destiny of the individual to the mercy of the destiny of society.

On the other hand, Ortega constantly asserts that society is only the organization and collectivization of usages and opinions formerly held by individuals. He goes so far in this direction as to explain social activities as the inert result of spontaneous personal behavior. Thus, for example, philosophy as a function in collective life, i.e., as a social fact backed by universities, publishers, etc., is the consequence of philosophy as a creative personal activity. Thus also the function of being a Caesar—at times an almost impersonal function—became possible because there was a man named 'Caesar' who possessed enough political genius to discover that a certain vacuum of power had to be filled by means of a new type of rule: so-called 'Caesarism.' Examples could easily by multiplied. All of them, however, would confirm the fact that society is never original and creative, that it limits itself to organizing and to administering previous original creations.[69] In other words, social usages are the *tardy* outcome of spontaneous forms of personal life. But this means that social forms bear the same relation to personal forms as the bark of the tree bears to its stem and even to its sap. Society is, as it were, the petrification of personality. No wonder Ortega has often spoken of the 'tyranny of society.'[70] No wonder too that he has even defined society as an 'irresponsible *ego*,' as the omnipotence and omnipresence of the 'one'—the ever present '*one* says,' '*one* hears,' '*one* does.' The 'social mode' is defined accordingly as an inauthentic albeit an inevitable mode.[71] Therefore we must be careful not to confuse what automatically belongs to us and what merely belong to the 'one' in us. We must, in short, be prepared to recognize that although estrangement is inevitable for the human being, he must always strive for withdrawal into himself.[72]

It has been suggested that the above difficulties sprang from Ortega's growing concern with spontaneity and authenticity. Filled with enthusiasm for the struggle against estrangement and falsification he seems to have attached but little importance to what some German philosophers have called 'the objective mind.' His remarks on how difficult or, in his vocabulary, how problematic and illusory it is to bear someone else's company seem to provide a confirmation not only of his excessive zeal for the authenticity of the self,[73] but also of his deficient treatment of 'the others,' or more generally, of society.

It is only fair to say that Ortega was quite aware of these difficulties, and that he did his best to overcome them. The missing link between pure authenticity and radical estrangement he tried to find in what he called 'inter-individual life.'

Ortega had warned his reader that the expression 'man is a social being' is true only in a certain measure. As a matter of fact, man's social dispositions are constantly matched by his antisocial impulses.[74] Here lies the explanation of Ortega's paradoxical statement, 'Society is utopia.' For society does not work with the precision of a good watch; it usually works deplorably and lamentably. Furthermore, collective life appears as a pure falsification only when we forget that every social fact is interlocked with other social facts and, therefore, when we omit to emphasize that a given society must be taken as a whole. The relationship between society and the individual is then more complex than it would seem from the viewpoint of the contrast 'estrangement-authenticity.'

On the other hand, society must not be confused with what Ortega calls 'co-living'—*coexistencia, convivencia.* True, he did assert on one occasion that 'coexistence and society are equivalent terms.'[75] But he made it clear immediately afterwards that society must not be confused with association.[76] Indeed, 'co-living' in itself is not sufficient to make up a society.[77] Individuals may live together without necessarily bringing forth social rules and norms. This is the case with 'inter-individual life.' In love, friendship, ties of kinship, etc., we find that individuals are not related to 'the others' as simply 'others,' but to this or that individual. 'The individual in love falls in love of himself—that is, in the intimate genuineness of his person—with a woman who is not woman in general, nor any woman, but precisely *this* woman.'[78] As a matter of fact, the social appears not when contrasted with the individual (or personal) but rather with the inter-individual (or inter-personal).[79]

Ortega's theory of inter-individual life may have arisen as a consequence of his wish to find a missing link between authenticity and estrangement. But such a theory is not a hasty addition to the doctrine of society; it is based upon a careful description of the ways in which 'the world' is given to the only authentic and 'radical' reality: myself. No doubt, since 'human life in its radicality is only *mine*' everything else will appear as questionable or, as Ortega says, merely presumed.[80] This does not mean, of course, that only *I* exist; it only means that reality is everything with which *I* have to deal. To say that the presumed realities are not radical is not to say that they are not realities;

it is to say that they are interpretations of the radical reality that *I* am. Now, whereas things, and the world at large, are not only second-degree realities (as compared with the reality of life as *mine*), but are lived as such, other men are second-degree realities which may be lived as radical realities. Ontologically speaking, there is nothing closer to me than 'the other.' Inter-individual life is, therefore, as Ortega puts it, 'quasi-radical.' Hence we can conclude that between the inauthenticity of society at large and the authenticity of the individual as he exists for himself is the half-authenticity of the 'personal coexistence.' There are, of course, degrees of personal coexistence, from the mere awareness of 'the other' to this 'closeness in mutual dealing' that we call 'intimacy.' There may even be no solution of continuity between the individual and society, between man as a radical reality and 'this unseizable, indeterminate, and irresponsible subject, *people.*'[81]

NOTES

1. III, 270–80 (1924).

2. The expressions 'vital reason' and 'historical reason' are very often found in Ortega's writings from 1924 on. For 'living reason' see V, 135 (1933) [*Man and Crisis*, p. 176]. For 'ratio-vitalism' see VI, 196, note (1934) [*Concord*, p. 164]. It should be noted that *razón vital* (vital reason) appears translated also as 'living reason' in *Concord, loc. cit.*

3. VI, 23 (1936) [*Toward a Philosophy of History*, from here on cited as *Toward*, p. 183].

4. VI, 46 (1936 [*Toward*, p. 226].

5. *loc. cit.*

6. IV, 58 (1929); VI, 16 (1936) [*Toward*, p. 170]; V, 384 (1934); VII, 117 (1958) [*Man and People*, pp. 62 ff.]; VII, 407 ff. (1958) [*What is Philosophy?*, pp. 205 ff.].

7. V, 85 (1933).

8. IV, 108 (1930); V, 307–8 (1939); V, 530 (1941) [*Concord*, p. 64].

9. IV, 58 (1929).

10. Julián Marías, *Reason and Life. The Introduction to Philosophy.* New Haven: Yale University Press, 1956, p. 188.

11. VI, 351 (1932); VI, 391 (1942) [*Concord*, p. 199].

12. IV, 108 (1930).

13. IV, 108 (1930); V, 307–8 (1933–39).

14. V, 88 (1933) [*Man and Crisis*, p. 107].

15. V, 70 (1933) [*Man and Crisis*, p. 87].

16. V, 381–409 (1934). Also: V, 87 (1933) [*Man and Crisis*, p. 111]; VI, 11 (1936) [*Toward*, p. 174]; VI, 61 (1940) [*Concord*, pp. 18–9].

17. V, 304 (1933–39); VI, 391 (1942) [*Concord*, p. 99].

18. III, 260–4 (1924); III, 245–54 (1924); III, 281–316 (1924); V, 495 (1940); VI, 385–8 (1942) [*Concord*, pp. 92–6].

19. V, 9–164 (1933) [*Man and Crisis, passim*]; V, 492–507 (1940). Also *Invertebrate Spain, The Revolt of the Masses* and, to a certain extent, *The Dehumanization of Art.*

20. See Eduardo Nicol, *Historicismo y existencialismo*, México: El Colegio de México, 1952, pp. 308–31. On Ortega's account of Dilthey see V, 165–214 (1933–34) [*Concord*, pp. 129–82].

21. Julián Marías, *Reason and Life*, pp. 186–92, 369.

22. V, 83, 95 (1933) [*Man and Crisis*, pp. 104–5, 122]; V, 347 (1932); VI, 13, 32 (1936) [*Toward*, pp. 165, 198]; VI, 347 (1932); VII, 99 ff. (1957) [*Man and People*, pp. 38 ff.]; VII, 407 ff. (1958) [*What is Philosophy?*, pp. 205 ff.].

23. VI, 34 (1936) [*Toward*, p. 203].

24. III, 180 (1923) [*Theme*, p. 72].

25. III, 291 (1924).

26. III, 607 (1924) [*Toward*, p. 14].

27. IV, 400, 426 (1932).

28. V, 384 (1934).

29. IV, 411 (1932); VIII, 468 (1950).

30. VI, 32 (1936) [*Toward*, p. 200].

31. V, 96 (1933) [*Man and Crisis*, pp. 123–4].

32. IV, 399 (1932).

33. On the 'authentic ego' as the 'unbribable basis' of our life, see also II, 84–5 (1916).

34. IV, 406 (1932).

35. VI, 400 (1942) [*Concord*, p. 108, note].

36. IV, 403 (1932).

37. IV, 366 (1932); IV, 414 (1932); V, 341 (1933–39) [*Toward*, p. 116]; VI, 13 (1936) [*Toward*, p. 165]; VI, 421 (1942).

38. VI, 33 (1936) [*Toward*, p. 202].

39. IV, 171 (1930) [*Revolt*, p. 52].

40. VI, 37 (1936) [*Toward*, p. 208].

41. V, 23 (1933) [*Man and Crisis*, p. 23].

42. II, 645 (1929); IV, 77 (1930); IV, 400 (1932); V, 239 (1935).

43. II, 350 (1924) [*Toward*, p. 18].

44. *La redención de las provincias y la decencia nacional*, Madrid: Revista de Occidente, 1931, Chap. vii.

45. I, 480 (1910).

46. IV, 254 (1930) [*Revolt*, p. 170]; IV, 321 (1930) [*Mission of the University*, p. 56]; IV, 397, 412 (1932); V, 472 (1932); V, 24 (1933) [*Man and Crisis*, p. 25].

47. I, 354–6 (1914) [*Meditations*, pp. 94–6]; IV, 397 (1932).

48. See specially *Theme, Revolt* and *Mission of the University*. Also V, 13–54 (1933) [*Man and Crisis*, pp. 9–66] and V, 493–507 (1940).

49. See, however, V, 78 (1933) [*Man and Crisis*, p. 99]. Ortega seems to imply here that culture *always* ends by stifling the authentic life of the individual.

50. IV, 77 (1930); IV, 194 (1940) [*Revolt*, p. 86]; IV, 400 (1932); V, 31, 37 (1933) [*Man and Crisis*, pp. 32, 41]; V, 305 (1933–39); VI, 32 (1936) [*Toward*, p. 200]; VIII, 468 (1950).

51. VI, 350 (1932); VII, 407 ff. (1958) [*What is Philosophy?*, pp. 205 ff.].

52. V, 37 (1933) [*Man and Crisis*, p. 41]; VI, 421–2 (1942).

53. VI, 22 (1936) [*Toward*, p. 182].

54. IV, 425 (1932).

55. IV, 540 (1928); IV, 56–9 (1929); IV, 70 (1930); IV, 345 (1932); V, 95 (1933) [*Man and Crisis,* p. 122]; VI, 49 (1936) [*Toward,* p. 230].

56. VI, 49 (1936) [*Toward,* p. 230].

57. IV, 156 (1930) [*Revolt,* p. 31].

58. VI, 35 (1936) [*Toward,* pp. 205–06].

59. VI, 38, 43 (1936) [*Toward,* pp. 210, 220]; V, 487 (1936); IV, 297 (1937); V, 296 (1939); VI, 53 (1940); VI, 88 (1940) [*Concord,* p. 105]; VII, 212–32 (1957) [*Man and People,* pp. 176–91].

60. VII, 214 (1957) [*Man and People,* p. 195].

61. VII, 228 (1957) [*Man and People,* p. 215].

62. V, 219 (1935); VI, 88 (1940) [*Concord,* p. 22]; VI, 397 (1942) [*Concord,* p. 105].

63. III, 103 (1922).

64. V, 485–7 (1936).

65. IV, 295 (1937).

66. IV, 221–8 (1930) [*Revolt,* pp. 127–36].

67. VI, 83–107 (1940) [*Concord,* pp. 32–47].

68. VI, 61 (1940) [*Concord,* p. 19].

69. V, 174 (1934); V, 232 (1935); VI, 38 [*Toward,* p. 210]; VI, 395–9 (1940) [*Concord,* pp. 103–7].

70. II, 745–8 (1930) [*Invertebrate Spain,* pp. 166–71]; V, 201–5 (1935).

71. VI, 400 (1942) [*Concord,* p. 109].

72. V, 60, 61, 74 (1933) [*Man and Crisis,* pp. 74–6, 92–3]; V, 293–315 (1939).

73. VI, 61 (1933) [*Man and Crisis,* pp. 75–6].

74. VI, 72–3 (1940) [*Concord,* pp. 24–5].

75. IV, 117 (1930) [*Toward,* p. 49].

76. *loc. cit.* [*Toward,* p. 50].

77. VI, 38 (1936) [*Toward,* p. 211].

78. VII, 203 (1957) [*Man and People,* p. 178].

79. *loc cit.* [*Man and People,* p. 179].

80. VII, 114 (1957) [*Man and People,* p. 114]. See also VII, 141–73 (1957) [*Man and People,* pp. 94–138].

81. VII, 199 (1957) [*Man and People,* p. 173].

Chapter Five

Thought and Reality

1 THE IDEA OF BEING

As the basic reality or, as Ortega often puts it, as 'the radical reality,' human life is the foundation or the 'root' of all other realities. Not, of course, in the sense that human life 'contains' all things. The relation in Ortega's philosophy between human life and other realities is quite different from the relation in idealistic tendencies between, say, consciousness and the world. It is also different from the relation in realistic and naturalistic philosophies between an entity—the world, matter, etc.—that is supposed to be an 'absolute' and particular beings. Hence to inquire about reality is not the same as to inquire about whether there is or is not something 'human' in 'things.' Nor is it the same as to inquire about what reality *qua* reality is. There is no such thing as reality *qua* reality, or as being *qua* being. What there is and, in general, being, emerges as an answer to man's questioning about it. Indeed, nothing can be said to be 'real' unless man raises the question 'What is reality?' But the fact is that man does not raise such a question simply because of his human condition. There is nothing specifically human in asking questions about what is properly speaking real or, in a more semantic vein, about what the predicate 'is real' means. Man is not necessarily a 'philosophical animal'; as a matter of fact, most of the time he seems to behave quite unphilosophically.

Despite some features of his language, Ortega cannot be considered an existentialist. Existentialists, or at least some of the philosophers thus called, have claimed that man is, in the final analysis, Nothing, and that Nothingness lies in the core of Being. But Ortega has pointed out that the existentialists' claims are due to their one-sided view of human life. For if it is certain that human life does not exclusively consist in knowledge, it is no less certain

179

that it does not exclusively consist in anguish, or dread, or care, or being unto death. It may also consist in generosity, spontaneity, and even gaiety. Human life therefore is not reducible to any of the usual 'existential characteristics.' If human life has a characteristic, it is its openness to many possibilities. Life possesses, as Ortega says, 'infinite tastes.' In other words, life is 'a many-sided affair.'

Nor can Ortega be considered a follower of Heidegger despite his recognition of Heidegger's philosophical greatness. For instance, Heidegger has claimed that being human is the same as wondering about Being—and perhaps also the same as wandering about Being. This seems to indicate that Being is essentially 'questioning'—an opinion that Ortega maintains as his own. But two things must be taken into account in this connection. First, even if we equate Being with questioning, we are still not allowed to presume that man wonders incessantly about Being. Second, the equation of Being with questioning is accepted by Ortega only as 'a starting point for a dialectical movement.' Ortega does not, of course, deny that man at times raises the questions 'What is Being?' and 'What is reality?' But he often indicates that man raises such questions only when confronted with certain vital situations. We cannot discuss here the entangled philosophical relationship between Ortega and Heidegger, as we cannot discuss the no less entangled relationship between Ortega and Dilthey, and Ortega and Husserl. Let it suffice to point out that although neither Heidegger, Dilthey, nor Husserl—or, for that matter, neither Scheler nor Bergson—is alien to Ortega's thought, the latter has often developed quite independently from the thought of all these philosophers. Ortega's philosophy is probably more akin to Dilthey's than any other, but aside from having reached some of Dilthey's conclusions by quite different ways, it sharply differs from it in one fundamental respect: Ortega's philosophy is not based, as was Dilthey's, upon the idea that consciousness is the basic relation between subject and object. Consciousness, Ortega claims, is a 'hypothesis'; only human life, or rather 'my life,' is a fact—a 'radical fact.'

Although Ortega developed some of his ideas about reality and being very early in his philosophical career, he did not formulate them rigorously until 1925.[1] He discussed these ideas again and again[2] until they gained a central importance in his thought.[3] We can even conclude that Ortega's ideas on reality and being—which we shall abbreviate as 'Ortega's ontology'—have always been the guiding thread of his philosophical adumbrations. Thus, they can be considered as the most important unifying factor throughout all the phases of his intellectual development.

Blending humility with pride Ortega did not consider his ontology as a particular theory which he had discovered by a lucky stroke.[4] He rather described such an ontology as 'the present state of philosophy' or, to use his own words, as 'philosophy at the present day level.' Since philosophy develops historically, and is itself a historical event, Ortega's ontology must also be 'historical.' However, this does not make it relative. To be sure, any philosophical theory is only partially true. But it is at the same time 'absolute.' A given 'level' in philosophy—the 'Aristotelian level,' the 'Stoic level,' the 'Cartesian level,' etc.—is not just another philosophical event in the history of thought, but *the* philosophy that has ensued from years, or perhaps centuries, of strenuous philosophical speculation and debate. As Ortega has put it, 'the philosophies of the past have all contributed to the formation of our own philosophy.'[5] Philosophy today—any 'today' for that matter—is possible only because of philosophy yesterday, and so forth until we reach the very origins of philosophy. All this does not means that the entire history of philosophy is the development of some kind of 'internal necessity.' Contrary to Hegel, who proclaimed that history is rational, Ortega asserts that reason is historical.[6] Therefore, there is no need for philosophy to have developed the way it did. The philosophical past is a collection of errors as well as a collection of truths. The philosopher must then 'assume' and, as Hegel would say, 'absorb' the past, but without making it a necessary antecedent of the present.[7] On the other hand, the philosophical present need not be what it is, but it would not be a 'present' unless integrated with the entire past.

Now, integrating the present with the past is not tantamount to accepting all of the past philosophical doctrines, and even less to blending them more or less eclectically. The present is integrated with the past only when the latter is assumed by the former. Now, to 'assume' the past is not to stand for it, but rather to stand by it. It is, in short, to determine the position, namely the historical position, of the present. But there would be no possibility of determining our own position unless we were convinced that we have a 'position.' This position is necessarily different from the others, for otherwise there would be no philosophy but simply an 'ideology'—or, as Ortega writes, some kind of 'scholasticism,' which is not a 'real position' but a mere repetition. At the same time, any position is necessarily ahead of all the preceding positions, for if such were not the case it would reduce to one of them. Hence the need for discovering where we stand in philosophy, that is to say, the need for ascertaining our own 'philosophical level.' Understandably enough, a more advanced level always lies 'under' any preceding level, for philosophy more nearly resembles digging than constructing. Progress in philosophy consists, indeed, in showing that what was once considered extremely original now has been shown to be utterly trivial and what was the work of genius has now become mere common sense. Now, a philosophical idea becomes trivial and commonsensical when we can easily describe the assumptions on which it is based. These assumptions were invisible not only to the philosophers who produced such an idea but also (or perhaps even more so) to the philosophers who sincerely embraced such an idea as an incontrovertible truth. These philosophers did not in fact possess such an idea; it was rather the idea that possessed them.

Hence to find our own 'level' in philosophy implies to accept all the preceding 'levels' but the same time to reject them as too 'superficial' and as too 'trivial.' Since the predicates 'is superficial' and 'is trivial' are equated by Ortega with the predicate 'is not philosophical enough' (or perhaps with the predicate 'has not gone far enough in philosophy'), we may reach the startling conclusion that all the preceding levels, or rather the assumptions underlying such levels, had *been* philosophical, but are no longer. To be sure, it may be proved later that our own assumptions, which we cannot discover, are also superficial and trivial, but nobody will be able to deny that they have not been superficial and trivial for us.

It must be conceded that Ortega's ideas on the nature of philosophical ideas are rather paradoxical, for they force us to admit that philosophy has been done only because it has not been done. But Ortega may, after all, have been perfectly aware of this embarrassing paradox since he declared that philosophy is 'a permanent failure.' An 'honest' failure because philosophers *qua* philosophers have never claimed that they have really 'solved' any problem. Philosophers claim that they solve problems only when they forget that philosophy is no more but no less than an inquiry, namely, an 'attempt.'

We shall refer to Ortega's idea of philosophy in more detail in our next section. What we said above was only intended to clarify why Ortega revolted against all the philosophies of the past while at the same time he 'followed' them. It was not so much because he wanted to say something new, but because he *had* to say something new. Ortega's ontology is in this sense, as he often put it, 'radical,' namely, an ontology that goes 'to the root'—'to the root of the problem of Being,' that is.

Ortega's approach to ontology is, of course, 'historical' in the sense at least that it presents itself as endowed with historical consciousness. His constant reference to the history of philosophy, and in particular his investigation of the various basic 'forms of thought' developed throughout history, is not therefore a consequence of mere historical curiosity. Human history in general and the history of philosophy in particular is not simply 'what has happened' and still less a record of what has happened; it is what makes it possible for all of us to exist, and to think, meaningfully. Ortega treated some aspects of the history of philosophy in considerable detail precisely because he did not consider them to be the sole concern of the historian; the analysis of the historical past, and of its inevitable failures, is one of the ways, if not the only decent way, of determining our position in the present. We must not be misled then by Ortega's blasts against this or that philosopher. In some cases Ortega is indeed enjoying himself when dealing blows to philosophers. As, for example, when he fustigates Kierkegaard in a manner that some will consider deplorable, but that others may consider only implacable. In many instances, however, Ortega's whipping of philosophers and philosophical doctrines has only one aim: to 'integrate' them by making them really 'alive.'

Now philosophers and philosophical doctrines come really alive only when their hidden assumptions are unearthed and, as if it were, unmasked. The most important of these assumptions is the corresponding theory of being—the theory which is supposed to elucidate what Being (or Reality) is. Ortega rejected the theories of Being—the ontologies—of the past as 'insufficient' and, in the sense in which we have used these terms, as 'superficial' and 'trivial.' These ontologies were, or rather prove now to be, insufficient, because they were based on ideas that are presently too 'obvious.' Let us confine ourselves to three examples.

Some philosophers have thought that being must be 'something'—some sort of 'thing,' that is, be it material or spiritual. Some other philosophers have claimed that being is, besides, some kind of 'stable' or 'permanent' entity, even to the point of asserting that if x is not stable and permanent, then x is not 'truly real.' To this claim they have added another one: being exists only behind the so-called 'appearances.' The vast majority of philosophers, finally, have reached the conviction that the proper task of man is to do his utmost to discover, or rather to uncover, what is hidden behind such appearances. The being thus uncovered has often been equated with 'truth.' This 'truth' may be conceived as something given to man (or to a particular human faculty) or as something forever out of the reach of the human mind.

It may now be argued that not all of these ideas about being have been so naively accepted by philosophers. The history of philosophy is not that simple. For instance, some philosophers have surmised that being is not necessarily stable, and even that being (or reality) is only in so far as it is constantly changing. We need not even refer to such 'lovers of change' as Heraclitus and Bergson; Aristotle himself, who had an undeniable fondness for 'permanence,' made several great efforts to conceive of being as other than a stable entity. Now, when all is considered, none of the ontologies of the past has succeeded in freeing itself from the conceptual framework devised by the first Greek philosophers. As if this were not enough, all philosophers until the present time have presupposed that being is something that 'is'—although it may well happen that man will never know what it is. In other words, no philosopher thus far has dared to proclaim what Ortega considers to be the basic discovery in philosophy today: the idea that being is not this or that entity, that it is neither permanent nor changeable, material nor spiritual, real nor ideal. Being, indeed, 'is' nothing. This is not to say that being is Nothingness; it is only to say that being is no thing at all, but only a hypothesis.

Being is, in short, a human invention. It has not been given to man so
that he may occasionally uncover it or declare that it is unattainable. It is the
result of a bold imaginative act that some men had to perform in order to face
some otherwise untractable vital—and, no doubt, historical—situation. Some
men therefore 'invented' the idea of being (and of reality as such) as a hypothesis once other hypotheses to account for human existence and the existence
of the world had failed. In some respects there is no difference between
imagining that what there is is God, or the gods, and imagining that it is
being, namely, that there is something we call 'reality.' Because the gods
ceased to play a part, or at least ceased to play the part that was expected of
them, the idea of being or reality had to come to the rescue. Being is thus
'something' invented for a purpose, and probably 'something' contrived to fill
a gap. If the idea that, after all, 'there is Reality' had not been 'necessary' it
would have occurred to no one. For men need not think that there is reality;
it may suffice for them just to live, or work, or love, or pray.

To say that being is a human invention may seem to be almost the same
as saying that being is some kind of entity superimposed by man as a thinking
reality upon the chaos of appearances in order to account for phenomena, and
in particular for the orderly succession of natural phenomena. If such were
the case Ortega's ontology would end by being a reformulation in 'existential'
terms of some type of Kantianism. Now, although Ortega always firmly believed
that no philosopher worthy of the name could dispense with a careful study
of, and even some sort of 'immersion' in, Kant's philosophy, his ontology was
far from being Kantian.[8] At any rate, it would be unfair to read 'invented' as
'posited.' To begin with, the entity whose activity as a thinking entity consists
in 'positing' is ordinarily what we call 'consciousness'—in the philosophical,
and sometimes specifically epistemological, meaning of this word. On the
other hand, the entity that happens to have invented the idea of being is not
consciousness: it is 'human life.' And human life is not reducible to any of its
operations, including intellectual operations. We have already pointed out
that according to Ortega human life is 'many-sided.' Therefore, human life is
not reducible to consciousness, or to thinking, or to 'positing,' etc. Thus, to
assert that man has invented the idea of being by questioning about reality
is not the same as to affirm that man must order the 'chaos of sensations' by
means of a system of categories. At any rate, to recognize that being is
fundamentally a human hypothesis is quite different from defining 'being' in
a manner only slightly different from that of all the other philosophers. In
point of fact, it is to jump to, or perhaps dive into, another philosophical
'level.' From the new viewpoint thus gained, being does not appear as some
essential feature that things have only because they happen to exist, but as
'that which has to be done.'

A number of difficulties arise here. Ortega seems to presuppose that we are no longer obliged to subscribe to past doctrines of being because there is no such thing as being. Then he claims that being 'is' rather some sort of activity. It would seem then that being is more similar to thought than to anything else. But Ortega of course disclaims any idealist affiliation.[9] Furthermore, he contends that, as we shall see in our final section, the word 'thought' must not be interpreted as possessing a purely intellectual meaning. As if all this were not enough, he refuses to adhere to any position that would smell of irrationalism, intuitionism, etc. To make things more perplexing, he talks sometimes about being, and some other times about reality. The temptation is strong to declare that although Ortega's ontology may not be trivial it is far from being as clear as crystal.

Nevertheless, Ortega himself has dropped some hints that may help us understand at least the nature of the philosophical upheaval he was proposing.

Some philosophers have assumed that something is real only when it is, or can become, an object of possible experience. These philosophers have accordingly accepted to abide by the following principle: 'to be is to be experienced.' Some other philosophers, on the other hand, have assumed that something is real only when it is not self-contradictory and when its existence is not contradictory with any other existing reality. These philosophers have accepted as an axiom the principle: 'to be is to be rational.' Both groups of philosophers—which comprise practically all the philosophers that have ever existed—have subscribed to an idea which is at the same time a theorem in modal logic: the idea, that is, that something is real if and only if it is possible. For even the philosophers who have relied mostly, if not exclusively, on experience, have never had the slightest doubt that if something is or can be experienced, it is because it was in principle possible to experience it. Therefore, the idea in question looks so evident that it would seem foolish to throw doubts upon it.

Let us, however, allow for this apparent absurdity, and dispense with the whole body of beliefs concerning the relation between reality and possibility. To begin with, let us question whether what is can be. Not only should we then be tempted to change the theorems of modal logic—a feat at which only a few people will be alarmed—but also the whole of the so-called classical ontology—an attempt which will produce (among philosophers, to be sure) more disquiet. It may now be argued that all this is wishful thinking, and that we are not allowed to throw to the winds basic principles honored by hundreds of philosophers merely because of some sudden whim. But it happens that the principles in question are not as basic as they seemed to be; they are themselves founded upon an idea of being that has been left unquestioned for more than twenty-five hundred years. According to this idea, something is when it is self-sufficient, for nothing indeed would be if it were not what it is.

But the case is that this idea is far from being an obvious truth. In any case, it does not make room for some types of being which are not self-sufficient—types of being which are only 'an attempt to be' without any assurance that they will 'succeed in being.' It is even conceivable that for some types of being their attempt to be only shows that their being is impossible— impossible, of course, as 'being what they are.' The most outstanding example of such types of being is 'human life'—or, again, 'my life.' This example suffices to show that the time-honored relation between what is, or is sup- posed to be, real, and what is possible is far from being evident. It also suffices to show that it is not necessary to describe reality in terms of the contrast between the real and the possible, and, in general, in terms of 'being.' Ortega has not elaborated this theme further, but it can easily be seen that merely wondering about it is equivalent to trying to break a chain that had seemed to be truly unbreakable: the very same chain that Lovejoy has called 'the Great Chain of Being.'

2   THE IDEA OF PHILOSOPHY

Philosophers have tackled many problems. But the most disturbing one has always been the problem of philosophy. What is philosophy: Is it a necessity? Is it a luxury? Is it a rigorous science? Is it an unwarranted set of assumptions? Implicitly or explicitly, many great philosophers have been bewildered by these questions. In the last decades, furthermore, even a new philosophical discipline has loomed up: the 'philosophy of philosophy,' to which Nietzsche and Dilthey, among others, have contributed many keen insights. We have seen in the preceding section that Ortega is no exception to this trend. He was aware that philosophy is not something to be taken for granted but something we must justify and account for unceasingly. He pointed out that a philosopher becomes more authentic as he insistently demands its own credentials from philosophy.

We shall conclude this book with a few remarks on Ortega's idea of philosophy. This idea is intimately related to his ontology and, of course, to his doctrine of human life. It is also, and above all, related to the question of the role played by knowledge in human life. The reader will probably remem- ber that in Ortega's opinion knowledge is not the automatic release of psy- chological mechanisms but rather a human acquisition. Running counter to Aristotle's celebrated principle, 'All men by nature desire to know,' he claims, or rather implies, that if 'Man has a nature' is a preposterous saying, then 'Man has a knowing nature' is a senseless one. All things considered, however, it is easy to see that the word 'knowledge' in the above sense is hopelessly ambiguous. On the one hand, knowledge is defined as a vital function. On the other hand, knowledge is considered *also* as a conventional cognitive process. How is one to account for the undeniable difference between the former and the latter? Ortega has come to think that a terminological device may caste some light on this tangled question. Let us introduce it here, for it will prove useful for an understanding of the meaning of philosophy, that is, of the role that philosophy plays or can play in human existence.

The device in question roughly consists in introducing a distinction between knowledge—or cognition—and thinking.[10]

What is thinking? Like everything which has some bearing on human life, thinking does not appear to us in its 'naked truth.' It appears to us masked by all kinds of deceiving realities. The expression 'deceiving realities' must be understood in its full and literal sense: the realities masking the genuine phenomenon of 'thinking' are deceiving and confusing precisely because they are very similar to what they *pretend* to be without being it in the least. Among these concealing realities two deserve special mention. One is thinking as a psychological process; the other, thinking as a set of logical rules.

Thinking as a psychological process is open to the same objections already singled out when, after examining the meaning of knowledge for human life, we concluded, following Ortega, that the question 'What is knowledge?'—now reformulated as the question 'What is thinking?'—cannot be answered by means of a description of the psychological mechanisms which make it possible for us to think. Psychological mechanisms are merely instrumental in the production of thinking, because in its primary sense thinking is the fact that we put those mechanisms *in use* for some purpose. Man must dedicate himself to thinking, *because* he has to free himself of doubts. Thinking takes on different forms, and what we call 'knowledge' or 'cognition' is only one among them. The fact that it is *for us* the outstanding form does not mean that it is the only possible one.

Another reality masking the genuine phenomenon of thinking is, according to Ortega, logic. It has been held that thinking is primarily logical thinking, namely, thinking according to certain rules—the very rules to which classical logicians have given the name of 'principles.' But logical thinking is, again, one among the many possible forms of thinking. In fact, it is a very restricted one. If the limitations of logical thinking had not been discovered earlier, it was because philosophers had shown an unbounded confidence in a certain type of logic. Implicitly or explicitly the assumption had been made that the principles of classical logic were the only trustworthy guiding norms of human thought. This confidence was shaken as soon as it was discovered that the foundations of traditional logic can no longer rely upon the ontological assumptions predominant for more than two thousand years in the history of Western philosophy. Like the foundations of all sciences, the foundations of logic—and of mathematics—have undergone a momentous, and healthy, crisis. Mathematical logic in particular has shown that old concepts such as 'principle,' 'truth,' and so on must be drastically revised. Indeed alternative logics are nowadays held possible. Thinking must not, therefore, be confused with logical thinking, inasmuch as the expression 'logical thinking' has lost most, if not all, of its traditional connotations.

If thinking is neither a psychological process nor a set of logical rules, it will no longer be plausible to say that it is always a cognitive act. Thinking has thus a broader meaning than knowledge. In fact, knowledge is only *one* form in the rich morphology of thinking. And as neither psychology nor logic nor, for that matter, philosophy or science, can tell us what knowledge is, we are compelled to look elsewhere for an answer to our question. This answer we find, according to Ortega, in that element permeating all human reality: history.

The phenomenon we call 'knowledge' or 'cognition,' namely, the particular way of thinking that makes use of concepts and of reasoned analyses and arguments, has come out at a certain stage of man's historical development. When? Only when certain presuppositions had been fulfilled. Ortega mentions two of them: (1) the belief that behind the chaos of impressions there is a stable reality called the 'being' of things, and (2) the belief that human intellect is the sole possibility of grasping the nature of such a stable reality. Now, it is commonly agreed that only the Greek philosophers held these beliefs in a sufficiently radical manner. The circumstances that prompted Greek philosophers to reach them would require considerably more space than is available here. Let it suffice to point out that, as is always the case with human life, the Greeks arrived at those beliefs because some other previous beliefs had been shaken to their foundations. Thus the Greek philosophers became, as Ortega puts it, 'cognizers' *par excellence.* They transmitted to us a splendid heritage which we have since spent lavishly. As a consequence, the idea has been held for more than two thousand years that cognition and, therefore, philosophy as a purely cognitive activity are something man can always lay hands on, and accordingly scarcely in need of special justification. The use of concepts and of reasoned arguments has become so 'natural' in our Western culture, and in the areas influenced by it, that we have come to the conclusion that philosophical activity is, to speak, inborn and can be easily cultivated by means of proper education. The philosophers in particular have often wondered how it is possible for some people to dispense altogether with philosophy, the 'nonphilosophical existence' being, in their opinion, far less complete and endurable than the philosophical one. These thinkers have, in short, taken philosophy for granted and have paid little or no attention to the very motives from which philosophy itself springs.

Now to be a 'cognizer' is by no means something connatural with human existence. There have been, and there still exist, many types of men who, for better or for worse, do not place on cognition the emphasis which has been a matter of course in Western culture. A case in point is the Hebrew way of life before any contact with cognitive cultures had been established. The Hebrews believed, for instance, that reality was identical with God—with a God who was pure will, arbitrary power, having in principle no relation whatsoever with what we call the rules of morality or the laws of nature. Such rules and laws, if they existed at all, were a pure gift of God that God could withdraw with the same facility—and incomprehensibility—as He bestowed them. Everything that happened to the human creature depended, therefore, upon the inscrutable decrees of God. How in this case was one to adopt a cognitive attitude? It would be entirely useless. In the face of that overwhelming God prayer is far more rewarding and even far more enlightening than reason. No wonder prayer becomes in that case a form of thinking, having its own technique and its own rules. But this changes not only the fundamental ways of life but also the meaning of certain terms. It changes, for instance, the meaning of the word 'truth.' What we call 'truth' is then no longer the discovery of the stable being hidden behind the unstable appearances of reality; it is the 'discovery' of what God might have decided or the understanding of what God might have revealed. Let us call this discovery by its proper name: prophecy. In other words, what we call a 'true statement' will not be, as it was among the Greek philosophers, a 'description' of 'what really is' but an announcement of 'what it will really be.'

Some other examples might, of course, be quoted. As a matter of fact, a careful description of the main features of Western culture would show that even this culture has not always given cognition a free hand. But the above example, being considerably more extreme than many others, will help the reader to understand that while man cannot escape thinking as a way of getting along with the difficulties of his life, he is able, and above all he has been able, to solve the riddle of his life by means other than knowledge. Whether this is desirable or even possible in the present stage of history is, of course, another question—and a very difficult one, indeed. We cannot here dwell on this problem, nor can we raise and still less debate the question of whether the meaning of the propositions upheld by science or philosophy can be reduced to the role that science or philosophy as such play in human existence. Even if this reduction proves impossible, it remains undeniable that Ortega's historical idea of knowledge and his subsequent historical account of philosophy may cast a vivid light on certain aspects of both that have been deplorably neglected. At any event, what philosophers can learn from Ortega is that 'the first principle of a philosophy is the justification of itself.' Ortega himself never lost sight of this necessity.

NOTES

1. Particularly in University lectures.

2. IV, 48–59 (1929); V, 81–6 (1933) [*Man and Crisis*, pp. 102–9]; VII, 407 ff. (1958) [*What is Philosophy?*, pp. 205 ff.].

3. Particularly important in this respect are VIII, 13–58 (1958) [*Prólogo para alemanes*] and VIII, 61–356 [*La idea de principio en Leibniz y la evolución de la teoría deductiva*].

4. In what follows we shall draw upon material abstracted from the writings mentioned in the preceding two footnotes. For the sake of brevity we will abstain in this section from specific references, except when using writings other than those already mentioned.

5. IX, 354 (1960).

6. IX, 366 (1960).

7. IX, 359 (1960).

8. Except in so far as underlying Kant's notion of 'pure reason' there may be some notion of a 'vital reason' (See IV, 59 [1929]).

9. Fichte's philosophy would probably raise a problem here, but it is only fair to remind the reader that the present book is only an 'outline.'

10. V, 517–47 (1941) [*Concord*, pp. 49–82]. See also V, 88 (1933) [*Man and Crisis*, p. 113]; VII, 314 (1958) [*What is Philosophy?*, pp. 68–70].

Ortega y Gasset

BIOGRAPHICAL NOTE

1883   Born in Madrid, May 9th.

1898–1902   Student at the Universidad Central (University of Madrid). Took degree of *Licenciado en Filosofía y Letras*. Previous studies of *Bachillerato* in Colegio de Jesuítas de Miraflores del Palo (Málaga) and one year in Deusto.

1904   Took doctor's degree in the University of Madrid with a dissertation entitled *Los terrores del año mil (Crítica de una leyenda)*.

1905–1907   Post-graduate studies in Germany: Leipzig, Berlin, and Marburg.

1910   Professor of Metaphysics in the University of Madrid (until 1936).

1915   Founded *España,* in cooperation with some other writers.

1916   Lectures in Argentina.

1917   Gave up writing articles for *El Imparcial.* Associated with the new periodical *El Sol.*

1923   Founded *Revista de Occidente.* Publication suspended in 1936, but books by Ediciones de la Revista de Occidente are still being published.

1931   Founded Agrupación al Servicio de la República (with R. Pérez de Ayala and G. Marañón). Delegate at the Chamber of Deputies *(Cortes Constituyentes).* Ceased to contribute to *El Sol* and began writing articles for *Crisol* and *Luz.*

1936–1945   Residence in France, Holland, Argentina, Portugal.

1945–1954   Residence in Spain and Portugal, with frequent trips and residence abroad.

1948   Founded in Madrid, with Julián Marías, the *Instituto de Humanidades,* a private institution.

1949   Lectures in the U.S.

1949–1951   Lectures in Germany and Switzerland.

1951   Doctor *honoris causa,* University of Glasgow.
1955   Died in Madrid, on October 18th

ORTEGA Y GASSET'S WORKS

Only books are listed. Dates refer to the first printing.

Meditaciones del Quijote (Madrid, 1914)
Vieja y nueva política (Madrid, 1914)
Personas, obras, cosas (Madrid, 1916)
El Espectador, I (Madrid, 1916)
El Espectador, II (Madrid, 1917)
El Espectador, III (Madrid, 1921)
España invertebrada. Bosquejo de algunos pensamientos históricos (Madrid, 1921)
El tema de nuestro tiempo. El ocaso de las revoluciones. El sentido histórico de la teoría de Einstein (Madrid, 1923)
Las Atlántidas (Madrid, 1924)
La deshumanización del arte e ideas sobre la novela (Madrid, 1925)
El Espectador, IV (Madrid, 1925)
El Espectador, V (Madrid, 1926)
El Espectador, VI (Madrid, 1927)
Espíritu de la letra (Madrid, 1927)
Tríptico. I. Mirabeau o el político (Madrid, 1927)
El Espectador, VII (Madrid, 1929)
Kant (1724-1924) Reflexiones de centenario (Madrid, 1929)
Misión de la Universidad (Madrid, 1930)
La rebelión de las masas (Madrid, 1930)
Rectificación de la República (Madrid, 1931)
La redención de las provincias y la decencia nacional (Madrid, 1931)
La reforma agraria y el Estatuto Catalán (Madrid, 1932)
Goethe desde dentro (Madrid, 1933)
El Espectador, VIII (Madrid, 1934)
Notas (Madrid, 1938)
Ensimismamiento y alteración. Meditación de la técnica (Madrid, 1939)
El libro de las misiones (Madrid, 1940; includes *Misión de la Universidad)*
Ideas y creencias (Madrid, 1940)
Estudios sobre el amor (Madrid, 1940; includes some essays published in earlier books)
Mocedades (Madrid, 1941; includes some essays published in *Personas, obras, cosas*)
Historia como sistema y Del Imperio Romano (Madrid, 1941)
Teoría de Andalucía y otros ensayos (Madrid, 1942)

Esquema de las crisis (Madrid, 1942)—(lessons V–VIII of *En torno a Galileo,* 1956)

Dos prólogos. A un tratado de montería. A una historia de la filosofía (Madrid, 1944)

Obras completas, I, II (Madrid, 1946)

Obras completas, III, IV, V, VI (Madrid, 1947)

De la aventura y la caza (Madrid, 1949)

Papeles sobre Velázquez y Goya (Madrid, 1950)

Velázquez (Madrid, 1955)

Posthumous works

Al pie de las letras (Madrid, 1956)

En torno a Galileo (Madrid, 1956; completes the book *Esquema de las crisis*)

Viajes y países (Madrid, 1957)

Caracteres y circunstancias (Madrid, 1957)

El hombre y la gente (Madrid, 1957)

¿Qué es filosofía? (Madrid, 1958)—(Revised edition in Madrid: Alianza, 1997)

La idea del principio en Leibniz y la evolución de la teoría deductiva (Madrid, 1958)

Idea del teatro (Madrid, 1958)

Meditación del pueblo joven (Madrid, 1958)

Prólogo para alemanes (Madrid, 1958)

Goya (Madrid, 1958)

Velázquez (Madrid, 1959)

Apuntes sobre el pensamiento (Madrid, 1959)

La caza y los toros (Madrid, 1960)

Una interpretación de la historia universal. En torno a Toynbee (Madrid, 1960)

Meditación de Europa (Madrid, 1960)

Origen y epílogo de la filosofía (México, 1960)

Vives-Goethe (Madrid, 1961)

Obras completas, VII (Madrid, 1961)

Obras completas, VIII, IX (Madrid, 1962)

Pasado y porvenir del hombre actual (Madrid, 1962)

Misión del bibliotecario (y otros ensayos afines) (Madrid, 1962)

Unas lecciones de metafísica (of the year 1932–33) (Madrid, 1966)

Obras completas, X, XI (Escritos políticos) (Madrid, 1969)

Sobre la razón histórica (Madrid, 1979)

Obras completas, XII (Madrid, 1983)

¿Qué es conocimiento? (Madrid, 1984)

Sobre la caza, los toros y el toreo (Madrid, 1986)

Meditaciones sobre la literatura y el arte (Madrid, 1987)

Epílogo . . . : notas de trabajo (Madrid, 1994; ed. José Luís Molinuevo)

La vida alrededor (Madrid, 1998)

Several of the books published in the series "El Arquero" (Madrid: *Revista de Occidente*) incorporate material not included in earlier books often bearing the same titles. As examples we mention:

En torno a Galileo, 1956.
Historia como sistema, 1958.
Ideas y creencias, 1959.
Apuntes sobre el pensamiento, 1959.
Estudios sobre el amor, 1959.

EDITION OF WORKS

Obras completas, 12 volumes (1946–1983), ed. Paulino Garagorri, Madrid: *Revista de Occidente*.

The *32 volumes (1979–1988)* of *Obras de José Ortega y Gasset*, published by Alianza Editorial under the direction of P. Garagorri contain a remarkable number of unpublished pages and the volume *¿Qué es conocimiento?*

Ortega y Gasset. Antología, ed. Pedro Cerezo Galán, Madrid, 1991.

Textos sobre el 98: antología política (1908–1914), Madrid, 1998.

CONTENTS OF "OBRAS COMPLETAS"

Volume I

Pp. 11–264   Artículos (1902–1913)
265–308   Vieja y nueva política (1914)
309–400   Meditaciones del Quijote (1914)
401–416   Artículos (1915)
417–574   Personas, obras, cosas (1916)

Volume II

Pp. 13–748   El Espectador, vols. I–VIII (1916–1934)

Volume III

Pp. 9–34   Artículos (1917–1920)
35–128   España invertebrada (1921)
129–140   Artículos (1923)
141–242   El tema de nuestro tiempo (1923)
243–280   Artículos (1924)
281–316   Las Atlántidas (1924)

317–336	Epílogo al libro 'De Francesca a Beatrice' (1924)
337–349	Artículos (1925)
351–428	La deshumanización del arte (1925)
429–510	Artículos (1926–1927)
511–599	Espíritu de la letra (1927)
601–637	Mirabeau o el político (1927)

Volume IV

Pp.	9–21	Artículos (1929)
	23–59	Kant (1929)
	61–109	Artículos (1930)
	111–310	La rebelión de las masas (1930)
	311–353	Misión de la Universidad (1930)
	355–379	Artículos (1931–1932)
	381–541	Goethe desde dentro (1932)
	543–554	Artículos (1933)

Volume V

Pp.	9–164	En torno a Galileo (1933)
	165–206	Artículos (1934–1935)
	207–234	Misión del bibliotecario (1935)
	235–287	Artículos (1935–1937)
	289–375	Ensimismamiento y alteración (1939)
	377–489	Ideas y creencias (1940)
	491–549	Artículos (1940–1941)
	551–626	Estudios sobre el amor (1941)

Volume VI

Pp.	9–107	Historia como sistema y Del Imperio Romano (1941)
	109–214	Teoría de Andalucía y otros ensayos (1942)
	215–244	Brindis (1917–1939)
	245–512	Prólogos (1914–1943)

Volume VII

Pp.	9–23	Prospecto del Instituto de Humanidades (1948)
	25–31	Enviando a Domingo Ortega el retrato del primer toro (1950)
	33–37	Prólogo a "Teoría de la expresión" de Karl Bühler (1950)
	39–55	Prólogo a "El collar de la paloma" de Ibn Hazm de Córdoba (1952)

57–67   Prólogo a "Introducción a las ciencias del espíritu" de
          Wilhelm Dilthey (1946)
69–272   El hombre y la gente (1957)
273–438   ¿Qué es filosofía? (1957)
439–501   Idea del teatro (1958)
503–573   Goya (1958)

                          Volume VIII

Pp. 11–58   Prólogo para alemanes (1958)
     59–355   La idea de principio en Leibniz y la evolución de la
               teoría deductiva (1958)
     357–449   Meditación del pueblo joven (1958)
     451–661   Velázquez (1959)

                          Volume IX

Pp. 9–242   Una interpretación de la historia universal (1960)
     243–313   Meditación de Europa (1960)
     315–343   Otros escritos afines:
     317–326   La sociedad europea (1941)
     327–331   Tocqueville y su tiempo
     332–338   Vistas sobre el hombre gótico
     339–343   Algunos temas del "Weltverkehr" (1954)
     345–434   Origen y epílogo de la filosofía (1960)
     435–438   Para los niños españoles
     439–446   Boletín núm. 1 del "Instituto de Humanidades"
     447–473   La caza y los toros (1945)
     475–501   Pío Baroja: anatomía de una alma dispersa (ca. 1914)
     503–612   Vives-Goethe (1940–1949)
     613–746   Pasado y porvenir para el hombre actual:
     617–624   Conferencias (1952)
     625–644   Anejo: En torno al "Coloquio de Darmstadt, 1951" (1953)
     645–663   Pasado y porvenir para el hombre actual (1952)
     665–675   Apuntes sobre la educación para el futuro (1961)
     677–690   Individuo y organización (1954)
     691–706   Las profesiones liberales
     707–725   Un capítulo sobre la cuestión de cómo muere una creencia
               (1954)
     727–746   Una vista sobre la situación del gerente o "manager" en la
               sociedad actual (1954)
     747–784   Comentario al "Banquete" de Platón (1946)

Volume X

Pp. 9–681   Escritos polícos, I (1908–1921):
     15–628   1908–1914
     269–681   1915–1921

Volume XI

Pp. 9–681   Excritos políticos, II (1922–1933):
     11–124   1922–1930
     125–180   1931–1933
     181–332   La redención de las provincias y la decencia nacional (1931)
     333–454   Rectificación de la República (1931)
     455–539   El Estatuto Catalán (1932)

Volume XII

Pp. 15–144   Unas lecciones de metafísica
     145–332 Sobre la razón histórica:
              —La razón histórica (Buenos Aires, 1940)
              —La razón histórica (Lisboa, 1944)
     333–456 Investigaciones psicológicas
     457–480 Para un diccionario filosófico

CORRESPONDENCE

Epistolario, ed. Paulino Garagorri, 1974.
Epistolario completo Ortega-Unamuno, ed. L. Robles, 1987.
Cartas de un joven español (1891–1908), ed. S. Ortega, 1991.

ENGLISH TRANSLATIONS OF ORTEGA Y GASSET WORKS

The Modern Theme. Translated by James Cleugh. London: C. W. Daniel, 1941. New York: W. W. Norton, 1933. Torchbook Edition. New York: Harper & Brothers, 1961, with an introduction by José Ferrater Mora. [a translation of *El tema de nuestro tiempo*].

The Revolt of the Masses. Authorized translation. London: Allen and Unwin, 1923. New York: W. W. Norton, 1932. New York: New American Library of World Literature, 1950. Often reprinted.

Invertebrate Spain. Translated by Mildred Adams. New York: W. W. Norton, 1937. New York: Howard Fertig, 1974.

Contents:

Pp. 19–87: 'Invertebrate Spain' (some passages of the original Spanish edition
have been deleted).

Pp. 88–102: 'A theory about Andalusia.' A translation of an article originally
published in 1927 and reprinted in *Teoría de Andalucía y otros ensayos* and
in *O. C., VI,* 111–120.

Pp. 103–115: 'Castile and the Asturias.' A translation of parts of 'De Madrid
a Asturias o los dos paisajes,' originally published in 1915 and reprinted
in *El espactador, III* and in *O. C., II,* 249–265.

Pp. 116–142: 'The Meaning of Castles in Spain.' A translation of parts of
'Notas del vago estío,' originally published in 1925 and reprinted in *El
Espectador, V* and *O. C., II,* 413–450.

pp. 143–157: 'A Topography of Spanish Pride.' A translation of parts of 'Para
una topografía de la soberbia española (Breve análisis de una pasión),'
originally published in 1923 and reprinted in *Goethe desde dentro* and in
O. C., IV, 459–466.

Pp. 158–165: 'Arid Plains, and Arid Men.' A translation of parts of 'Temas
de viaje (Julio de 1922),' reprinted in *El Espectador, IV* and in *O. C., II,*
367–383.

Pp. 166–171: 'The Increasing Menace of Society.' A translation of the article
'Socialización del hombre,' originally published in 1930 and reprinted in
El Espectador, VIII and in *O. C., II,* 745–748.

Pp. 172–189: 'Against the Economic Interpretation of History.' A translation
of 'La interpretación bélica de la historia,' originally published in 1925
and reprinted in *El Espectador, VI* and in *O. C., II,* 525–536.

Pp. 190–201: 'On Fascism.' A translation of 'Sobre el fascismo,' originally
published in 1925 and reprinted in *El Espectador, VI* and in *O. C., II,*
497–505.

Pp. 202–212: 'Meditation in the Escorial.' A translation of parts of 'Meditación
del Escorial,' originally published in 1915 and reprinted in *El Espectador,
VI* and in *O. C., II,* 553–560.

History as a System. Translated by Helene Weyl and William C. Atkinson.
New York: W. W. Norton, 1941.

Toward a Philosophy of History. New York: W. W. Norton, 1941.

Contents:

Pp. 11–40: 'The Sportive Origin of the State,' translated by Helene Weyl
from 'El origen deportivo del Estado,' originally published in 1924 and
reprinted in *El Espectador, VII,* and in *O. C.,* 607–623.

Pp. 41–83: 'Unity and Diversity of Europe,' reprinted from Eleanor Clark's translation of 'Prólogo para franceses' (1937), included a new edition of *La rebelión de las masas* and in *O. C., IV,* 113–139.

Pp. 85–161: 'Man the Technician,' translated by Helene Weyl from *Meditación de la técnica,* a series of lectures given in 1933, published in *Ensimismamiento y alteración* and in *O. C., V,* 317–375.

Pp. 163–233: 'History as a System,' reprinted from William C. Atkinson's translation of 'Historia como sistema,' originally published (in English translation) in *Philosophy and History. Essays presented to Ernst Cassirer,* edited by Taymond Klibansky and H. J. Paton. Oxford: Clarendon Press, 1936, pp. 283–322. The Spanish text was published later in *Historia como sistema y Del Imperio Romano,* and has been reprinted in *O. C., VI,* 2–50.

Pp. 235–273: 'The Argentine State and the Argentinian,' translated by Helene Weyl from 'El hombre a la defensiva,' originally published in 1929 and reprinted in *El Espectador, VII* and in *O. C., II,* 643–666.

Mission of the University. Translated by Howard Lee Nostrand. Princeton: Princeton University Press, 1944. London: K. Paul, Trench, Trubner, 1946. New York: W. W. Norton, 1966.

Concord and Liberty. Translated by Helene Weyl. New York: W. W. Norton, 1946.

Contents:

Pp. 9–47: 'Concord and Liberty.' A translation of 'Del Imperio Romano,' a series of articles originally published in 1940 and reprinted in *Historia como sistema y Del Imperio Romano* and in *O. C., VI,* 51–107.

Pp. 49–82: 'Notes on Thinking—Its Creation of the World and Its Creation of God.' A translation of 'Apuntes sobre el pensamiento: se teurgia y su demiurgia,' orginally published in 1941 and reprinted in *O. C., V,* 517–546.

Pp. 83–128: 'Prologue to a History of Philosophy.' A translation of a long preface to the Spanish translation of E. Bréhier's *Histoire de la philosophie.* Ortega's 'Prólogo' was originally published in 1942 and has been reprinted in *Dos prólogos* and in *O. C., VI,* 377–418.

Pp. 129–182: 'A Chapter from the History of Ideas. Wilhelm Dilthey and the Idea of Life.' A translation of 'Guillermo Dilthey y la idea de la vida,' originally published in 1933–1934, reprinted in *Teoría de Andalucía y otros ensayos* and in *O. C., VI,* 165–214.

The Dehumanization of Art and Notes on the Novel. Translated by Helene Weyl. Princeton: Princeton University Press, 1948. Reprinted New York: P. Smith, 1948.

The Dehumanization of Art and Other Writings on Art and Culture. New York: Doubleday Anchor Books, Garden City, 1948. (As well as the essay *The Dehumanization of Art* it includes a translation of *Sobre el punto de vista en las artes, O. C.* IV, *Pidiendo un Goethe desde dentro, O. C.,* IV, and *Ensimismamiento y alteración, O. C.,* V).

The Dehumanization of Art and Other Essays on Art, Culture and Literature. Translated by Helene Weyl et al. Princeton, N.J.: Princeton University Press, 1968.

Velazquez. Translated by C. David Ley. New York: Random House, 1954 [a translation of *Introducción a Velázquez*].

On Love, Aspects of a Single Theme. Translated by Toby Talbot. New York: Meridian Books, 1957 [a translation of *Estudios sobre el amor*].

Man and People. Translated by Williard R. Trask. New York: W. W. Norton, 1957.

Man and Crisis. Translated by Mildred Adams. New York: W. W. Norton, 1958. Paperback edition: The Norton Library, 1962 [a translation of *En torno a Galileo*].

What is philosophy? Translated by Mildred Adams. New York: W. W. Norton, 1960.

History as a System, and Other Essays Toward a Philosophy of History. Translated by Helene Weyl, with an afterword by John William Miller. New York: W. W. Norton & Company, 1961.

The Mission of the Librarian. Translated by James Lewis and Ray Carpenter. Boston: G. K. Hall & Company, 1961.

Meditations on Quixote. Translated by Evelyn Rugg and Diego Marin, with Introduction and notes by Julián Marías. New York: W. W. Norton, 1961.

The Origin of Philosophy. Translated by Toby Talbot. New York: W. W. Norton, 1967.

Some Lessons in Metaphysics. Translated by Mildred Adams. New York: W. W. Norton, 1969.

The Idea of Principle in Leibniz and the Evolution of Deductive Theory. Translated by Mildred Adams. New York: W. W. Norton, 1971.

Velázquez, Goya, and the Dehumanization of Art. Translated by Alexis Brown, with an introduction by Philip Troutman. London: Studio Vista, 1972.

An Interpretation on Universal History. Translated by Mildred Adams. New York: W. W. Norton, 1973.

Phenomenology and Art. Translated and with an introduction by Philip W. Silver. New York: W. W. Norton, 1975.

Historical Reason. Translated by Philip W. Silver. New York: W. W. Norton, 1984.

Meditations On Hunting. Translated by Howard B. Wescott. New York: Scribner's, 1985.
Psychological Investigations. Translated by Jorge García-Gómez. New York: W. W. Norton, 1987.

SELECTED BIBLIOGRAPHY ON ORTEGA Y GASSET

Rukser, Udo. *Bibliografía de Ortega.* Madrid: *Revista de Occidente,* 1971.
Jiménez García, A. "Bibliografía," *Aporía. Revista de actualidad filosófica,* 21–24 (1983–1984).
Donoso, A., H. Raley. *José Ortega y Gasset: A Bibliography of Secondary Sources.* Bowling Green, Ohio: Bowling Green State University/Philosophy Documentation Center, 1986.

SELECTED SECONDARY SOURCES

It consists of the secondary bibliography of the last edition of Ferrater Mora's *Diccionario de Filosofía,* Barcelona: Ariel, 1994, plus some additional bibliography.

Aníbal Sánchez Reulet, 'El pensamiento de Ortega y Gasset' (*Cursos y Conferencias,* Parte I, vol. 9, no. 3, 1937. Parte II, vol. 11, no. 6, 1937. Parte III, vol. 12, nos. 7 and 8, 1937. Parte IV, vol. 12, nos. 9 and 10, 1937 and 1938).
Humberto Díaz Casanueva, *Das Bild des Menschen bei Ortega y Gasset und seine Beziehung zur Erziehungswissenschaft,* 1938.
Joaquín, Iriarte, *Ortega y Gasset, su persona, su pensamiento y su obra,* 1942.
Joaquín Iriarte, *La ruta de Ortega. Crítica de su filosofía,* 1949.
José Sánchez Villaseñor, *Pensamiento y trayectoria de José Ortega y Gasset. Ensayo de crítica filosófica,* 1943.
J. D. García Bacca, *Nueve grandes filósofos contemporáneos y sus temas,* t. II, 1947.
Miguel Ramis Alonso, *En torno al pensamiento de José Ortega y Gasset,* 1948.
Julián Marías, *La filosofía española actual. Unamuno, Ortega, Morente, Zubiri,* 1948.
———. *Ortega y la idea de la razón vital,* 1948.
———. *Ortega y tres antípodas. Un ejemplo de intriga intelectual,* 1950 (analysis and critique of the books by Iriarte, Sánchez Villaseñor and Roig Gironella against the thought of Ortega, with a critical appendix to the book by J. Saiz Barberá, *Ortega y Gasset ante la crítica,* 1950).

———. *Ortega. Circunstancia y vocación*, vol. I, 1960.

———. *Las trayectorias*, vol II, 1983.

———. *Acerca de Ortega*, 1991.

Manuel Granell, *Lógica*, 1949, part IV.

———. *Ortega y su filosofía*, 1960.

J. H. Walgrave, *De wijsbegeerte van Ortega y Gasset*, 1949.

Domingo Marrero, *El centauro*, 1951.

Fray M. Oromí, *Ortega y la filosofía. Seis glosas*, 1953.

Juan Uribe Echevarría, *Estudios sobre Ortega y Gasset*, 3 vols., 1955–56.

J. M. Hernández Rubio, *Sociología y política en Ortega y Gasset*, 1956.

José Gaos, J. Marías, D. Marrero et al., articles on Ortega y Gasset in *La Torre*, IV, nos. 15–16 (1956) [similar extraordinary issues in the magazines *Sur, Clavileño, Atenea, Insula*, etc.].

Gosé Gaos, *Sobre Ortega y Gasset y otros trabajos de historia de las ideas en España y la América española*, 1956.

———. *La filosofía de la historia*, 1989.

Ch. Cascales, *L'humanisme d'Ortega y Gasset*, 1957 (tesis).

E. Frutos, M. Mindán, C. París, J. Zaragüeta et al., articles on O. y G. in *Revista de Filosofía*, 16 (1957), nos. 60–61.

J. D. García Bacca, M. Granell, L. Luzuriaga, E. Mays Vallenilla, A. Rosenblatt, *Homenaje a Ortega y Gasset*, 1958.

Paulino Garagorri, *Ortega: Una reforma de la filosofía*, 1958.

———. *Relecciones y disputaciones orteguianas*, 1965.

———. *Unamuno, Ortega, Zubiri en la filosofía española*, 1968.

———. *Introducíon a Ortega*, 1970.

———. *La filosofía española en el s.XX: Unamuno, Ortega, Zubiri; dos precursores, Clarín y Ganivet; y cuatro continuadores*, 1985.

J. L. Aranguren, *La ética de Ortega*, 1958; 2nd rev. ed., 1959.

Brigitta (Gräfin von) Galen, *Die Kultur-und Gesellschaftsethik J. O. y Gassets*, 1959.

Fernando Salmerón, *Las mocedades de Ortega y Gasset*, 1959.

J.-P. Borel, *Raison et vie chez Ortega y Gasset*, 1959.

Francisco Romero, *Ortega y Gasset y el problema de la jefatura espiritual*, 1960.

Alfonso Cobían y Macchiavello, *La ontología de Ortega y Gasset*, 1960.

Fernando Vela, *Ortega y los existencialistas*, 1961.

Antonio García Astrada, *El pensamiento de Ortega y Gasset*, 1961 [with 'Léxico orteguiano' by Susana Gordillo de García Astrada].

Ubaldo Casanova Sánchez, *Ortega, dos filosofías*, 1961.

Ugo Log Bosco, *Filosofía e diritto in Ortega y Gasset*, 1961.

Franco Díaz de Cerio Ruiz, *José Ortega y Gasset y la conquista de la conciencia histórica. Mocedad: 1902–1915*, 1961.

Francisco Xavier Pina Prata, *Dialéctica da razão vital: Intuição originária de José Ortega y Gasset*, 1962.

Arturo Gaete, *El sistema maduro de Ortega*, 1962.

Hernán Larraín Acuña. *La metafísica de Ortega y Gasset I: La génesis del pensamiento de Ortega*, 1962.

Alain Guy, *Ortega y Gasset, critique d'Aristote: L'ambiguité de mode de pensée péripatéticien jugé par le ratiovitalisme*, 1963.

Francisco Goyenechea, *Lo individual y lo social en la filosofía de Ortega y Gasset, con una línea sistemática de su saber filosófico*, 1964.

José Hierro Sánchez-Pescador, *El Derecho en Ortega*, 1965.

Francisco Soler Grima, *Hacia Ortega, I. El mito del origen del hombre*, 1965.

José Luis Abellán, *Ortega y Gasset en la filosofía española: Ensayos de apreciación*, 1966.

Ciríaco Morón Arroyo, *El sistema de Ortega y Gasset*, 1968.

Guillermo Araya, *Claves filológicas para la comprensión de Ortega*, 1971.

Harold C. Raley, *José Ortega y Gasset. Philosopher of European Unity*, 1971.

Julio Bayón, *Razón vital y dialéctica en Ortega*, 1971.

N. Orringer, *Ortega y sus fuentes germánicas*, 1979.

Pelayo H. Fernández, *Ideario etimológico de José Ortega y Gasset*, 1981.

A. Rodríguez Huéscar, *La innovación metafísica de Ortega. Crítica y superación del idealismo*, 1982.

M. Ortega, *Ortega y Gasset, mi padre*, 1983.

Sergio Rábade, *Ortega y Gasset, filósofo. Hombre, conocimiento y razón*, 1983.

Varies. *Ortega vivo*, 1983 [*Revista de Occidente*, 24–25].

Varies. *Monográfico a Ortega en el primer centenario de su nacimiento*, 1983–84 [*Aporía*, 21–24].

Pedro Cerezo Galán. *La voluntad de aventura. Aproximamiento crítico al pensamiento de Ortega y Gasset*, 1984.

———. 'De la crisis de la razón a la razón histórica,' in *Historia, Literatura, Pensamiento*, 1990, vol. I, 307–343.

A. Elorza, *La razón y su Sombra. Una lectura política de Ortega y Gasset*, 1984.

F. López Frías, *Etica y política. En torno al pensamiento de Ortega y Gasset*, 1984.

F. L. Molinuevo, *El idealismo de Ortega*, 1984.

Varies, *Presencia de Ortega*, 1985 [*Revista de Occidente*, 48–49].

Durán, Manuel, ed., *Ortega, hoy: estudio, ensayo y bibliografía sobre la vida y la obra de José Ortega y Gasset*, 1985.

Pedro J. Chamizo Domínguez, *Ortega y la cultura española*, 1985.

H. Pelayo Fernández. *La paradoja en Ortega y Gasset*, 1985.

I. Sánchez Camara, *La teoría de la minoría selecta en el pensamiento de Ortega y Gasset*, 1986.

J. M. García Mouriño, *Ortega y Gasset: el raciovitalismo*, 1988.

J. M. Osés Gorraiz. *La sociología en Ortega y Gasset*, 1989.

A. Regalado García, *El laberinto de la razón: Ortega y Heidegger*, 1990.

Juan Marichal. *El Intelectual y la política en España: 1898–1936: Unamuno, Ortega, Azaña, Negrín*, 1990.

Luís Jimémez Moreno. *Práctica del saber en filósofos españoles: Gracián, Unamuno, Ortega y Gasset, E. d'Ors, Tierno Galván,* 1991.

Anna M. Fernández. *Teoría de la novela en Unamuno, Ortega y Cortázar,* 1991.

Manuel González Burón. *La historia de la naturaleza: ensayo sobre Ortega,* 1992.

Juan José Abad Pascual. *El método de la razón vital y su teoría en Ortega y Gasset,* 1992.

Juan Francisco García Casanova. *Ontología y sociología en Ortega Gasset,* 1993.

Serafín M. Tabernero del Río. *Filosofía y educación en Ortega y Gasset,* 1993.

Antonio Rodríguez Huéscar. *Semblanza de Ortega,* 1994.

José Luis Molinuevo (ed.). *Ortega y La Argentina,* 1997.

Maria Teresa López de la Vieja (ed.). *Política y sociedad en José Ortega y Gasset,* 1997.

Eduardo Martínez de Pisón. *Imagen del paisaje: la generación del 98 y Ortega y Gasset,* 1998.

Gregorio Morán. *El Maestro en el erial: Ortega y Gasset y la cultura del franquismo,* 1998.

SELECTED SECONDARY BIBLIOGRAPHY IN ENGLISH

Monographies

Ceplecha, Christian. *The Historical Thought of José Ortega y Gasset.* Washington D. C.: The Catholic University of America Press, 1958.

Díaz, Janet Winecoff. *The Major Themes of Existentialism in the Work of José Ortega y Gasset.* Chapel Hill: University of North Carolina Press, 1968.

Dobson, Andrew. *An Introduction to the Politics and Philosophy of José Ortega y Gasset.* Cambridge: Cambridge University Press, 1989.

Fernández, Pelayo H., et al., eds. *Ortega y Gasset Centennial/University of New Mexico.* Madrid: José Porrúa Turanzas, 1985.

Graham, John T. *A Pragmatist Philosophy of Life in Ortega y Gasset.* Columbia: University of Missouri Press; London, 1994.

Holmes, Oliver W. *Human Reality and the Social World: Ortega's Philosophy of History.* Amherst: University of Massachusetts Press, 1975.

Marías, Julián. *Generations: A Historical Method.* Translated by Harold C. Raley. University: University of Alabama Press, 1970.

————. *Ortega y Gasset: Circumstances and Vocation.* Translated by Frances López-Morillas. Norman: University of Oklahoma Press, 1970.

Marval-McNair, Nora de (ed.). *José Ortega y Gasset: Proceedings of the "Espectador Universal."* International Interdisciplinary Conference. New York: Greenwood Press, 1987.

McClintock, Robert. *Man and His Circumstances: Ortega as Educator.* New York: Columbia University Teachers College Press, 1971.

Mermall, Thomas. *The Rhetoric of Humanism: Spanish Culture after Ortega y Gasset.* New York: Bilingual Press, 1976.

Ouimette, Victor. *José Ortega y Gasset.* Boston: G. K. Hall, 1982.

Raley, Harold C. *Ortega y Gasset: Philosopher of European Unity.* University: University of Alabama Press, 1971.

Ramos Mattei, Carlos. *Ethical Self-Determination in Don José Ortega y Gasset.* New York: Lang, 1987.

Rockwell, Gray. *The Imperative of Modernity: An Intellectual Biography of José Ortega y Gasset.* University of California Press, 1989.

Rodríguez Huéscar, A. *José Ortega y Gasset's metaphysical innovation: A critique and overcoming of idealism.* Translated and edited by Jorge García. Albany: State University of New York Press, 1995.

Sánchez Villaseñor, José. *Ortega y Gasset, Existentialist.* Translated by Joseph Samall, S. J. Chicago: Henry Regnery, 1949.

Silver, Philip W. *Ortega as Phenomenologist: The Genesis of "Mediations on Quixote."* New York: Columbia University Press, 1978.

Tuttle, Howard N. *The Dawn of Historical Reason: The Historicality of Human Existence in the Thought of Dilthey, Heidegger and Ortega y Gasset.* New York: Lang, 1994.

———. *The Crowd Is Untruth.* New York: Lang, 1996.

University of New Mexico. *Ortega y Gasset Centennial: University of New Mexico.* Madrid: Ediciones J. Porrúa Turanzas, 1985 (English and Spanish).

Varies, *Ortega y Gasset and the Question of Modernity,* 1989.

Weigert, Andrew J. *Life and Society: A Mediation on the Social Thought of José Ortega y Gasset.* New York: Irvington, 1983.

Wyatt, John. *Commitment to Higher Education: Seven West European Thinkers on the Essence of the University: Max Horkheimer, K. Jaspers, F. R. Leavis, J. H. Newman, José Ortega y Gasset, Paul Tillich, Miguel de Unamuno.* Buckingham Bristol: Society for Research into higher Education & Open University Press, 1990.

Articles

Albright, Gary. "The Person in the Thought of José Ortega y Gasset," *International Philosophical Quarterly* (Fordham University, New York), 15 (1975), 279–292.

Alluntis, Felix. " 'The Vital and Historical Reason' of José Ortega y Gasset," *Franciscan Studies,* 15 (1955), 60–78.

———. "Social and Political Ideas of José Ortega y Gasset," *The New Scholasticism,* 39 (1965), 467–490.

———. "Radical Reality according to José Ortega y Gasset," *Studies in Philosophy and the History of Philosophy,* 4 (1967), 191–206.

————. "Origin and Nature of Philosophy According to José Ortega y Gasset," *Studies in Philosophy and the History of Philosophy,* 6 (1973), 65–76.

Asheim, Lester. "Ortega revisited," *The Librarian Quarterly,* vol. 52, n. 3 (1982), 215–226.

Conant, H. "Ortega y Gasset's Dehumanization Concept and the Arts of the 1970's," *Intellect* 105 (1976), 179–183.

Dietz, Conrad R. "Ortega's Attempt to Restore the World," *Laval Theólogique et Philosophique,* 26 (1970), 131–146.

Dixon, J. W., Jr. "Ortega and the Redefinition of Metaphysics," *Cross Currents* (New York) 29, 3 (1979), 281–299.

Donoso, Antón. "Ortega on Philosophy," *Minerva's Owl* (Detroit) 4 (October 1977), 13–14.

————. "Ortega on the United States: A View from the Outside," *Philosophy Today* (Celina, Ohio, USA) 21 (1977), 143–153.

————. "Problems for Research in the Philosophy of José Ortega y Gasset," *Los Ensayistas* (Athens, Georgia, USA) 3 (1978), 39–46.

————. "José Ortega y Gasset: His Sources and Influences," *International Philosophical Quarterly,* vol. 22, n. 2 (1982), 203–207.

Dust, Patrick H. "Style of Thought and Style of Expression in Ortega's Amor en Sthendal," *Hispania,* 62 (1979), 266–274.

————. "Freedom, Power, and Culture in Ortega y Gasset's Philosophy of Technology," *Research in Philosophy and Technology,* 11 (1991), 119–153.

Dworwin, Martin S. "Ortega y Gasset: Praeceptor Hispaniae," *Journal of Aesthetic Education,* 6 (1972), 43–48.

Gracia, Jorge J. E. "Notes on Ortega's Aesthetic Works in English," *Journal of Aesthetic Education,* 11 (July 1977), 117–125.

Graham, John T. "Historical Research and Discovery in Private Libraries: Positivism in Comte, Donoso and Ortega," *Journal of the Rutgers University Libraries,* 41 (June 1979), 20–50.

Gray, Rockwell. "Ortega and the Concept of Destiny," *Review of Existencial Psychology and Psychiatry* (New York) 15 (1977), 173–185.

Hall, David L. "The Humanization of Philosophy through the Bhagavad Gita: Antonio de Nicolás and Ortega y Gasset," *Philosophy Today* (Celia, Ohio, USA), 25 (1981), 149–175.

Herzberger, David K. "Ortega y Gasset and the 'Critics of Consciousness,' " *Journal of Aesthetics and Art Criticism* (Baltimore, USA), 34 (summer 1976), 455–460.

Martínez, Marie Louise. "The Historical Relativism of Ortega y Gasset," *Proceedings of the American Catholic Philosophical Association,* 22 (1947), 193–211.

McClintock, Robert. "Ortega or the Stylist as Educator," *Journal of Aesthetic Education,* 3 (1969), 59–80.

Nicolas, Antonio T. de. "The Americanization of Ortega y Gasset," *Main Currents*, 28 (1972), 180–185.

O'Connor, Robert. "Ortega's Reformulation of the Husserlian Phenomenology," *Philosophy and Phenomenological Research* (Buffalo, USA), 40 (September 1979), 53–63.

Orringer, Nelson R. "Nobles in 'La rebelión de las masas' and Related Works: Ortega y Gasset's Sources," *American Hispanist*, 1 (January 1976), 6–12.

———. "Life as Shipwreck or as Sport in Ortega y Gasset?," *Romance Notes*, 17 (1976), 70–75.

———. "Luminous Perception in 'Meditaciones del Quijote': Ortega y Gasset's Source," *Revista Canadiense de Estudios Hispánicos*, vol. 2, n. 1 (1977), 1–26.

———. "Don Juan in the Evolution of Love: Ortega y Gasset and Lucka," *American Hispanist*, 2 (February 1977), 5–10.

———. "Simmel's 'Goethe' in the Thought of Ortega y Gasset,' *Modern Language Notes* 92 (March 1977), 296–311.

———. "Depth Perception in the History of Painting: Ortega y Gasset and Jaensh," *Comparative Literature Studies*, 14 (1977), 53–73.

Read, Herbert. "High Noon and Darkest Night: Some Observations on Ortega y Gasset's Philosophy of Art," *Journal of Aesthetics and Art Criticism*, 23 (1964), 43–50.

Rogers, W. Kim. "Ortega and Ecological Philosophy," *Journal of the History of Ideas*, 55 (July, 1994), 503–522.

Romanell, Patrick. "Ortega in Mexico: A Tribute to Samuel Ramos," *Journal of the History of Ideas*, 21 (1960), 600–608.

Shin, Un-Chol. "Ortega''s Concept of Artist," *Journal of Aesthetic Education*, 20 (Fall, 1986), 19–29.

Stern, Alfred. "Ortega y Gasset and the Modern World," *The Southern Journal of Philosophy* (Memphis, USA), 13 (1975), 255–269.

Tuttle, Howard N. "Some Issues in Ortega y Gasset's Critique on Heidegger's Doctrine of Sein," *Southwest Philosophical Studies*, (Spring, 1991), 96–103.

———. "Ortega's Vitalism in Relation to Aspects of 'Lebensphilosophie' and Phenomenology," *Southwest Philosophical Studies*, 6 (April 1981), 88–92.

Part III

Ferrater Mora
Chapter 3 of *Being and Death*

EDITOR'S NOTE

The text published here corresponds to chapter three of the book *Being and Death: An Outline of Integrationist Philosophy* (University of California Press, Berkeley and Los Angeles), that came out in 1965, and was basically the translation of a work written in Spanish and published in Madrid in 1962 (*El ser y la muerte: Bosquejo de una filosofía integracionista,* ed. Aguilar). In the preface to the English edition Ferrater asserts:

> It is not, however, a mere duplicate, in another tongue, of the original version. It differs from the latter in various important respects. To begin with, I have revised the text throughout in order to make it more concise without loss of meaning. I have added a number of paragraphs on some crucial points which I felt needed clarification. I have entirely rewritten half a dozen sections, and in many cases I have changed the order of presentation.
>
> As a consequence, I hope that, while still fundamentally a translation, the book has been considerably improved. Indeed, if a new Spanish edition of the book is produced, I will probably rewrite large portions of it in accordance with the present English text.

Ferrater wrote the notes at the end of the text. But in order to keep the symmetry with the two former texts of this volume, we have added a biographical note, the list of works by Ferrater and a selective bibliography of commentary on his work.

Chapter Three

Human Death

20 MAN AND HIS BODY

For many centuries it has been assumed that man possesses, as a defining characteristic, some "element" or "principle" substantially different from his body. This "element" or "principle" has been given various names: 'mind,' 'reason,' 'spirit,' 'soul,' and so on. A few daring thinkers have even gone so far as to conclude that, if the element in question is the defining characteristic of man, and if it does not necessarily entail the existence of the body, then the body does not belong to the essence of a human being. More cautious philosophers have claimed that the body is still a significant element in man, but since it is, so they believe, an element substantially different from the rational or spiritual part, then there must be some way of explaining the undeniable interactions between soul, spirit, or reason, on the one hand, and the body, on the other hand. A host of metaphysicians, particularly since the time of Descartes, have spent much time and ingenuity in providing elaborate explanations of such interactions.

The numerous blind alleys up which all these philosophers—both daring and cautious—have stumbled, have led some thinkers to hoist the flag of naturalistic, even materialistic, reductionism. Since man, they argue, is at bottom a natural being, and since natural beings are material entities, man's nature and activities must be thoroughly accounted for in terms of material organization. We may, if we wish, talk about mind, soul, spirit, and so on, but these are only epiphenomena of the material body. Naturalistic and materialistic reductionism explains away the so-called "spiritual manifestations," "mental events," and, it goes without saying, "spiritual substances," as mere appearances, if not plain forgeries.

The above account of the philosophical controversies on the mind–body problem is, of course, a deplorable oversimplification. But it may help us to understand the nature of the difficulties encountered when man has been defined either as only a soul (or a mind, a spirit, etc.), or as only a body, or as some uneasy combination of both. In contrast to the doctrines sketched above, some thinkers have tried to view man's body in a different light, for instance, as man's inalienable property and at the same time as a reality which cannot be accounted for only as a material system. Curiously enough, some efforts in this direction were made by thinkers who are customarily described as thoroughgoing spiritualists. Such is the case with Thomas Aquinas, who followed here in the footsteps of Aristotle, and subscribed, *mutatis mutandis,* to the Aristotelian definition of the soul as "the form of the organic body having the power of life."[1] To be sure, Thomas Aquinas concluded that the human soul is a spiritual substance, not just an "organic form," but nevertheless his philosophical starting point was a conception of the soul which seemed to entail an idea of a certain way of being a body. Such is also the case with St. Augustine, at least when he declared that "the way in which the body attaches to the soul . . . is man himself" (*hoc tamen homo est*).[2] These opinions—or rather, a certain (no doubt, somewhat biased) interpretation, of these opinions—are quite similar to some of my own. Unfortunately, the former have been expressed at times obscurely, and often, as it were, half-heartedly, for practically all the thinkers I praised as my possible predecessors have ended by defending the doctrine that there is in man some principle substantially different from the body.

The first point I wish to put forward is this: man does not have a body, but *is his* body—his *own* body. Another way of expressing it is: *Man is a way of being a body.* Thus, I seem to subscribe now to naturalistic or materialistic reductionism. I hope to be able to prove that I am not so rash. If my philosophical anthropology has some analogues, they can be detected in a number of contemporary philosophical elucidations.[3] This does not mean that my ideas are derived from such elucidations, and the ensuing contentions; it only means that they are often in tune with some of them. Like a certain number of contemporary philosophers, but with vastly different assumptions, I try to shun both classical monism (spiritualistic or materialistic) and classical dualism, such as that exemplified in the Cartesian, or Cartesian–Augustinian, idea of an entirely spiritual substance more or less uncomfortably lodged in the body. Basically, what I contend is that nothing can be detected *in* man that absolutely transcends his body; *and* that man is not reducible to a material substance. A human being is not a reality, or a cluster of realities, unified by a certain element or principle existing "beyond" or "beneath" it. Man can be defined tentatively as *his* living. If man is formally defined as a set, he is a set whose only subset is himself.

21 BIOLOGICAL LIFE AND HUMAN LIFE

Let me put it this way: living things—"organisms"—*live;* man, on the other hand (or rather, besides) *makes his own life.* This distinction looks overly subtle, or perhaps merely verbal. Could it not be asserted that organic systems, and in particular higher organisms, also make their own life? After all, organisms behave, as pointed out earlier, "spontaneously." This does not necessarily mean that their behavior is uncaused; it only means that it springs forth from them and yet is reflected upon them. This latter meaning is not to be dismissed lightly, for it conveys the interesting idea that organisms possess an "inside" as well as an "outside."[4] To be sure, 'inside' and 'outside' are also names of attributes of inorganic systems. However, whereas in the latter 'inside' and 'outside' primarily designate spatial attributes, in the former they principally designate behavioral characteristics. Organisms are capable of revealing, and of concealing, attitudes, purposes, impulses, emotions. Furthermore, they do that, not just accidentally, but constitutively. Rather than *having* an "outside" and an "inside," organisms *are* an "outside" and an "inside."

The terms 'outside' and 'inside' designate here, so to speak, ultimate behavioral attributes of organisms. Organisms reveal and conceal *themselves* instead of being "revealed" and "concealed" to a knowing subject, as is the case with inorganic realities. Organisms express "what they are" no less than "what they are not." They are capable of deceit and of dissimulation. They express themselves not only impulsively, but also cunningly. In *this* sense, organisms also make their own life. But the expression 'to make one's own life' must have a stronger meaning than the one surmised above if it is to serve as a feature capable of distinguishing human life from biological life *in genere.* Should we say that the expression 'to make one's own life' easily acquires such a meaning when it is made synonymous with 'to behave rationally' or 'deliberately'? I do not think so. We have experimental proof that some higher animals display an impressive amount of intelligence in their behavior. Not even tool-using and tool-making are exclusive attributes of human beings; some prehuman primates discovered that certain stones, sticks, and bones could be used as tools and even as tool-making tools.[5] The same may be said, even if less confidently, with respect to language. If the term 'language' designates a set of signals, expressed by means of bodily behavior, to impart information, then the bees use language. If, however, 'language' has a stronger meaning than the one just indicated, then its existence can be very intimately tied up with the human meaning of 'making one's own life.'[6]

The difference between "to live" and "to make one's own life" must be based, therefore, on less controversial features. One of them I consider noteworthy: it is the one revealed through a study of the type of relationship existing between living beings and their world, both the inanimate and the animate world.

All organisms develop within the frame of a more or less definite biological species. Each one of the species is adapted, or becomes adapted, to a certain "world" by means of a fixed system of challenges and responses. The behavior of each individual organism fits almost perfectly into the structure of its world, to the extent that the latter can be defined conversely by the set of operations which each individual organism can perform within it.

The dependence of each individual organism on its species is practically complete. The individual organism limits itself to performing those actions which become biologically possible within the species to which it belongs. When an individual organism attempts to perform actions of a quite different character, its survival as an individual is gravely impaired. If I may be permitted to use a formula infected with Platonic realism, "the species prevents the individual from acting otherwise." The well-known expression 'the genius of the species' summarizes metaphorically this almost consummate adaptability. Without such a "genius" the species would fade away or would change so drastically as to become a different species. Far from making its own life, each individual organism is "making" a part of the life of the relevant species. This I call "to live" *simpliciter.* In order to make, or be able to make, its own life it would be necessary for an individual organism to deviate from the perpetual cyclical movement of the species. If the individual organism succeeded without perishing, and if enough individual organisms followed suit, then the species would no longer be a species: it would be a community.[7] An essentially different type of relation between the individual organism and the species would then emerge. For such an event to happen, two basic conditions are required: on the one hand, the subordination of a certain number of primary impulses, among them the sexual impulse, to communal needs;[8] and on the other hand, and quite paradoxically, the possibility of a further inadaptability to, and even revolt against, communal patterns. Yet these conditions would still prove insufficient for the emergence of a full-fledged society. For such an emergence it would be necessary for the individual organism to invent and put forward new ways of life capable of transforming the behavioral structure of the community. Then, and only then, would the individual organism make its own life or have the possibility of making it. This happens, however, only with human beings. They belong to their community in a sense different from the one in which even prehuman primates belonged to their species. Human beings can, as a consequence, have a history, and not merely a temporal development. And in the course of history, behavioral changes occur which are, to be sure, based on biological processes, but which are not exclusively subservient to them. To make one's own life requires, thus, the transcendence of biological conditions. On the other hand, to live *simpliciter* looks more like sinking into life.

Individual organisms not only adapt to the conditions imposed by their biological species; they are also subordinated to the specific biological world corresponding to the species. This world is not an "objective world"; it is a biologically conditioned world. If we are ready to make 'reality' synonymous with 'objective reality,' then the world in question is not a "real world." The reality peculiar to the biological world is determined by the sum of biological needs and impulses shaped by a definite physical environment. The various biological worlds can be intertwined, and together can constitute one world, the so-called "biosphere." But there is no world transcending these various worlds, that is, no objectively transbiological world. For an organic world to trespass beyond its own limits it would be necessary for the individual organisms belonging to it to stop, at least intermittently, acting according to a definite challenge-and-response pattern. They would have to be capable of refusing to fulfill biological demands for the sake of values of a more objective character.

That is what the human beings do, at times. They repress their biological drives in the name of possible actions having some end in themselves, for instance, in the name of knowing for knowing's sake. We may call the result of these actions "cultural achievements." Now, although such achievements must draw their energy out of the sublimation of biological processes, they cannot be measured solely in terms of this sublimation. Max Scheler wrote that man is the only animal capable of saying "No," or, as he put it, he is "the ascetic of life."[9] He was right but only up to a point, because refusal is not enough; otherwise what we call "culture" would become a rather uncomfortable display of asceticism. In point of fact, "culture" can also mean fostering life, including biological life. But in such a case, this is not to be done in the name of biological life (if it can be said that it should be done "in the name of" anything); it is to be done in the name of vital *values*. What, therefore, ultimately counts, is not what the individual does, but the purpose with which he does it. A nonascetic life permeated by values—for instance, beauty—is as cultured as any other, and sometimes even more so. Thus, we must not hastily conclude that cultural values are solely obtainable by the repression and sublimation of biological drives, for in such a case they would not possess values of their own. Yet without some transformation of biological impulses there would be no possibility of an "objective world"; there would only be what we may call a "subjective-biological world": the world of the species.

To make one's own life can now be defined as follows: as the possibility of making the biological-subjective interests of the species, and of each one of its members, serve as the energetic basis for the final recognition of objects as objects. This may in principle seem to lead to a type of existence in which the subjective drives of individual organisms are stifled so as never to recur. Nevertheless, the subservience of subjective-biological drives to objective realities and/or values need not be love's labor lost. The transformation of the self-enclosed biological world into an open objective world may be—it has, indeed, been—the necessary condition for a later much more effective fulfillment of biological impulses. The demands imposed upon men by the recognition of reality as objective reality have, in fact, led them to a mastery of the same biological world in which they were originally confined. Thus, to recognize reality as it is, and not as our whim takes it, has become—through science, for example—the most efficient means of mastering it. One of the many paradoxes of the human condition is that men may have to emphasize reality to the utmost in order to fulfill more completely the demands of their subjectivity.

22   BEING, BECOMING, EXISTING

The concepts thus far introduced can now be translated into an ontological vocabulary. Inorganic matter I understand as "being in itself," namely, being what it is. Organic reality I understand as "being for itself," namely being for the sake of its own fulfillment—the development and survival of biological species. Inorganic matter I conceive as "something that already is"; organic reality, as "something that is in the process of being." In some sense, organic reality can also be conceived as "that which is not yet what it is."

The term 'being' must not be construed here as designating something forbidding or recondite. In the present context 'being' means 'way of behaving,' in the general sense of 'way of being actualized.' To say that inorganic matter is already given is tantamount to saying that it is actual, or nearly so. The expression 'nearly so' I cannot adequately clarify here; suffice it to say that I am assuming the following ontological postulate: no reality is absolutely actual; and its counterpart, no reality is absolutely potential. In my ontological scheme there is no room for absolute attributes (or entities) of any kind; there is, at most, room for some concepts—which then become limiting concepts—of (equally limiting) absolute attributes or realities. Inorganic reality is, from this viewpoint, the most actual of all types of reality. If it is not purely actual, it "behaves"—or rather, it appears—*as if* it were so. Whenever there is something determinate, and determinable, that is the inorganic world. This is, by the way, the reason why it lends itself so easily to description in that language in which, according to Galileo, the "Book of Nature" is written: the language of mathematics.

Inorganic realities undergo a number of stages. Organic realities, and in particular higher organisms, undergo a number of phases. The former endure a series of processes; the latter, a series of developments. Terms such as 'state,' 'phase,' 'process,' and 'development,' are, of course, utterly inadequate. Furthermore, the distinctions which these terms are meant to convey do not in any way presuppose that organic realities cease to behave in the way inorganic realities behave. After all, there is only one species of matter: the so-called "physical matter." But organic realities, or, as I have also called them, "organisms," do something that inorganic realities do not: they realize, and constitute, themselves in the course of their development. They bring themselves, successfully or not, to an issue. They appear, much more than inorganic realities, as a set of potentialities which may or may not become actual. In principle, an organism could be expressed (ontologically) as a τὸ τί ἦν εἶναι— the well-known Aristotelian expression, sometimes translated, rather hastily, as 'essence.' But, of course, organisms are not essences. They are existences developing according to certain forms and patterns which, no doubt, change in the course of evolution. In *this* sense, organisms are even more "determined" than inorganic realities, if the semantics of 'determined' is duly clarified. They possess, as it has been put, a "determined future," and abide by a "certain generic and specific cycle."[10] Organic life, and in particular complex organic life, has, thus, a "direction." Which, of course, does not mean, even if it seems to mean, that life always and necessarily follows a preconceived plan, or develops according to a preestablished finality. We need not presuppose the existence of immanent final causes in the evolution of the organic world as a whole. We need only presuppose that organisms become what they are within a certain temporal-cyclical pattern, and according to certain laws of structural transformation.

When all is said, however, one thing remains certain: that both types of reality tally (ontologically) with the concept of "being." To be sure, one of these two types of reality is more aptly describable (ontologically, again) as "becoming" than as "being." Yet the concept of becoming is still indebted to the concept of being. At any rate, both inorganic and organic realities can be understood as "things" of some sort—things which move and change; and things which, besides moving and changing, grow, develop and reproduce themselves.

The most striking characteristic of human life, as we view it ontologically, is that it can scarcely be called a "being," namely, a "thing." Following, deliberately or not, in Fichte's footsteps, some contemporary philosophers have emphasized that human life as *human* life is not a thing, not even a "thing that becomes." In the sense in which I have employed such terms as 'to be,' 'being,' 'it is,' 'they are,' and so on, it can be said then that human life, properly speaking, "is not." It is not what it is. But neither is it what it becomes. Can we then talk about it at all? If we were very particular about language, we would conclude that we obviously cannot. Happily enough, language is a somewhat pliable tool; we can make its terms mean, if not all that we wish, at least some things that we very much want. In consequence, we can also say that human life "is." But we must hasten to add that it is not a "something," but rather a "someone." A few philosophers have even gone so far as to define it as some sort of absolute in which everything that is or becomes remains, as it were, "enclosed"—at least insofar as it is, or becomes, perceivable, knowable, and so on. I cannot go along with them. But I am ready to admit that if human life is some sort of thing, it is a very unusual thing indeed. This thing which is not a thing, may be called "an existent," not, however, in the simple sense of "something that exists," but rather in the sense partly uncovered by some traditional metaphysicians when they coined, for another purpose, the expression 'the pure actuality of existing.'

The natural sciences and the social sciences contribute valuable information about human life. It would be unwise to dismiss all these sciences with a stroke of the pen, claiming that they touch only the "ontic" realm while in no sense reaching the "ontological" realm, as Heidegger puts it.[11] For these two realms are not incommunicable. It has been said that, after all, we are quite uncertain about where one such realm ends and where the other begins.[12] I heartily subscribe to this view. Translated into a somewhat less esoteric vocabulary, it simply means that metaphysical speculation and ontological analysis, while they do not need to follow scientific research blindly, should never proceed stubbornly against scientific results. If for no other reason than that science is here to stay (§ 3), philosophers would do well to resign themselves to the facts that it may set certain bounds and exert certain controls on metaphysics (the converse may, of course, also be the case). The frontiers between metaphysics and science will eventually change; after all, neither one nor the other is a ready-made system of knowledge. Now, setting bounds to metaphysical speculation is far from equivalent to determining the direction such speculation must take. Metaphysical speculation and, a fortiori, ontological analysis use concepts wrought by science and by common sense, but do not meekly conform to all the meanings established by them. That this is so we will verify at once. I will introduce a few terms whose ontological meanings will prove to be quite different from, albeit somehow related to, their usual meanings. Among such terms, one is notably singled out for distinction: it is the term 'property,' considered here as designating the positive and concrete aspect of a yet undefined concept: the concept "selfhood," a rather clumsy translation of the German Selbstheit and of the Spanish mismidad.

23 MAN AS SELFHOOD AND AS PROPERTY

To begin with, I will distinguish between "ipseity" (ipseitas) and "selfhood." The term 'ipseity' is meant to designate the fact that any given thing is what it is, namely, the identity of any given thing with itself. Since such an identity is accomplished only when we arbitrarily disregard the temporal element in a thing, pure "ipseity" is an attribute only of the so-called "ideal objects"— mathematical entities (if there are such), concepts, and perhaps values. However, it can be said that all things as things display a greater or lesser tendency to be what they are, and therefore to be "identical" in the above sense. This tendency to self-identity among existing realities reaches its maximum in inorganic systems for reasons that should now be moderately clear. It is much less perceptible in organisms, insofar as these are in the process of becoming what they are according to temporal and cyclical patterns. Nevertheless, all beings are in some ways what they are, even if at times their being is, to use the well-known Aristotelian expressions, a "coming to be" and a "passing away."

In a way, the term 'selfhood' purports to designate a type of attribute similar to the one designated by the term 'ipseity.' Furthermore, if we define 'selfhood' as "being itself" or as "becoming itself," then 'selfhood' is just another name for 'identity.' Thus, we may conclude that all realities, insofar as they are identical with themselves, possess the attributes of ipseity and selfhood.

Unfortunately, all these terms behave like the meshes in Eddington's fishing net: they let some interesting fish escape easily. At any rate, they let human reality quickly jump into the sea again. This happens in particular with the terms 'identity' and 'ipseity.' Does it also happen with the term 'selfhood'? Not necessarily, provided that we employ it the way scientists and, above all, philosophers handle a number of expressions—by twisting or, at least, stretching their meaning.[13] 'Selfhood' may mean more than just "being itself"; it may mean "being oneself." It may serve as a formal answer to the question: "Who is it?" rather than an answer to the question: "What is it?" In this sense it may describe a specifically human attribute. In order to avoid confusions, however, I propose the following terminological device: whenever 'selfhood' is used to refer to human beings, I will replace it by 'property,' in a sense of 'property' which I will soon clarify.

Besides being denounced as barbaric, the proposed vocabulary will in all likelihood be declared superfluous. Why not use in this connection the more respectable terms 'spirit' and 'person,' already tested through centuries of philosophical experience? The term 'person' in particular looks quite handy. Yet, I prefer to avoid it, or rather, to use it only after it has been purged of many of its traditional connotations. Should the occasion arise we could, if we really wanted to, use the terms 'spirit' and 'person,' provided that the two following conditions were fulfilled: First, that these terms would not refer to any realities absolutely transcendent to human life, and still less running counter to the material—inorganic and organic—constituents of human life. Second, that they would not designate any indissoluble and inalienable attributes, namely, any supposedly eternal predicate which man would, so to speak, "share" and of which he could be definitely assured. By the way, similar reservations could be made when the attributes called "rationality" and "emotivity" (some higher forms of emotivity) are chosen as denoting specific characteristics of human existence.

At most I will agree to say that man *becomes* personal and *becomes* spiritual, without ever completely succeeding. Man is making himself constantly as man, and that is what I meant by saying that he makes his own life. A certain biological structure and a number of psychological dispositions are in this respect necessary conditions. They are in no way merely contingent facts, purely circumstantial elements which man can take or leave as he pleases. A certain human body and a certain human mind are also a certain given man. Each man thus makes his own life with his body and his mind, which are not solely "things," but basic elements of man's existence.

Here lies one reason why human beings are not identical with, even if in some respects they are comparable to, servomechanisms. It is quite probable that the more we know about the structure and behavior of nervous systems— and above all, about the structure of the human central nervous system—the more similar they will appear to a complex servomechanism. The psychosomatic structure of human beings can be explained largely in terms of complicated mechanical states in stable equilibrium. The so-called "organic self-control" (homeostasis) can be described as a kind of thermostatic control. We may even go so far as to admit that servomechanisms can think, remember, learn, and so on. When all is said, however, there still remains the problem of whether a servomechanism, no matter how human-like we imagine it to be, can indeed perform operations of a really human character. Professor Mario Bunge has pointed out that "irrespective of their degree of automatism [computers] are all characterized by the fact that *they do not perform mathematical operations,* but only physical operations which we coordinate with mathematical ones."[14] Computers "do not add pure numbers; they add turns of cogwheels, electric pulses, etc."[15] That some functions can be described in terms of automatic control operations is one thing; that they are identical with such operations is another. In any case, it would be pure fantasy to claim that servomechanisms make themselves the way human beings do; that, therefore, they belong to themselves. This does not mean that servomechanisms could not in principle "think" or even reproduce themselves (if von Neumann's blueprint for a self-reproducing machine proves feasible, we will eventually witness such a stupendous ceremony);[16] it only, but significantly, means that their reality will never be *theirs,* but something else's, and actually, someone else's reality.

"Man belongs to himself" is a way, albeit a rather awkward one, of saying that man is his own property. I mean not only the fact that the body and the mind of human beings belong to them, instead of being something alien and contingent. I mean also, and above all, that men possess their own lives, so that they are ontologically, and not only morally, responsible for themselves. Man is not a being *that* lives; he is *his own* living. However, since man is not anything definite except the constant effort to become man, it may even be risky to say that he is his own living; let us then say that he constantly tries to make his living his own. Making one's own life—for this is ultimately what all this boils down to—is then something different from, although somehow correlated to, the biological processes of growing and developing. What such "self-making" most resembles is a series of efforts to reach and, as it were, to conquer one's own reality while stumbling all along the way.

The above may cast some light on the perplexing paradox of man as a free being. On the one hand, man as man is necessarily free. The arguments adduced in favor of this view by authors such as Ortega y Gasset[17] and Sartre[18] are quite pertinent, even if they are not always altogether convincing. On the other hand, freedom is not given to man in the sense in which it might be given to a thing as one of its unassailable, or at least normal attributes. As a consequence, the paradox of freedom is still more puzzling than it has been claimed. Let me put it this way: man acquires his own freedom insofar as he freely develops as man. Thus, freedom is a requisite for the existence of man—who must himself provide this requisite. Man is that type of reality that can make itself while it can also unmake itself. Man, in short, has the possibility of being himself, and of not being himself, of appropriating himself and of alienating himself.

Human reality is, therefore a "being for itself" in a much more radical sense than the being for itself proper to organisms. No organic reality as such can move away from itself. Ceasing to be itself is for such a reality equivalent to becoming another. To use, and by the way to distort, the Hegelian vocabulary—to which I and many others are indebted nowadays, no matter how much we try to put this fact out of our minds—an organic reality is never an *Anderssein* and can never become, strictly speaking, an *Aussersichsein*. If we persist in applying the expressions 'being for itself' and 'being other' to the behavior of organic realities, we should give them quite different meanings from the ones just intimated. To the extent that we are taking an ontological point of view on human reality, we are not interested in forms of being as being but rather in ultimate possibilities of existence. Whereas organic reality can be in many different ways, it never ceases to be what it is. On the other hand, man can cease to be himself and, as a rule, never becomes entirely himself. Yet, not being himself is also one of the ways of being a man. The reason for this paradoxical condition of human existence is, again, that man is never "a thing that is."

It may now be contended that I have gone too far in my attempt to deny that man is a "being" or a "thing." First, man is obviously also a thing, an organic thing and many inorganic things together. Second, we may view man, from the religious angle, as a creature, and therefore as a type of reality that could never make is own existence, or even simply exist, unless God produced him, and perhaps helped him to exist. Such claims are not lightly to be dismissed. The former is based upon facts; the latter is founded on a belief. Nevertheless, I need not consider these claims as unduly embarrassing. The first claim I have already rebutted; although man, through his body and mind, is a fact, or a collection of facts, what makes him a man is not these facts but what he does with them. In human life it is the meaning of the facts that counts. As to the second claim, it is sufficient to say that even if man received his being from God it could still be argued that he is not properly speaking a man unless he maintains himself in existence. If man is a created being, he is such in a sense quite different from the one in which we say that things, or for that matter, pure spirits, are created. The freedom that constitutes man and by means of which he constitutes himself must be his very own. To express it in Nietzsche's words: man is an acrobat walking over an abyss;[19] it is up to him to fling himself down or to keep his balance. In order to be able to walk over the abyss with a reasonable degree of poise he does all sorts of things; for example, he creates "culture" and "history." There is little doubt that "part of every culture is 'defense mechanism,'" and that "the function of culture and psychosis alike is to be 'homeostatic,' to maintain preferred equilibriums."[20] But this is only part of the story. As I have tried to establish, culture is also, and above all, the result of the attempt to make man's world an objective world, independent from, albeit attached to, his basic drives and instincts. There is no harm, however, in admitting that man is fundamentally a cultural and historical being. He does not produce culture and history just because he finds it fun, but because he desperately needs them. But this question leads us to the heart of our present problem: the problem of "where" man is heading.

24 THE DEFINITION OF MAN

Let me briefly recapitulate my argument. The concepts "being" and "becoming" apply to human reality only insofar as this reality is part of a continuum—the "continuum of Nature." I have never denied, but rather emphasized, that man is also an inorganic and an organic being, to the extent that he really *is* a body. But as we wish to distinguish human reality ontologically from other realities of the said continuum, the ontological vocabulary must be stretched when it is not twisted. Thus, terms such as 'selfhood,' 'property,' and others come to the rescue in order to allow us to have a glimpse of what it means to say such odd things as "man is not a being, but a maker of himself."

I could have also said that the reality of human life is, properly speaking, the meaning of human life if I had been given the opportunity to introduce the term 'meaning' (or perhaps "sense") with any likelihood of not being utterly misunderstood. I will confine myself to a less controversial vocabulary, and will say that human reality is "intentional" in character. 'Being intentional' here means "going toward, wending or directing one's course." But a question now arises: "Where" is he going? "To what" is he wending or directing his course?

If I say "toward something outside him," or "toward something inside him," I will not go very far indeed. To proceed to the outside is tantamount to adapting to the surrounding world—a world in turn constantly shaped by the adaptive efforts. To proceed to the inside is tantamount to self-regulating the individual structure. In both cases we are talking about biological and psycho-biological processes. These have, in man and in higher animals, a firm basis in two types of nervous systems: the cerebro-spinal nervous system, which coordinates the knowledge and action relations with the external world; and the sympathetic nervous system, which regulates the so-called "inner processes" of the organism and which is split into as many independent systems as prove necessary for the proper functioning of the various parts of the organism. Where, then, does man as man proceed to? No doubt, we can still use such expressions as 'toward the outside' and 'toward the inside,' but the terms 'outside' and 'inside' acquire quite a different meaning here.

The "outside" toward which human beings proceed is the world as a world, namely, the world as an objective reality, independent in principle from strictly biological and psycho-biological needs. This "intentional openness" to the objective world, as phenomenologists would put it, is the foundation of knowledge. To be sure, men know and think to some purpose. But the contents of thinking and knowledge must be objectively valid, and not only subjectively useful. Human beings project themselves toward a world outside that transcends any subjective purpose. Human beings may have, so to speak, invented and promoted knowledge for the sake of "life," of "human *praxis*," and so on. But here we can modify a celebrated formula: *propter cognitionem cognitionis perdere causas;* we must sacrifice knowledge (knowledge as an end). Or, rather, we must promote the former only because we hope to reach the latter. This does not mean, of course, that knowledge as an end is necessarily incompatible with knowledge as a tool; after all, action has often been all the more successful when disinterested contemplation—or so-called "pure theory"—has preceded it. On the other hand, knowing is not the only possible intentional attitude; acting and evaluating are also important, and sometimes even more so than knowing. In any case, man exists as man insofar as he fulfills himself, not by directly responding to the challenges of the environment, but by making the environment an objective world. Therefore, when man proceeds toward an outside, he does not confine himself either to adapting to it completely, or to refusing it completely. He goes back and forth from subjectivity to objectivity—which helps explain why the cultural world, which man creates as he springs up from the natural world, is at the same time a world which he must objectively recognize.

On the other hand, the "inside" toward which man wends his way is not only the inner biological or psycho-biological structure. It is not equivalent to, even if based on, the process of self-conservation and self-regulation of the organism, but rather to some sort of reality which may be called "oneself," "one's own reality," and "one's authenticity." There is also a projecting movement here. But man does not project something; he rather projects "someone"—namely himself. When he thus projects himself, man searches for—without necessarily finding—his "authentic being," or, as it has also been called, somewhat pathetically, his "destiny." To be sure, all realities, and in particular all highly developed organisms, exist in some way as self-fulfilling and self-projecting entities; they all are, consciously or not, intent on realizing themselves. But whereas the pattern for self-realization is given to them in the forms and/or laws of nature, man is not given any such definite pattern. Each one of us, whether he knows it or not, or even cares for it or not, is on the lookout for his own pattern, without knowing whether it will ever be discovered, or even whether there is one. All realities, except man, can be, or can become, in the sense of 'being something' or 'becoming something.' Man can, besides, cease to be, in the sense of 'ceasing to be himself.' Here is why the concepts "being" and "becoming" have proved inadequate to describe ontologically human reality. In that sense Sartre was correct when he contended that human life—or, "consciousness," the "being for itself"—is not what it is, and is what it is not. In view of this, we could now assert that man is not even doomed to be free. Man is not, properly speaking, doomed to anything, not even to be man. This does not necessarily mean that freedom is neither good nor bad. In fact, unless he is, or rather, struggles to become, free (in many senses of 'free,' including 'morally free,' 'free from alienation,' etc.), man is not worthy of being called a human being. But he does not receive his freedom ready-made; he must make it. Or, more precisely, he makes it as he (freely) makes himself. This is no doubt, a deplorably vicious circle, for it amounts to saying that only freedom makes a certain type of reality, which makes itself through freedom. But I see no way of escaping this circle. It may well happen, as we have already pointed out (§ 8), that some vicious circles are philosophically inevitable. On the level of the ontology of human life, we must often acknowledge that some consequences may play at the same time the role of principles.

Human life can be defined as a kind of unceasing march toward oneself, which can often become a march against oneself. Paradoxically, not being oneself is as good an attribute of human life as being oneself.

This is the meaning of the attribute called "property": that human life is always man's *own* life. Man owns his life even when he seems to be on the verge of annihilating himself as man, whether going back to his purely animal living, or transcending himself and becoming, as it were, ecstatic in front of pure objectivity. This last point deserves brief elucidation. Let us imagine that man consists, as some say, in being a spiritual substance, and that such a substance is defined as the possibility of bowing to objectivity—to objective reality and to objective values. Even in such a case, spiritual reality cannot be conceived except as *existing*. And in order to exist it must undergo all sorts of experiences, private and public, personal and historical, individual and social. To live as a man is to undergo what makes one be what one is. As a consequence, man as a personal reality tends to yield to the impersonal, but he is no longer a man when he yields to the impersonal to the point of fusing with it. This is, of course, another paradox which, I am afraid, must be allowed to remain. Let me simply say that man continually hesitates between the realm of pure objectivity and the realm of pure internal experience. He cannot come to a halt in his constant shift from one extreme point to the other. Reality and values are objective to man only insofar as they are subjectively experienced. Human experience, on the other hand, is lived through what some philosophers have called "situations." And since situations, whether individual or collective, are historical in character, human living is always historical, namely, irreversible, and in some sense at least, "dramatic." Anything done, thought, or felt by man in order to live authentically is irretrievable. It may be claimed that some acts or decisions sink so deeply into the living root of human reality that they transform it from the ground up. As an example I may cite repentance, usually followed by some kind of conversion (in various senses of 'conversion,' the religious sense being extremely important, but by no means unique). In contra-distinction to mere remorse,[21] repentance makes possible some sort of rebirth, traditionally, but not always aptly, called "spiritual rebirth." The past is not actually wiped away, but it becomes so transfigured by the present as to make it appear entirely different from what it was. Yet, even these "extreme situations" are possible only because the facts which they transform have existed the way they did. In other words, for repentance to be even conceivable, something to repent from is necessary. The very possibility of a fundamental change in human life is based on life's basic irreversibility. No human act is entirely alien to man. Hence the dramatic character of human existence. I do not inject the word 'dramatic' here just because I wish to make readers shudder, for I feel certain that readers, if they happen to be philosophers, will hardly shudder. I use the term 'dramatic' only to emphasize the temporal, experiential, and historical character of human reality. To say "life is a drama," on the other hand, is one of the ways of saying "life is mine." No drama is such if it is not the exclusive property of the character who displays it.

The source out of which the "dramatic" actions and decisions of human individuals spring, is therefore, not of a purely spiritual nature, nor is it of a permanent nature. Ortega y Gasset has pointed out that human life is at all times "circumstantial"; [22] each man does what he does, or abstains from doing what he abstains from doing, in view of specific and very concrete circumstances. I must say that I agree, but with one important reservation. Ortega y Gasset thought, as did Sartre later, that the body and mind (the character and temperament) of man belongs to the circumstances of human life, so that man makes his choice with, and, if necessary, against his own body and mind. If such were the case, however, the human reality would boil down to pure nothingness. The body and mind of an individual would never be his own. He would become a disembodied ghostly "chooser." Furthermore, he would be an infinitely plastic and malleable reality. By dint of making every natural reality in him appear as a purely contingent "facticity" (as some philosophers have put it), the very human reality would entirely dissolve. By means of depriving man of everything, he would not even be someone who would act with, for, or against any circumstances. On the other hand, if we conclude that only man's body and mind constitute man, we again risk making man a thing among other similar things. I will now turn to this difficulty.

Some philosophers have tried to determine "who" ultimately man is as distinct from ascertaining "what" he is. A few have contended, moreover, that man is his irreducible "authenticity," his "inner call," his "destiny." And they have added that we may choose to be faithful or not to our "incorruptible (in the sense of 'absolutely reliable and unchangeable') core." Theirs is an exquisite and refined doctrine. It is not, however, a very illuminating doctrine. To say that "whoness" (if I may be allowed to use this word) is equivalent to authenticity and nothing else is to put forward a purely nominal definition of the expression 'oneself.' It is equivalent to saying that one is (at bottom) what one (at bottom) is. No consequences, moral or otherwise, ensue. It may be argued that in view of the above difficulties it is preferable to subscribe to a more traditional definition of man—at any rate, to a formula defining man as a really permanent "someone." But when philosophers have started defining or describing this supposedly more enduring reality, they have been caught in the trap of all classical substantialist theories. They have been compelled to define man as some kind of "invariable nature," and often as someone possessing a "rational nucleus." In other words, they have again defined human reality in terms of such categories as "thing" and "being" which I have taken so many pains to discard.

Is the question at all solvable? The general ontological framework that supports the philosophical views brought forth in this book comes to the rescue. In this ontological framework no "Absolutes," and hence no absolute modes of being, are allowed. Each reality is supposed to bend toward some of the so-called "Absolutes" without ever reaching any of them. Now, the infinite plasticity and malleability of the human reality, on the one hand, and its invariable and permanent character, on the other, are absolute modes of being. As such, they must be viewed only as limiting realities describable by means of limiting concepts. We can talk about them, but only if we are careful enough to allow them a mere quasi-existence. Thus, concrete human reality perpetually oscillates between two ideal poles. Man is not to be defined either as a pure possibility of choice or as a purely invariable entity; he unceasingly rebounds from one to the other in order to make himself. Human reality is not like an unbordered river. Neither is it comparable to a waterless riverbed. It is not pure nature. Neither is it pure history. It is both, but in a constantly shifting—perhaps I should say, "dialectical"—way.

In some respects I have tried to put traditional metaphysics and modern ontology together. The former insisted on substance; the latter was emphasized function. The former argued in favor of a "rational" core of man; the latter has underlined "history," "experience," "drama." If we now reintroduce the time-honored term 'person' and try to put it to some use, would we not say that the unforeseeable and irretrievable history of the human being is inscribable within the frame of the notion of person? We would not then say that man is a person having a history, but rather a person constituting himself historically. According to a celebrated formula, the human person is "an individual substance of a rational character,"[23] subsisting in its own right. Provided that we interpret the term 'substance' in the light of the preceding considerations as a self-making reality, we can conclude that man is "an individual substance of a historical character."[24] It is most improbable that my formula will ever become as influential as Boethius'. But perhaps, it is only because nowadays philosophers are much harder to please.

25   A BUDGET OF PARADOXES

We have assumed that to be real is to be mortal, in a very broad and, indeed, "analogical" sense of 'mortal.' The converse is, of course, true: to be mortal is to be real. Furthermore, we have assumed that for any given reality, R, the nature of R is parallel to the type of mortality—or, in general, "ceasability"—of R. In other words, R is what it is because of the way in which it ceases to be, and R ceases to be in such and such a way because R is what it is. These assumptions we have consistently maintained throughout our elucidation of the nature and mode or modes of cessation of inorganic and organic realities. The same must be the case with human reality.

The philosophical anthropology sketched above (§§ 20–24) is meant to convey the idea that, although man is also an inorganic reality (a cluster of inorganic systems) and, to be sure, a biological organism, his existence is not entirely explicable in terms of purely inorganic and organic substances. As a

consequence, man's mode of cessation—his peculiar kind of "mortality"—
should not be entirely explicable in terms of the modes of cessation of such
substances. It is now the moment to show that man's peculiar mode of cessation confirms, as well as supports, the main results of our philosophical
anthropology. To this question we will devote the remaining sections of the
present chapter.

Before we proceed to scrutinize in more detail the nature of human
death, we wish to call attention to a few paradoxes, as startling as they are
enlightening.

1. On the one hand, human death—which we will henceforth simply call
"death"—seems to be so deeply embedded and, as it were, "internalized" in the
human being that we are tempted to conclude that man is an essentially mortal
being. In other words, to die seems to be something truly "inherent" in the
human reality. This aspect of human death we will name "the interiority of
death." In addition, death seems to "belong" to the very nature of man, so that
it can be concluded that the death of any given man is truly "his own"—or
otherwise said, that death is man's inalienable "property." On the other hand, men
often act and think as if it were their aim to overcome death at all costs; after all,
man is the only being who has ever dreamed that he could be "immortal."

2. On the one hand, death is an event which possesses the same meaning,
or, as the case may be, the same lack of meaning, for all men. On the other
hand, human death is an event which is strictly individual or, more precisely,
strictly personal.

3. On the one hand, death seems to make its presence felt only "at the
other end of life"; thus, death emerges truly "outside of," and has little to do
with, human life. To be sure, some thinkers have surmised that man is, as it
were, perpetually dying, for he begins to die from the very moment when he
begins to live. Yet once a man is dead, his death is, in fact, "beyond his life."
Death is not simply dying, but "that which has died." Hence to die is, as Paul
Ludwig Landsberg has put it, "to set foot into the ghostly, chilly world of
absolute death."[25]

From this point of view, we were able to say little, if anything at all about
death. 'Death' is a name which merely designates the complete absence of life.
Since the complete absence of life (or, for that matter, of anything) is nothingness, it would seem only wise to abstain from talking about it, for nothingness
is not a proper subject of meaningful talk.

On the other hand, death "refers to"—in the senses of 'points at,' 'calls
attention to'—life, even if it is only "a life that was." Something remains for
a time after death which can be regarded as "that which death has left behind": the "dead one," the corpse. Thus, it is hard to believe that death refers
to nothing; as the saying goes, it "preys upon" living beings.

Now, the expression 'death refers to life' can be given two meanings. First, the expression in question may describe the trivial fact that death is, in every case, the end of life. Second, it may imply that death is somehow inherent in— and thus "internal to"—life. 'Being inherent in life' may again have two meanings: (1) It may mean that 'death' describes or designates the culmination of the biological process called "aging," at least in highly developed organisms. (2) It may mean that human life calls for and, as it were, necessarily implies death, which is nearly the same as saying that human life would become meaningless without death, and indeed without "his own" death.

In what follows I will take the above "paradoxes" and "contradictions" into account. In tune with a form of thinking on which nothing less than a general ontology is based, I will not try to avoid, but will even occasionally emphasize, a number of conflicting statements and positions. Thus, it will be shown that each man dies for himself, but at the same time that the death of each human being can be taken as a symbol of human mortality in general. It will also be shown that death is an event internal to man's life while not being ever *completely* "his own." It will be shown finally that the predicate 'is basically mortal' is not necessarily synonymous with the predicate 'is (or exists) unto death.'

26 THE INTERIORITY OF DEATH

The expression 'the interiority of death' is meant to describe the following state of affairs: death is not simply the end of life but an event which shapes and constitutes life. Correspondingly, the expression 'the exteriority of death' is meant to designate the fact that death falls outside the scope of life. Now then, it is my opinion that no matter how much death may belong to man as his "property," it is never completely interior (or, as we shall also say, "internal") to man's life. If such were the case, man's life would be explicable solely in terms of his death. On the other hand, I maintain that a complete exteriority of death with respect to life is most improbable and, indeed, inconceivable, for in this case human death would be an entirely meaningless event. We must assume, then, that death is partly internal, and partly external, to human life. The question is now, to what degree does the interiority of death noticeably prevail over its exteriority in human beings?

The answer is, to a considerable degree. As has been shown in the preceding chapters, cessation is not equally fundamental and significant in all types of realities. We have been able to disclose that even within the sole realm of organic beings, some entities are "potentially immortal"; for them, cessation is primarily, although never entirely, external and, therefore, primarily, although never entirely, accidental. In highly developed organisms, death seems to be more deeply anchored in their existence; they inevitably die, or nearly so. Now, the death of highly developed organisms is biological death; it is a fact but has yet no meaning, or, more precisely, if it has a meaning it is not yet meaningful enough to be seriously taken into account. That is, of course, due to the fact that even highly developed organisms are (at least relatively) value-free—which is, of course, different from saying that they are valueless. At any rate, their value and, consequently, their meaning is not sufficiently internal to their being. Thus, death puts an end to these organisms but does not "realize" or "fulfill" them; they are not made what they are because of the way in which they happen to die. In fine, for any purely biological organism, O, the fact that O dies is always more important than what it means (or may mean) for O to die. In human beings, on the other hand, death is already an essentially meaningful event; it not only puts an end to their existence but, as intimated, it constitutes their very existence to a considerable extent.

Highly developed organisms can be said to be potentially mortal. Death is, therefore, internal to these organisms—not, of course, completely, but, so to speak, sufficiently. If we now claim that death is internal to human beings, and add that it is not completely so, then we might seem to be led to conclude that human beings are also potentially mortal. Accordingly, it would seem that there is no difference worth mentioning between biological organisms as such and human beings, at least insofar as their degree of mortality is concerned: both are potentially mortal, and death is internal to both of them. Yet we persist in affirming that, although human death is also in a high degree biological death, the former is not entirely reducible to the latter.

The above puzzle can be solved as soon as we realize that we have been surreptitiously identifying the meaning of 'potentially mortal' with the meaning of 'death is internal to life.' Now then, these expressions are far from having exactly the same meaning. To say that death is internal to life is not in the least like saying that death is in life potentially, for instance, as "that which is bound to happen sooner or later." If a being is potentially mortal, then it is potentially mortal. Being potentially mortal means only that death is contained, as it were, in life, perhaps in the manner in which an organism is contained in its seeds. Only in a very metaphorical sense can we affirm that death is then internal to life. On the other hand, although it is true that, as a biological organism, man is also potentially mortal, it is no less true that death is not merely contained in this existence. Death, as potential death, brings pressure to bear upon man's life, and so becomes a decisive factor in it.

We can thus affirm that death gives human life not so much its being, as that which constitutes it primarily, although not, it must be acknowledged, exclusively: its meaning, or, to say it another way, its being as meaning. For human life exemplifies superlatively that form of reality in which meaning predominates over being—over facts as facts—to such a degree that it may even be said that facts exist for man only to the extent that they possess meaning for him. This is only another way of saying that death constantly "points at" life. Thus, death truly "belongs" to human life, which is the same as saying that it makes it possible for human life to achieve its own reality.

In his "metaphysics of death" Simmel pointed out that a distinction must be made in human life between "process" and "contents."[26] The term 'process' designates the course of life and, therefore, its pure and simple temporal development. The term 'contents' designates all that is, or can be, experienced in the course of life: feelings, thoughts, judgments of value, and so on. Now, according to Simmel, it would be totally impossible to distinguish between "process" and "contents" if life had no end. If a life continued endlessly, none of its "contents" would make any great difference, and, therefore, all the "contents" would become identified with the "process." It would be all the same if one embraced this or that particular thought, made this or that particular judgment of value, underwent this or that particular experience. In fact, no thought, no feeling, no experience would be "particular" at all; they would all be the same and, as a consequence, they would all be "indifferent." Now, if we wish each and all of the contents to have a meaning, we must assume that life is not endless but always limited and bound by death.

It is then the continual presence of death in life, its "hidden presence," which makes all the contents of life, and life itself, meaningful. This is why, as Simmel indicated, we do not die at one particular moment; death is not, properly speaking, an event but an "element" continuously shaping our existence. Death may not be the only thing that really matters, but in any case, nothing matters very much without it. We can thus conclude that death is internal to life in a sense of 'being internal,' which is not to be confused with the sense of 'being potentially mortal.' The expression 'the interiority of death' has a definite and more precise meaning now; it means that in human life, death is not only a limit (no matter how inevitable) but also a kind of "dividing line." This "line" performs two functions: it puts an end to a process, and gives this process a meaning. Now, if having some meaning is what specifically differentiates man from all other kinds of reality, then it can be said that an adequate understanding of human life depends, *a tergo,* on death. To express it in plain language, human death is a fact—or an event—that really counts.

27 THE EXPERIENCE OF DEATH

To say that death is—or, more precisely, tends to be—internal to human life is, of course, a very general statement. In point of fact, it is so general as to be quite unenlightening. In order to make it more specific, and thus more informative, we must have recourse to what is often called the "experience of death."

To be sure, we all know what we mean when we use such expressions as 'X' is mortally ill, and is about to die,' 'X died yesterday,' and so on. But, although we know that there is such a thing or such an event as death, that death is inevitable, that we all must die, and so on, we still do not realize in full measure what death is and what it means until we somehow "experience" death.

Now, how is an "experience of death" ever possible? We can "see" that people die; we can think of our own death as an event which will take place sooner or later, but we do not seem to be able to experience death in the same way as we do other "events" such as pleasure, pain, good health, illness, senility. All we can "see" of death is its "residue," for example, a corpse. Even a corpse is not only, or exclusively, a testimony of death, for it may equally well call attention to life. A corpse is not only a reminder of "that which is no longer," but also a reminder of "that which was." Thus, death as such seems to be outside all possible experience. As Karl Jaspers has written, "death as an objective fact of existence is not itself a limiting situation."[27]

According to Heidegger, we cannot experience another's death, or what is sometimes called "the death of the Other"; at most, we can "witness" it.[28] Death cannot be "substituted," "replaced," "transferred," "interchanged." No one can die in lieu of another. Although one can "die *for* another"; this does not mean that one can take the Other's *own* death.[29] It is characteristic of the *Dasein*'s death that each *Dasein* assumes it *a radice* for himself.

Heidegger's ideas in this respect should be understood in the light of his famous contention: the being of *Dasein* is a "being unto death."[30] Further on (§ 29) I shall explain more in detail why I disapprove of Heidegger's views on this question, or why I disapprove of them while considering them acceptable when duly integrated with other, seemingly contrary, views. Now, to reject *prima facie* Heidegger's contentions would seem to imply an acceptance of the criticisms against them which were formulated by Sartre.[31] Such, however, is not the case. Sartre points out that, if it is true that one cannot die for another, it is equally true that one also cannot, for example, love for another. He further maintains that, far from shaping and completing the being of human life, death completely alienates it and turns it into a sort of "prey of the living"[32]—one of those who may survive the dead person. Accordingly, it is not we ourselves who are mortal; it is "the Other" who is mortal "in his being."[33]

Now, whereas there is considerable truth in Sartre's views, they lead us, paradoxically enough, to conclusions very similar to those of Heidegger. If death were, as Sartre puts it, a "pure event," an "absolute contingency," something purely and simply "given," then it could not be experienced in any manner whatsoever, except perhaps as the absurd *par excellence*. Must we then resign ourselves to saying nothing about death because it is either absolutely one's own or absolutely another's? Is there no possibility of integrating these contrasting views so as to give each one its due?

The pages that follow are an attempt to give the latter question a positive answer. We shall endeavor to prove that we can indeed cast some light on death—to begin with, on the basis of the experience of another's death. I therefore agree with Gabriel Marcel's contention that the death of a human being, in particular the death of a loved one, cannot be considered as a purely external event; in some manner, it metaphysically affects the one who loves. "One can only lose," Marcel writes, "what one owns. Was this 'Other' *mine?* In what sense? Is my fellowman mine? He is with me; that is his way of being mine."[34] The relation to which Marcel refers does not need to be restricted to the relations "lover-beloved," "friend–friend," and so on; it can be extended to all human beings, and thus it becomes the general, but still very concrete, relation "fellow–fellow." Now, if such relationships are possible, then, it is also possible that the "complete disappearance"—the death—of one member of the relation can be experienced by the other member. As Roger Mehl has written, the experience of another's death "exhibits an aspect through which it is converted into an experience of one's own death," for "the Other's presence is never a quality that belongs exclusively to him."[35] Granted that such an experience is far from yielding a direct and complete grasp of the nature of death. But we should be reasonably satisfied with the possibility of drawing some inferences, which is exactly what I shall try to do in the pages that follow.

28 THREE CASES

The following three descriptions are to be taken as examples of another's death. They cover "cases" which, as happens in legal matters, can be considered "precedents."

The first "case of death" I witnessed was that of my maternal grandmother. She was not "just a relative." I was bound to her not only by blood but also by "togetherness," in the original, and hopefully deeper, sense of this much too dilapidated word. We had lived under the same roof, often seen the same objects, talked about the same persons, followed similar schedules. All this I call "participation in (or sharing) the same circumstances" or, more plainly, "sharing things in common." Now, to participate in the same circumstances means that some part, large or small, of the experience of one person is shared by another. But if one of the "participants" can no longer "share things in common" because he is dead, does, then, the participation of the survivor become exclusively *his own?* No doubt, this is the case to a great extent, and this explains, by the way, the "feeling of loneliness in the very presence of death" to which I shall later refer. Nevertheless, I find it difficult to believe that when a member of what I may be allowed to call "a community of participation" dies, the survivor is merely "present" at his demise. What was shared in common—objects, persons, even feelings and projects—still remains, often for quite a long period of time. It is still what it was, but at the same time it is no longer exactly what or how it was. It has been, as it were, "amputated," and, as happens with some physical amputations, a deep pain is felt where there should be no pain at all.

It may be argued that all this is a "mere question of feelings," and, thus, something "purely subjective." The deceased person is, indeed, deceased, namely, is no longer. On the other hand, we are still alive. Can it be said then that we are, or have been, "experiencing" his death in the sense of somehow "sharing" it? It would be preposterous to give this question an affirmative answer if the death in question were a "purely external event." Now, such would be the case if the deceased person carried with him, so to speak, to the grave whatever he had shared with another person. It is not the case, however, because, as intimated above, "what was shared" still remains—and it remains precisely as "something which we had shared with the deceased person." Therefore, there are times when we are not merely "watching" someone die but we are, or also are, "sharing" his death—at least to the degree in which we had "shared things in common." The obvious fact that we are not dead, but alive, does not in the least indicate that we have been totally unaffected by the beloved person's death. It is not, however, a "mere question of feelings"—such as sadness, anguish, resignation, despair, and so on—but a more fundamental question. Something which belonged to us—we may call it "a common stock of experiences (including projects of further experiences)"—is now irrecoverable and, for that matter, objectively, and not only subjectively, irrecoverable. To conclude from this that we are actually "sharing" another's death would be to go too far. But we may be allowed to say that we have in many cases an experience of another's death which is not reducible to the sheer fact of "just being there" when the beloved person died.

An experience of another's death is a complex affair. In fact, it is made up of a number of contrasting, or seemingly contrasting elements. Thus far we have emphasized "what is left behind," even if, as has been surmised, "what is left behind" has been "amputated." Yet it is also characteristic of death to be final and irrevocable. To experience a beloved person's death is like a departure. Now, human existence is made up to a considerable extent of situations in which we depart, or someone departs and takes leave of us. As a rule, departures are only temporary and seem to be somewhat fictitious. One takes leave of a lover whom one will see soon again. One sees a child off to school, and expects him to return home early in the afternoon. But, are departures and "leave-takings" always temporary? As a rule, we are certain that they are—so certain, indeed, that we do not even raise the question of whether the person whom we left will be seen again; confidence and routine take care of the question. Nevertheless, as soon as we think about it, we realize that any departure could be final. One leaves behind the house where one has spent his childhood. One wonders whether one will ever see it again. In some cases it looks extremely improbable, but then uncertainty—a different kind of uncertainty—floats before the eyes; won't there be a possibility of coming back and taking one more, perhaps final, look? All is possible, which means that all is uncertain. Now, leave-taking is final, and truly definitive, with those who die. Farewells are farewells; no matter how final they may seem, they are never definite. Therefore, those who take leave do not feel their being diminished insofar as their relation with whoever is left behind is concerned; after all, there is always the possibility that a personal relationship among living persons can be resumed. With that final and irrevocable "farewell" called "death," however, there is no such possibility. As a consequence, the being of the person who is "left behind"—in the present case, the "survivor"—is irretrievably diminished, and thus actually diminished. Not even the aforementioned possibility of continuing to share what remains of the personal community, of the "common stock of experiences," compensates for the absence of that person. Continuing to live in the deceased person's house, continuing to see the same people he knew, remembering him, paying homage to his memory, and so on, prove to be poor consolations, for in no case will the deceased person "return." This is one of the reasons why death seems to be so incomprehensible, so "unreasonable," even so "unnatural." It is not perhaps an unfathomable mystery, but it is certainly a most disquieting puzzle.

To be sure, habit and common sense soon come to the rescue. There seems to be nothing more "natural" and "reasonable" than for someone to die, especially when, as in the case I am now trying to elucidate, the deceased person had reached an advanced age, and the premonitory signs of her impending death were unmistakable. There was no doubt that her "hour" had come. But, why precisely *that* hour? This is what seems "unnatural," inexplicable, and, of course, "unreasonable." In order to explain why such and such a person died last Monday rather than last Tuesday, at eleven o'clock in the morning rather than at noon, many reasons can be adduced and many causes can be listed: the remedy did not produce the desired effect, the heart was too weak, and so on. None of these reasons and causes can completely obliterate the "surprise" caused by the person's death. Could not death have taken place some other day, which is the same as saying any other day, which in turn may mean no day in particular, that is to say, never? Perhaps this is not what we "should" think, but this is what we actually do think. Death was expected, and yet not expected, but when it finally took place, it was really and irrevocably "the end."

The experience of another's death is tinged with the idea of finality and irrevocability. It may be contended that such is not always the case. For those who believe in an eternal life, in which they will rejoin their loved ones, there seems to be nothing "unreasonable" in death. Death can be explained, and justified, as the "wages of sin," but also as a necessary condition for a later reunion free from any further partings. Yet it is far from true that the belief in an eternal life, even when such a belief is firmly and deeply rooted, not a half-hearted conviction or a search for comfort, solves the puzzle of death for those concerned.[36] Whether he believes in an eternal life or not, the person who experiences another's death cannot repress a feeling of bewilderment: death is obvious, yet elusive; it puts an end to the life of "the Other," as well as to something in us—our "common participation in life."

Among the teachings we derive from the experience of a beloved person's death is an understanding of the peculiar relation between the deceased and what we may be allowed to call "his world." This world does not solely consist of the objects which had surrounded him, for the manner in which he was related to them also make up his world. Since a living and changing relation is no longer to be expected, everything that had surrounded the deceased appears to be temporarily immobilized. On the one hand, things still seem to respond to the presence of the deceased. This strange feeling has been described by Jules Romains in his *Mort de quelqu'un.* "When the janitor, discovering Godard lying in bed, is about to draw the window shades, an impression crosses his mind. A gesture coming from the dead man had drawn the shades. He was not, then, completely dead, for things happened because of him." It may be argued that this is only metaphorical, and that, in the last analysis, inanimate things may produce similar effects. We could say, for instance, "I drew the window shades because of the wet paint in the room; too much sunlight might damage it." Now, although there is no real difference between the effects, there is in their meaning. We expect nothing from the deceased and yet we are ready to accept certain changes as taking place because of his former living presence. On the other hand, from the moment a person dies, the things—and, in general, the "circumstances"—which had surrounded him begin to fade away. This explains, by the way, the very common wish on the part of those who survive the loved one to keep, at least for a while, things the way the decedent had kept them, or to leave them the way they happened to be placed during his last moments, as if this could delay the final separation. The survivors would not act in this way if they considered such things as "mere objects," if they did not look upon them as a world of meanings. Thus, the actual displacement, removal, and dispersion of things symbolizes the demise and is, in some respects, a kind of delayed reenactment of it. For this reason, the experience of another's death may continue for some time, until the experience itself fades away.

The experience of death just described awakened, among others, the feeling of loneliness; I felt I was, as it were, "alone with death." Nevertheless, it did not produce the bewildering feeling of solitude which emerged so forcefully on another occasion, when I witnessed the sudden death of a man whom I did not know personally and who was, therefore, "just a fellow human being." It happened one day when, in the midst of battle, I saw the body of a man fall, mowed down by a bullet. I experienced neither grief nor—except in a very general way—anguish. It would seem then that another's *death* was merely the death of "*the Other.*" Something happened "outside there," something, so to speak, "objective," a mere fact. Was it not, to begin with, only the body of an unknown fellow creature that fell, like a marionette whose strings had suddenly been cut, with a dull and muffled thud, on the stone covered field? Enhancing this impression was the somewhat dramatic setting in which the event occurred: the dim light of dawn, the abrupt crack of rifle fire, the desolate landscape, and, within my gaze, as if lit by an invisible projector, the quiescent shape of the fallen man. Ever so gradually, there arose in my mind a myriad of impressions and thoughts which began to give meaning to the event just witnessed. There was no grief striking and gripping the soul, no anguish rising in the throat and rendering one helpless, yet the death of a nameless stranger was as enlightening as that of a close relative. In a way, it was even more enlightening. Paradoxically enough, that sudden death seemed entirely meaningless. The life of the unknown man had been snuffed out during a skirmish, in precisely that moment when it displayed unusual strength: when fighting. The fallen man had rushed—unless he had been rushed—into battle; he had probably hoped that he would weather the storm of steel and fire and come out alive. Strength and hope were imprinted on his body during and after his brief agony: the former showed in the compulsive twitching of his hand clutching the rifle; the latter in the remarkable serenity of his face. His fall gave the impression of having been at once expected and unforeseen; it had taken place in the course of a battle where life is always at stake, and yet it seemed to be the result of chance. This death left me perplexed. I experienced it as an event at once totally alien to me and in some ways also "mine." He had died; *I* might have died instead. I saw his death as a symbolic threat to my own life. I looked upon it as the death of a "martyr," that is to say, of a "witness" testifying to the universal and overwhelming presence of death. Precisely because he was no man in particular, he was a symbol of all human beings as mortal beings.

Yet, no matter how "symbolic" this death may have seemed, it was still meaningless. Let it not be said that his death could be accounted for in terms of a "cause," good or bad, for which the man, either voluntarily or by compulsion, gave up his life. Such "causes" can explain perhaps man's history, but not, or not entirely, man's existence. At most, one might know *from* what he died but not *for* what he died. Thus death appeared "unfair"—just ashes, dust, and silence. In the presence of this death, I felt more alone than ever, as if face to face with death itself, pervaded with disquietude and perplexity.

The meaninglessness of this death was revealed to me primarily in the form of a question: "Death, what for?" Such a question became even more pressing when I witnessed another death—or rather, many deaths—as a consequence of an air raid. I saw an indeterminate number of anonymous human beings slaughtered by an equally anonymous force which, seemingly, was directed against no one in particular and which could therefore be supposed to be directed against everyone. Death loomed strange and uncanny, almost without warning or, at best, with too sudden a warning, and hence with no time for anything other than fear and trembling, fright and flight. In this sense, this anonymous death in pursuit of an anonymous human multitude was unlike my grandmother's and even very different from the fighting soldier's. There was neither expectation nor commitment on the faces of the countless victims buried under the rubble. Resignation, distress, even pain—all had given way to an overwhelming and omnipresent sensation of terror, the terror felt when one is faced with impersonal mass extermination, the kind of death that gives no warning, neither choosing its victims nor making any distinction between them. It could not even be said that the rush to escape was the result of cowardice, for the latter is usually manifested before "something" or "someone." On the other hand, this was the terror before pure and simple annihilation, the kind of annihilation that leaves behind no trace, neither sorrow nor anguish, but only destruction. The air raid victims were not "martyrs," "witnesses." They were not "ready to die," but they died nonetheless—fortuitously, indiscriminately, meaninglessly.

In such a case, can we still speak of an "experience of another's death"? It would seem that we cannot, for here death was truly faceless and anonymous. To be sure, I knew little about the relation between the man shot down in battle and *his* death. My experience of these "cases" was, therefore, considerably limited. As to the air raid victims, my experience of *their* death was so restricted as to raise the problem whether there was any experience of another's death at all. Nevertheless, I think that not only was there an experience but a particularly enlightening one: it was the experience of the bewildering meaninglessness of death.

The moment has now come to ask this question: Can the various experiences of another's death yield some general idea which can apply to all possible cases of human death? The answer is, "Yes," provided that such an idea is supported by experience and can eventually apply to further experiences. I now proceed to unfold this idea.

From the experiences described and analyzed we can conclude that human death is meaningful—in varying degrees—insofar as we view it as an event capable of molding some fundamental structures of human life. This is not to say that death completely determines life, because if it did there would be no difference between life and death: to live would be, in the last analysis, to die, which is manifestly gloomy; and, conversely, to die would be to live, which is notoriously absurd. It is only to say that death must partly shape and complete a person's life. The adverb 'partly' must be taken literally. In fact, death never completes anyone's life; otherwise, everyone would die "at the right moment," and, as far as I know, no one ever does. On the other hand, death is never entirely alien to life as if it were something totally external to it, as a more or less deplorable "accident." Sartre was correct when he pointed out that we should not compare death to the final note of a melody.[37] He was only wrong in adding that, whereas the final note of a melody is not absurd, death is. To be sure, there are cases when death seems completely absurd. I have described and analyzed one such case, that of the victims of the air raid. But this was so because we were unable to discover any relation between the victims and their death: the anonymity of the deceased made death equally anonymous and thus engendered the impression of meaninglessness. It did not seem to be their death, but death purely and simply. Now, a death which is not the death of anyone is not, properly speaking, death but only "cessation."

In other words, human death is never completely meaningful, nor is it entirely meaningless. It is meaningful and meaningless in varying degrees. Insofar as death, or rather its possibility, is meaningful, it leads us to understand it. Insofar as it is meaningless, it leads us to rebel against it. Now, understanding of, and rebellion against, death are equally significant ingredients in human life. We may choose the ingredient we like best, or the one we dislike the least; in any case, our choice will disclose the basic structure of our existence, which includes our attitude before the possibility of death. As far as I am concerned, I hold that life would be scarcely worth living were it not for the hope of being able to fight against death. On the other hand, I believe that such a hope would be mere wishful thinking if we did not realize that, when all is considered, death still remains one of the possibilities of human life. Human life is largely, if not exclusively, made up of projects with which life anticipates itself. Nevertheless, these projects are constantly threatened by the possibility of remaining unfulfilled. Indeed, they are projects only insofar as they might not be accomplished. We have already intimated that human existence—and perhaps all reality—must be finite in order to be meaningful. Furthermore, human existence is finite not only "externally" (by circumstances, chance, and natural causes) but also "internally" (by the very nature of the human projects). As a constant possibility, death molds our behavior, whether we know it or not: anything we want to do must be accomplished within a certain, constantly decreasing, period of time.

Curiously enough, the basically finite character of human life helps to destroy the idea that the human person is, ontologically speaking, a thing of naught, a kind of "incarnated nothingness." For death bestows upon the human person a unique nobility. "The dead," says one of the characters in Marcel Aymé's novel, *La rue sans nom,* "have the right to have done all sorts of things. A dead man is not something to be cheerful about; nothing is left in him except what he has done." This idea is, by the way, the reason behind the respectful attitude in front of the dead adopted by the survivors. To be sure, sometimes the survivors despise, ridicule, discredit, or desecrate the dead. But then it is because they do not look upon the dead as dead but regard them as if they were still alive, as is the case with men who died in the name of a still vehemently hated cause. As a rule, however, all of a person's most objectionable deeds are forgotten the moment he dies. A unique nobility then emerges: the nobility which consists in having lived and "accepted," whether consciously or not, the possibility of death (§ 29, *ad finem*)— having "accepted" it while rebelling against it, for what is "accepted" here is not so much the sheer fact of death as the human condition which carries with it the possibility of mortality.

29   "LITERARY" TESTIMONY

The author's own experiences of another's death are, of course, limited in number and scope. For a more ample understanding of the nature and forms of human death we must have recourse to some accounts of other, similar experiences. We can find them in "literature," and thus we can speak of "literary testimony."[38]

In Book IV of his *Confessions,* St. Augustine describes his state of mind upon hearing of the death of a friend in Tagasthe. He informs us that everything he had experienced in the company of his friend suddenly acquired the opposite value. What had been happiness was turned into grief. "All that we had done together was now a grim ordeal without him."[39] Everything seemed intolerable and hateful in a world from which his friend was absent, because (as Landsberg has noted in his analysis of this passage)[40] his friend's death was to him not a mere absence but a symbol of the universality and omnipresence of death. "Wherever I looked," St. Augustine writes, "I saw only death."[41] As is often the case with St. Augustine, his account of a personal experience is permeated by metaphysical preoccupations. Thus, in the present case not one particular man but man as such appeared to St. Augustine illuminated by some kind of soul-subduing mystery. To be sure, in the mind of St. Augustine this "mystery" already had an explanation: it was not a matter of raising philosophical questions but of testifying to the existence and glory of God.[42] Yet in the experience of another's death St. Augustine could not help toppling over some kind of "existential mystery": death made its appearance under the guise of an *atrocissima inimica,* as something unjust and "unfair," without which, however, life itself could not be adequately explained. Furthermore, in experiencing the death of his friend, St. Augustine experienced at the same time the possibility of his own death. Witnessing another's death seemed to drain him of his own vital form and substance. Hence, the death of "half his soul," in the words of Horace, was to St. Augustine a step toward the experience of the death of any man, including, of course, himself. At some point Augustine felt that death served no purpose. Later on he was convinced that he had found the ultimate reason for death: when he was able to view his friend's death, or for that matter any death, as the result of a decree of the true God, who should not be questioned but worshiped.

According to St. Augustine, only after God has become manifest and the human heart purified can the death of a friend, as well as human death in general, acquire its true meaning. Grief and anguish should then be relinquished as manifestations of selfishness. As a result it becomes possible to love men, not only individually but humanly—*humaniter.* Such is the insight gained from the experience of another's death: each and any man can "be," at a most decisive moment, "everyman." Viewed in this manner, death is absolutely personal and yet completely universal; it is a fact, a symbol and a meaning all in one.

A similar insight can be found in a more recent "literary testimony." André Gide also described the death of a friend. He begins by warning us that "this time it is not the same thing," because the one who passed away was "somebody real."[42] His friend's death was for Gide, as it was for St. Augustine, a crushing experience. He describes it in his own style, clearly and serenely. "There he lies, so small on a large linen sheet, dressed in a brownish suit; very straight, very rigid, as if waiting for a call."[44] The mere presence of the body, so quietly stretched out in repose, generates an enormous and overwhelming vacuum. Around it, all emotions and gestures crystallize—grief, depression, despair, the urge for an impossible dialogue. These emotions and gestures are as individual and irreplaceable as the very friend who has passed away. Some consolation is sought by substituting the environment of the deceased for the deceased: this house was *his* house; this town, *his* town; this table was the table where *he* worked. Can we, then, speak of a man and his death instead of referring to a particular man and his particular death? Gide seems at first to oppose such a suggestion, and yet he ends up by fully accepting it. "I hardly admire those who cannot bear definition, who must be deformed by being seen askance. Philippe could be examined from all points of view; to each of his friends, to each of his readers, he seemed *one,* but not the *same one.*"[45] Thus, the late friend was truly a human person and, as such, he could not be replaced by any other person. At the same time, he had something disturbing and surprising within him which Gide describes as "something lasting." We can give it a name: "his attestation of human death as a human being." Upon his death, Gide's friend ceased to be a particular person in order to become a symbol—paradoxically, "a living symbol"—of man as man.

We do not fall short of "literary testimonies" of human death, but the two above will suffice for our purpose. As we go over other "literary descriptions" of someone's death, we notice that they often exhibit a most characteristic feature: they serve as points of departure for gaining an insight into the meaning of human death in general. The same happens with many descriptions of different "types" of decedents and "kinds" of deaths. Sometimes it is the death of a relative, a friend, or a stranger. Sometimes death is described as caused by illness, at other times as caused by an accident. The "type" described may have faced death with resignation, repentance, fear, even (as if abiding by the rules set up by many eighteenth-century "libertines" in order to "enjoy a good death") with arrogance and a hint of irony. In all these typical cases, the description of human death serves as the basis for an understanding of the nature of death in general. It is not surprising, then, that most authors agree in the main points.

Two points of agreement are quite obvious. On the one hand, there is a tendency to regard death as a sort of "fulfillment of life," even when death is considered premature and, as it were, "unfair." Before it occurs, and often immediately afterwards, death seems to be incomprehensible and meaningless. But once it is accepted as a *fait accompli,* against which there is no appeal, it tends to be regarded as one of the inalienable "possibilities" of human existence—a possibility which is both immanent and imminent. On the other hand, there is a tendency to view the death of any person as an event so truly "ultimate" as to be capable of investing the deceased with a certain irretrievable dignity: the dignity usually ascribed to a "martyr" in the original sense of a "witness." The deceased person testifies, willingly or not, to the constant presence of death as the setting of human life.

It would be unwise to consider any descriptions, and subsequent analyses, of human death as strict "proofs." They are not, however, entirely worthless. Reduced to their essentials, they make us notice the paradoxical character of human death: it is absurd, unjust, inexplicable, and yet it is somehow inherent in life, molding it. The conflicting statements of Heidegger and Sartre (§ 27) can now be reconciled and integrated. Death itself is meaningless, and yet it endows life with meaning. Death is, to a considerable extent, a "pure fact," totally contingent and completely outside my scope, and yet without it my life would not exhibit "contents" (thoughts, actions, decisions, etc.) essentially different from the mere "process" of living. It is not necessary to be always on the brink of death, or to be "unto death" in order to live authentically, but neither is it necessary to "choose" the moment in which our life will end in order to acknowledge that death belongs to us. Life does not derive its full meaning from death, but neither does life lose all meaning because of death. Death, in short, is one of the "possibilities" of life, but to live is obviously not the same as to die.

30 THE ATTITUDES REGARDING DEATH

Up to this point we have described and analyzed experiences of another's death. Is it possible to discourse on the experience of one's own death, or, as it is sometimes said, "my death"?

Death is the suppression of life and consciousness. It is obvious that no person has an experience of his own death. Nevertheless, in some sense we can speak meaningfully of "our own death." First, we can "anticipate" our death insofar as we can think of it, and even "imagine" it. Second, we can use analogy, and conceive of our death in terms of another's death. "Everything that applies to me," Sartre has written, "applies to the Other."[46] If we turn this sentence around, we obtain the following plausible statement: "Everything that applies to the Other applies (or can, in principle, apply) to me." Finally, and above all, we can tackle the problem raised here within the framework of our ontology. According to this ontology, there is no clear-cut distinction between "Absolutes," for the simple reason that there are no such "Absolutes." Accordingly, we must refuse to admit that there is "something" called "pure (or absolute) subjectivity" and, of course, that there is "something" called "pure (or absolute) objectivity." Another's death is both a subjective and an objective event. The same must be the case with one's own death. Therefore, if it is true that we cannot experience it exactly in the same sense in which we can experience love, friendship, sorrow, and so on, we can place ourselves, so to speak, in front of it (of its possibility). This I call "an attitude regarding death." A description and analysis of some typical attitudes regarding death can then cast some light on our subject.

Many of the attitudes regarding death are the product of reflection. A case in point is Epicurus' well-known argument against the fear of death: when death exists, we no longer exist; when we exist, death does not.[47] Epicurus seems to deny that there can be any experience of one's own death; the total impossibility of such an experience is precisely what makes it possible to face death fearlessly. Yet there is no denial of the fact that Epicurus is describing a (possible) experience of one's own death: the experience of a death without fear and trembling.

Another attitude regarding death ensues from the feelings experienced by those who have been on the point of dying: those who have been on the verge of drowning, those who have faced a firing squad, and so forth. It has been said that during the moments immediately preceding death (or at least its imminence) there is something like an automatic release of memories, as if his whole life were passing before the person concerned in rapid cinematographic succession. Without necessarily subscribing to Bergson's theory of memory, we could certainly explain, or at any rate discuss, the aforementioned automatic release of memories in terms of the relations between consciousness and life. It seems quite probable that, when consciousness is on the point of losing its foothold on life, it becomes particularly receptive to memory. Thus, one attitude regarding death may consist of what we may call "a recapitulation of one's own life." To be sure, such a recapitulation may not take place. The moments immediately preceding impending death may very well demand all of a man's vital energy. Instead of despair, abulia, indifference, paralyzing fear, recapitulation of memories, and so on, there may be a renewed, and maximumly increased, "will to fight." But then we would still be confronted with an "attitude regarding death." No doubt, an "attitude" is not exactly the same as an "experience." We are not claiming, therefore, that we can have a direct experience of our own death—that we can, for instance, "see" death in the same way in which we "see" a shape, a color, and so on. We are merely claiming that we can conceive, even if it is *a tergo,* of an experience of the possibility of our own death. We see our death somehow from the outside, but 'somehow from the outside' is not the same as 'completely from the outside.' In some respects we are looking at our death (or its possibility) from the inside; otherwise, we could not even take "an attitude" in front of our death (or its possibility).

Some readers will argue that we are going too far in examining the (possible) experience of one's own death from the point of view of the (possible) attitude regarding one's own death. Some readers, on the other hand, will complain that we are not going far enough. Among the latter are those who surmise that we can experience our own death by simply being always "prepared" to die, living as if each moment were the last moment. Stoic and Christian thinkers have developed this theme with verve and vehemence. Thus, for instance, Seneca wrote that death merely interrupts our life without taking it away from us. According to many Stoic philosophers, "the door is always open," so that the wise man can reasonably step across the threshold when the burden of life becomes intolerable.[48] Many Christian writers tell us that our death is in the hands of Providence, so that there is nothing for us to do but await it with both resignation and hope, endeavoring to live in such a manner that we will always be ready to face the fatal yet unpredictable moment. Curiously enough, similar attitudes have been adopted, or at least preached, by writers who have been neither Christian nor Stoic, as is the case with those who have relied on reason—some kind of "Universal Reason"—to convey the idea that death is always "around the corner," so that "the reasonable man calmly walks down the gentle, easy slope which should lead him to eternal rest."[49] Bertrand Russell has come close to the idea that death is, so to speak, "constantly approaching." The best way to face death, Russell argues, is to convince yourself that with advancing age one's interests gradually become less "individual" or "personal" and more "general." Russell compares individual life to a river which at first rushes violently from its narrow source, and finally overflows, thus abating as it flows into the proverbial "sea of death."[50] We may not think of "preparing for death" when we are young, but as soon as we grow old, or simply suspect that we are, we cannot help but conclude that death and life are beginning to walk hand in hand.

This brief examination of various attitudes regarding death has had a twofold purpose: first, to show that, properly speaking, one cannot have an experience of one's own death; second, to surmise that, when all is said, one can have an experience of the possibility of death, and thus, to a certain extent, of the imminence and immanence of death. The problem remains now whether we can talk meaningfully about an individual's death as "his own."

31   THE PROBLEM OF ONE'S OWN DEATH

As a natural being, as a member of society, as part of a social, family, or community group, man never dies completely alone. Furthermore, man's actions and, above all, man's creations—his "cultural achievements"—often endure and, as it is said, "transcend" his life and, consequently, his death. Therefore, when we use the expression 'one's own death' we do not thereby imply that a human being is an "impenetrable," and "incommunicable," monad; we confine ourselves to pointing out that the death of a human being is "his own" in the sense at least that it is—or, more cautiously, constantly tends to be— a truly personal and nontransferable event.

Since there is no scarcity of reflections on the theme that "the death of a human being is his own," we do not have to restrict ourselves to quoting Heidegger or Kierkegaard. We can go as far back as Seneca, who writes to his friend Lucilius, "Be convinced that all ignorant men err when they say, 'It is a beautiful thing to die your own death,' for there is no man who does not die his own death (*Nemo moritur nisi sua morte*). Besides which, you can reflect on the following saying: No one dies in any but his own way [in his own day: *nemo nisi suo die moritur*]."[51] Granted that Seneca does not interpret "his own way" in the manner of many modern philosophers. After all, Seneca's main purpose is to convince his friend and, through him, all men that "to live

in conformity with Reason (and Nature)" is the same as "to relinquish everything that does not belong to me." Thus, all the so-called "external goods"
(including our own body, with the exception of its basic needs) must be
forsaken in order to prepare ourselves to become one with the Cosmic Soul,
the all-pervading *pneuma*. Nevertheless, we find in Seneca, as well as in other
ancient writers, a penetrating insight into the nature of human death as "our
own," that is to say, of human death as man's inalienable "property." One does
not simply fuse with the Cosmic Soul or Universal Reason; one joins it by
incorporating *oneself* into it and by the acceptance of one's own death.

In addition to philosophical reflections, and at times even more enlightening, are "intuitions" of human death as "one's own." Many writers, and in
particular poets, have touched upon the subject. In an imaginary conversation
with his late friend Seytres, Vauvenargues writes, "Death slid into your heart,
and you carried it in your breast."[52] The first part of this phrase refers to the
ineluctability of death; the second, to its "authenticity." Many contemporary
poets have been more explicit and vehement than the concise and often
elliptic Vauvenargues. Jules Supervielle, for example, writes, "The death which
I shall become already moves in me freely."[53] García Lorca describes a bull-
fighter who walks courageously to meet *his* death, "Ignacio goes up the gradins
/ His death so heavy on his shoulders."[54] Whether for reasons of literary technique or of poetic "vision," death is portrayed in the last two examples as
"someone" who is waiting outside, as a "thief"—a "thief of human life"—who
is easily recognizable and whose presence is accepted without questioning. A
poetic vision of human death as a more internal "reality"—or "event"—is found
in a poet who is particularly fond of "things," "objects," namely, Pablo Neruda.
He has compared death with "an inward shipwreck"; death is "like drowning in
our hearts / Like falling from our skins into our souls."[55] Although death
"moves inward," it is still seen as a "subtle thief"; it glides silently with its "green
face" and its "green look," with its penetrating dampness like that of the leaf of
a violet / And its somber color like that of an exasperated winter."[56] The
"vegetality" of death does not, however, impair its "inwardness." After all, man's
nature is also somewhat "vegetal"—comparable to a plant, to a leaf, to a tree—
so that man and his death finally sink into the same abyss. Death, writes
Neruda, "lives recumbent, and suddenly exhales."[57] Not recumbent, however,
outside, but within man, like ivy twining around the human tree.

The above are only a few among the many examples of poetic descriptions
of "one's own death"; literary scholars are liable to find the subject inexhaustible. These examples would suffice here, however, were it not for the fact that
we have not yet said anything about a writer who has been rightly called the
"poet of death," namely, Rainer Maria Rilke. A few words on Rilke's views
are inescapable.

"I have found it puzzling," Rilke has one of his characters say, "that men spoke about death in a different way from all other events."[58] Death is a very strange thing, but it is not necessarily something sinister or uncanny. It exerts a mysterious attraction, which explains why most men "go somewhere to find it and, unknowingly, load it on their shoulders." Yet, what they look for is not death in general, but a particular death, their own. That is why the poet asks God to give him his own death.[59] In *The Notebooks of Malte Laurids Brigge,* Rilke offers us not only a poetic insight but a detailed description of what he believes to be one's own death. The death of Chamberlain Brigge is not like any other death because, strictly speaking, there is "no death like the others." Even children, writes Rilke, die as what they are and "as what they would have become." For this reason, Chamberlain Brigge "closes in upon himself" in order to die, so that his death and the end of his life can coincide. For Rilke this means that death always comes "in time," since even "what one would have become" or "what one might have become" is, as it were, "compressed" and "abridged" in the instant in which death strikes.

It is most unlikely that Rilke wished to prove that people always die at the very moment in which they "ought to die," so that death would be then thoroughly explained as well as "justified." All that Rilke means is that we always carry death within us, in such a manner that "the solemn death that each of us within him has / That is the fruit around which all revolves."[60] We should not confuse "the right time" with "our own time." No matter when a man dies, even if he dies prematurely, he dies his own death. Death does more than simply end a man's life; it realizes his life and reveals its ultimate structure. If this self-realization and self-revelation discloses a person's being as free, then it can be said that one's own death brings one closest to freedom.

32 THE ESSENCE OF HUMAN DEATH

The foregoing descriptions and reflections are as enlightening as they are provocative. They help us to realize to what an extent the death of each human being is, whether he knows it or not, his own death. Nevertheless, these descriptions and reflections must be taken neither literally nor unconditionally. We should avoid the temptation of thinking that the nature of each human being can be grasped fully only in terms of his death, for we would end by concluding that there are no bonds linking each man to his fellow man, as well as no bonds between humanity, as a whole, and Nature. This conclusion would be totally incompatible with our philosophical system, which strongly emphasizes both the peculiarity of the human being and his "continuity" with the rest of reality.

If the degree of mortality runs parallel with that of "inwardness," there is little doubt that the highest degree of mortality and the highest degree of "inwardness" coincide. On the other hand, since "maximum inwardness" is equivalent to "property" in the sense of 'property' discussed above (§ 24), it can be concluded that man, as the most mortal of all realities, is a being whose death is maximally "his own."

Now, as I have so often remarked, inwardness is never absolute. First, there are no "Absolutes," and hence no absolute properties. Second, if death were absolutely "internal" in each human being, it would end up by being completely external to him. In dying his own death, and nothing but his own death, it would seem as if each person achieves absolute freedom. But what kind of freedom is it that forces us to die our own death? It can only be an external compulsion and, for that matter, a general or universal type of compulsion, not an internal and completely individual property.

If I accept the idea of human death as "one's own death," I do so with important reservations. Some of these I will now point out.

First, the characteristic of human death called "property" does not stem solely from the supposedly unique and totally autonomous character of human life. Human death is ontologically linked to other forms of cessation; indeed, cessation "culminates" in human death. Therefore, the cessation of nonhuman realities can cast some light on human death. The reverse is, of course, also true: the phenomenon or process called "human death" can cast some light on other modes of cessation, including that of inorganic nature. Inorganic, and even organic, entities do not cease to be in the same manner as man does; their cessation is, to a considerable extent, external to them. It is not, however, completely external, and in this sense we can say that nonhuman entities die, however minimumly, "their own death" or, more properly, "undergo their own type of cessation." The intercrossing of two ontological directions (§ 9) is here apparent. From the point of view of man, inorganic entities cease to be minimally. All entities, however, whether human or nonhuman, cease to be within a "continuum of cessation" which is strictly parallel to the "continuum of reality." Thus, the characteristic of human death called "property" *also* stems from some of the characteristics which we ascribe to "cessation as such."

Second, the idea that each human being is in possession of his own death—the idea, namely, that death is man's "property"—must be understood in the light of the meaning of 'property' to which I have referred at the beginning of the present section. Thus, to say that man achieves his very being by means of his death is not to say that his being is only, or even primarily, "a being unto death," as if man's life hinged upon his death and nothing else counted. Nor is it to say that man has his death at his disposal, as a servant whom he can summon or dismiss at will. The apothegm, "Die at the right time," and the eulogy of one's own death as the "voluntary death, which cometh unto me because *I* want it," have little to do with the concept of "property" proposed here. To affirm that death "is mine" simply means that death "belongs to me"; it does not mean that "I belong to death." Only in this sense can it be said that man makes his own death. In fine, man makes his own death only to the extent that he makes his own life.

Third, no human death is absolutely "his own"; it is only a limiting event which he can try to make completely his without ever entirely succeeding. Moreover, the degree of "success" in this respect is not only an individual matter; it is also historical. As man begins to make himself in the course of his own life, which is historical, he also begins to make his own death historically. At certain periods men have viewed themselves as "duplications" of other men to such a degree that they were not certain of whether or not they were "themselves," and whether or not they themselves had performed such and such actions or had such and such thoughts. Thomas Mann vividly portrayed this uncertainty in the first part of *Joseph and His Brothers,* when he described the Beni-Israel as a people who felt deeply immersed in a tradition created by the entire community and which no one in particular had helped to produce. No one can claim that he, as an individual, has done something all by himself. El Eliezer, Joseph's preceptor, considers himself the same Eliezer who, for Isaac's sake, had gone after Rebecca. There is a startling resemblance between being a member of a closely knit social group and being a member of a biological species. For this reason, the relative "deindividualization" and complete "depersonalization" of death which is characteristic of a biological species seems to reappear in such a social group. Just as in a biological species, the death of an individual seems to be an accident, so in a group or clan, the death of one person may appear as a "repetition," and sometimes as a "rehearsal"; what counts here is primarily the species, the group or the clan, and not the individuals. On the other hand, when a particular death is intimately related to a particular person, then the death of such a person is never a "repetition"; his death is entirely different from the death of any other man. Proust probably had this idea in mind when he wrote: "The death of Swann! Swann, in this phrase, is something more than a noun in the possessive case. I mean by it his own particular death, the death allotted by destiny to the service of Swann. For we talk of 'death' for convenience, but there are almost as many different deaths as there are people . . ."[61] If we keep well in sight the role played here by the adverb 'almost,' we cannot help but acquiesce.

We can understand now why an excessive weakening of what might be called the "human tension"—the effort exerted by each man in order to continue to be a man, and especially a particular man—can result in such a marked subordination of an individual to his group that their ensuing relationship almost duplicates that of an individual organism and its biological species (§ 21). On the other hand, the excessive strengthening of the above "tension" could cause an individual to forsake completely his own humanity for the sake of supposedly impersonal and absolute values. In either case, man would cease to be man, and accordingly would cease to die as such. Now, to live as a man is to exist "between" organic reality and so-called "spiritual reality." The human "tension" that characterizes man's life is similarly reflected in his death.

Can we ever disclose the ultimate essence of human death? If we are asking whether we can ever offer a final and irrevocable definition of 'human death,' then the answer must be negative. Just as with anything real, the nature of human death can be grasped only by means of a "dialectical process" which must continually move from one polarity to another, from one absolute to another, from one limiting concept to yet another, with the hope that they can finally be integrated. Without relinquishing our distrust of "final definitions," we now offer a few conclusions.

Human death includes inorganic cessation as well as biological decease. Man does not die unless his body, and the material systems of which his body is composed, dies. Nevertheless, man's body is not just "a body," but "a way of being a body" (§ 20). To a considerable extent, this way of being a body is made up of "possibilities" which may or may not be fulfilled, but which in any case are "real." Now, a moment may come when all of a human's possibilities become closed to him—which is the same as saying that a man may become aware that he had no future before him. For a few instants the past and all its memories might fill the resulting vacuum. This can happen only because the individual still regards the past as a future or as something which points to the future in some way, "filling it." To live, then, basically boils down to reminiscing about things past. When even the image of the past projected toward the future fades, man has nothing left but his organic existence. When this happens, man ceases to be a man; he is then only a member of a biological species. At this point, then, he dies as a man. In other words, death hovers over us when our possibilities of living as men vanish. The man contemplating suicide, who sees his future as completely devoid of any and all possibilities—who has no future at all, and no longer finds any meaning in his life, or even in his death—does not really need to carry out the final and supreme act: he is already dead before perishing. On the other hand, when new possibilities which transcend biological death—such as creations and "cultural achievements" which are likely to exert an influence upon a future in which we are no longer present—offer themselves, then death seems to withdraw even if it has biologically annihilated us. The paradox is as obvious as it is startling: in some really limiting cases, it is possible to die without ceasing to be, or to cease to be without dying.

Ferrater Mora

NOTES TO CHAPTER THREE, *HUMAN DEATH*

1. *De Anima*, II, 1, 412 a 27 ff.

2. *De Civitate Dei*, XXI, 10. See Pascal's comment on this passage in *Pensées*, ed. Jacques Chevalier (Paris, 1936), § 84 (p. 847), and *Oeuvres*, ed. Léon Brunschvicg, XII (Paris, 1925), § 72, pp. 91–92.

3. For instance, in Gilbert Ryle's *The Concept of Mind* (London, 1949), and M. Merleau-Ponty's *The Phenomenology of Perception* (Paris, 1945). Also, but less obviously, in Gabriel Marcel's *Journal métaphysique* (Paris, 1927), 3d edition (Paris, 1955), pp. 224–226, 252, 261–264, and *The Mystery of Being*, vol. I (London, 1950), pp. 148–170. For interesting similarities between the phenomenological approach and the "linguistic approach" see C. Taylor and A. J. Ayer, "Phenomenology and Linguistic Analysis," *Proceedings of the Aristotelian Society*, suppl. vol. 33 (1959), 93–124, and John J. Compton, "Hare, Husserl and Philosophic Discovery," *Dialogue*, III (1964), 42–51.

It should be kept in mind that there is now a tendency among a number of "analytical philosophers" to argue in favor of a (moderate) type of "dualism," or, at least, a tendency to prove that a mild body–mind dualism is no less defensible than an antidualism. As an example of the aforementioned tendency we may mention Anthony Quinton's article, "The Soul," *Journal of Philosophy*, LIX (1962), 393–409. To be sure, the term 'the soul' is made synonymous here only with 'the nonphysical aspect of a person.' It is, in Quinton's words, "an empirical concept of the soul, which, like Locke's, interprets it as a sequence of mental states logically distinct from the body" (*op. cit.*, p. 397). "All I have tried to show," Quinton writes, "is that there is no necessary connection between the soul as a series of mental states linked by the character and memory and any particular continuing human body" (*op. cit.*, pp. 407–408).

4. The terms 'outside' and 'inside' have here, then, a more radical (and hence more controversial) meaning than in Weston La Barre's sentence: "It was the first organism which first brought the concepts of 'inside' and 'outside' into the universe" (*The Human Animal* [Chicago, 1954], p. 2; reprinted in Phoenix Books P45 [Chicago, 1955], p. 2).

5. See Sherwood L. Washburn, "Tools and Human Evolution," *Scientific American*, 203, no. 3 (September, 1960), 63–75.

6. Cf. Grace A. de Laguna, "The *Lebenswelt* and the Cultural World," *Journal of Philosophy*, LVII (1960), 781.

7. I use the terms 'community' and 'society' in a sense similar to, although not necessarily identical with, the one proposed by Ferdinand Tönnies in *Gemeinschaft und Gesellschaft. Grundbegriffe der reinen Soziologie* (Leipzig, 1887); 8th edition (Leipzig, 1935).

8. See Marshall D. Sahlins, "The Origin of Society," *Scientific American*, 203, no. 3 (September, 1960), 76–86.

9. Max Scheler, *Die Stellung des Menschen im Kosmos* (Darmstadt, 1928), p. 63.

10. See Pedro Laín Entralgo, *La espera y la esperanza* (Madrid, 1957; 2d edition [Madrid, 1958], p. 479).

11. M. Heidegger, *Sein und Zeit* (Halle a. d. S., 1927), § 4, p. 13, and § 10, pp. 45–50.

12. José Ortega y Gasset, *La idea de principio en Leibniz y la evolución de la teoría deductiva* (Madrid, 1958), § 29, p. 339. The distinction between 'ontical' and 'ontological' has been hailed as a useful one by Willard van Orman Quine (*Word and Object* [Cambridge, Mass., 1960], p. 120), but on the basis of a meaning of 'ontological' quite different from Heidegger's.

13. Twisting and stretching the meaning of terms borrowed from common speech is, of course, only part of the story. It is necessary that meaning-twistings and meaning-extensions should not function *in vacuo*. See, among many other contemporary writings in this respect, H. A. Hodges, *Languages, Standpoints, and Attitudes* (London, 1953), pp. 17–18 (University of Durham, Riddell Memorial Lectures, 24th Series), and in particular A. J. Ayer, *Philosophy and Language* (Oxford, 1960), p. 30 (An Inaugural Lecture, Oxford, Sept. 3, 1960; reprinted in Ayer's book, *The Concept of a Person and Other Essays* [New York, 1963], pp. 1–35). Among classical warnings against *illegitimate* meaning-twistings and meaning-extensions Berkeley is still the most valuable.

14. Mario Bunge, "Can Computers Think? in *Metascientific Queries* (Springfield, Ill., 1959), p. 129. (American Lecture Series, 41).

15. *Ibid.*, p. 133.

16. See John G. Kemeny, "Man Viewed as a Machine," *Scientific American*, 192, no. 4 (April, 1955), 58–67.

17. José Ortega y Gasset, *The Revolt of the Masses*, James Cleugh, trans. (New York, 1933), p. 52. On the meaning of this contention in Ortega y Gasset's thought, see José Ferrater Mora, *Ortega y Gasset: An Outline of His Philosophy* (London, 1956, and New Haven, Conn., 1957), pp. 52–53; new revised edition (New Haven, Conn., 1963), pp. 61 ff.

18. Jean-Paul Sartre, *L'Etre et le Néant* (Paris, 1943), pp. 508–642. It should be noted that, despite his adherence to Marxism, Sartre has not changed his views too drastically concerning the "primacy of freedom" in man, even during the so-called "period of exploitation." Sartre limits himself to pointing out that such freedom displays itself "within a certain given conditioning environment"; man is "what he succeeds in doing with what has been done to him" (*Critique de la raison dialectique*, vol. I [Paris, 1960], p. 63). Sartre himself claims that his later opinions can easily be

integrated with his earlier ones—a claim similar to the one made by Heidegger with respect to the relation between his "earlier" and "later" philosophies (see *Unterwegs zur Sprache* [Pfullingen, 1959], pp. 85–155, especially pp. 98–99).

19. Literally, a tightrope walker *(ein Seiltänzer): Der Mensch ist ein Seil, geknüpft zwischen Tier und Übermensch—ein Seil über einem Abgrunde. Ein gefährliches Hinüber, ein gefährliches Aufdem-Wege, ein gefährliches Zurückblicken, ein gefährliches Schaudern und Stehenbleiben— ... eine Brücke und kein Zweck ... "* (*Also sprach Zarathustra.* Zarathustras Vorrede, vol. 4. *Werke in drei Bänden,* Karl Schlechta, ed., vol. II [München, 1956], p. 281).

20. Weston La Barre, *The Human Animal,* p. 246.

21. On the difference between repentance and remorse, see Vladimir Jankélévitch, *La mauvaise conscience* (Paris, 1951), pp. 94–107, especially pp. 94–95.

22. See José Ferrater Mora, *Ortega y Gasset: An Outline of His Philosophy,* pp. 26–27, 49; new revised edition, pp. 25–26, 58.

23. *Persona est naturae rationalis individua substantia* (Boethius, *De duabus naturis et una persona Christi,* 3 [Migne, *Patrologia Latina,* 64, col. 1345]).

24. Further elucidations on this question and, in general, on "the problem of man" will be found in my article, "Images de l'homme," *Revue philosophique de la France et de l'Étranger,* XC (1965).

25. Paul Ludwig Landsberg, *Experiencia de la muerte,* Spanish translation of a hitherto unpublished German manuscript (México, 1940), p. 71.

26. Georg Simmel, "Zur Metaphysik des Todes," *Logos,* vol. I (1910–1911), p. 59, reprinted with revisions in *Lebensanschauung. Vier metaphysische Kapitel* (München, 1918), 2d edition München and Leipzig, 1922), p. 108, and *Brücke und Tür* (Stuttgart, 1957), p. 31.

27. Karl Jaspers, *Philosophie,* vol. II (Berlin, 1932), p. 220.

28. Martin Heidegger, *Sein und Zeit* (Halle a. d. S., 1927), § 47, p. 239.

29. *Ibid.,* § 47, p. 240.

30. *Ibid.,* §§ 51–53, pp. 252–267.

31. Jean-Paul Sartre, *L'Etre et le Néant,* p. 618.

32. *Ibid.,* p. 630.

33. *Ibid.,* p. 631.

34. Gabriel Marcel, *Présence et immortalité* (Paris, 1959), p. 60 ("Journal métaphysique, May 19, 1942").

35. Roger Mehl, *Le vieillissement et la mort* (Paris, 1955), p. 67.

36. See Irving E. Alexander, "Death and Religion," in Herman Feifel, ed., *The Meaning of Death* (New York, Toronto, and London, 1959), pp. 271–283.

37. Jean-Paul Sartre, *L'Etre et le Néant,* p. 431.

38. The "literary testimony" is only a part, albeit a most significant one, of what we may call "historical testimony." We will not be concerned with the latter, but we will mention a few works in which the reader will find an abundance of historical material: Alfons Schulz, "Der Sinn des Todes im Alten Testament," *Braunsberg Akademie. Verzeichnis der Vorlesung* (1919), 5–41. Alberto Tenenti, *Il senso della morte e l'amore della vita nel Rinascimento (Francia e Italia)* (Torino, 1957), especially about the works concerning the *ars moriendi* and the iconography of death. J. Huizinga,

Hersttij der middeleeuwen (Haarlem, 1928), chap. 11. Bernhard Groethhuysen, *Die Entstehung der bürgerlichen Welt- und Lebensanschauung in Frankreich*, 2 vols. (Halle/ Saale, 1927–1930), part I, chap. 2, § 2.

39. *Confessions*, IV, iv, 9.

40. Paul Ludwig Landsberg, *Experiencia de la muerte*, pp. 92, 98.

41. *Confessions, loc. cit.*

42. *Ibid.*, IV, vi, 11: *Non enim tempus quaerendi nunc est, sed confitendi tibi.*

43. André Gide, "Mort de Charles Louis Philippe," in *Journal* [1909] (Paris, 1939), p. 278.

44. *Ibid.*, p. 280.

45. *Ibid.*, p. 287.

46. Jean-Paul Sartre, *L'Etre et le Néant*, p. 617.

47. Diogenes Laërtius, X, 127. Also Lucretius, *De Rerum Natura*, III, 830 ff.

48. Diogenes Laërtius, VII, 130. Also Epictetus, *Encheiridion*, 5. The Stoics' fearless attitude in the face of death may conceal a "fear of life." See, on this question, José Ferrater Mora, *Man at the Crossroads* (Boston, 1958), part I, chap. 2.

49. Choderlos de Laclos, *De l'éducation des femmes*, chap. 7 (*Oeuvres complètes*, ed. Maurice Allen [Paris, 1951], p. 419).

50. Bertrand Russell, *New Hopes for a Changing World* (London, 1951), p. 210.

51. *Epistolae morales*, LXIX.

52. *Éloge de Seytres.*

53. *La mort que je serai bouge en moi sans façons* (*Choix de poèmes* [Buenos Aires, 1944], p. 234).

54. *Por las gradas sube Ignacio / Con toda su muerte a cuestas* ("Llanto por Ignacio Sánchez Mejías. 2. La sangre derramada" [1935], in *Obras completas*, IV [Buenos Aires, 1944], p. 155).

55. *. . . como ahogarnos en el corazón / Como irnos cayendo desde la piel al alma* ("Sólo la muerte," in *Residencia en la tierra 1931–1935*, vol. II [Santiago de Chile, 1939], p. 21).

56. *. . . con la aguda humedad de una hoja de violeta / Y su grave color de invierno exasperado (loc. cit.).*

57. *. . . vive tendida y de repente sopla (loc. cit.).*

58. In the *Geschichten des guten Gottes.*

59. *O Herr, gib jedem seinen eignen Tod / Das Sterben, das aus jenem Leben geht / Darin er Liebe hatte, Sinn und Not (Das Stundenbuch* [*Gesammelte Werke*, vol. II, Leipzig, 1927], p. 273).

60. *Der grosse Tod, den jeder in sich hat / Das ist die Frucht, um die sich alles dreht* (*Das Stundenbuch*, p. 273).

61. Marcel Proust, *La prisonnière*, in *A la recherche du temps perdu*, eds. Pierre Clarac and André Ferré, vol. III (Paris, 1954), p. 199.

José Ferrater Mora

BIOGRAPHICAL NOTE

1912   Born in Barcelona, October 30.

1922–25   Completes *Bachillerato* in Col·legi de Santa Maria del Collell.

1925–29   Works as a clerk in a bank, in a public service company and in a car agency while studying.

1929–36   Works as a freelance translator and editor for several publishing houses to support his studies for the *Bachillerato* degree and his future studies in philosophy at the University of Barcelona.

1932   Receives degree of *Bachillerato* and enters the University of Barcelona.

1935   Publishes his first book, *Cóctel de verdad.*

1936   Completes Licenciado en Filosofía degree.

1936–39   Enlists in the Republican Army, Eastern Front. He serves in the Intelligence Section of the Advanced Headquarters of the Republican Army in the East. He spends four months in a sanitarium in the Pyrenees.

1939   Crosses the Spanish-French border when Catalonia is occupied by Franco's troops. He lives in exile in Paris for three months.

1939–41   Travels to Cuba and resides in Havana, where he lectures, translates, teaches summer courses and prepares the first edition of the *Diccionario.*

1941–47   Goes to Santiago de Chile to teach a summer course at the University of Chile. Several months later, he is appointed Professor of Philosophy at the University of Chile.

1943   Awarded "Concepcio Rabell" Prize for *Les Formes de la vida catalana,* Chile.

1947–48   Comes to the U.S. on a Guggenheim Scholarship and resides in New York City.

1948–49   Guggenheim Scholarship is renewed. He resides in Princeton and Baltimore.

1949–50	Lecturer of Spanish and Philosophy, Bryn Mawr College.
1951–54	Associate Professor of Philosophy, Bryn Mawr College.
1955–80	Professor of Philosophy, Bryn Mawr College.
1957–58	Visiting Professor, Princeton University.
1960	Becomes an American citizen.
1960–61	Senior Scholar, American Council of Learned Societies.
1961	Lindley Lecturer, University of Kansas.
1962–63	Visiting Professor, Johns Hopkins University.
1963	John Gordon Stipe Professor, Emory University.
	Special guest of the Mexican Government, XIIIth International Congress of Philosophy.
1965	Member of the Hispanic Society of America.
1967–68	Visiting Professor, Temple University.
1969–74	Director, Program in History and Philosophy of Science, Bryn Mawr College, in collaboration with Pennsylvania University and the American Philosophical Society.
1971	President, The International Symposium of Logic and Philosophy of Science, València, Spain.
1973	"Everydayness" wins First Prize, Movies on a Shoestring.
1974	Special guest, First National Congress of Philosophy, Morelia, Mexico.
	First recipient of the Fairbanks Chair in the Humanities, Bryn Mawr College.
	"The Suit of Night" wins Honorable Mention, Photographic Society of America, Motion Picture Division.
1975	"The Skin of the Earth" wins Honorable Mention, Photographic Society of America, Motion Picture Division.
1976	The Christian R. and Mary F. Lindback Foundation Award for Distinguished Teaching, Bryn Mawr College.
1977	"Venice 23" wins Certificate of Appreciation, Metropolitan Motion Picture Club.
1979	Doctor *honoris causa,* Autonomous University of Barcelona.
1981	Emeritus Professor, Bryn Mawr College.
	Special guest, National Congress of Philosophy, Guanajuato, Mexico.
	Cultural Merit Award from the Spanish Government.
1982	Awarded Isabel la Católica Cross.
	Medal from the Menéndez y Pelayo International University, Sitges, Spain.
	Member of the American Academy of the Spanish Language.
1983	Doctor *honoris causa,* Tucuman University, Argentina.
	Doctor *honoris causa,* University of Uruguay.

Doctor *honoris causa,* National University of Colombia, Bogotá, Columbia.

Member of Miguel Lillo Foundation, Argentina.

Conference in his honor, "Homage to a Humanist," Syracuse University.

1984   Awarded the Sant Jordi Cross, highest civil distinction of Catalonia.

Awarded Alfonso el Sabio Great Cross, Spain.

1985   Awarded the Prince of Asturias Award in Humanities, Spain.

Guest, Argentine Government.

"Lux Perpetua" wins Cinematography Award, Silver Medal, Best Travel Film, and Special Recognition, Photographic Society of America, Motion Picture Division.

1986   Doctor *honoris causa,* UNED (Spanish Open University).

Doctor *honoris causa,* University of Salta, Argentina.

Special guest of the Argentine Government. Lectures in Buenos Aires and other cities.

1987   Juan Carlos Chair, New York University.

Member of The Academy of Chile.

Nadal Prize Finalist for *El juego de la verdad.*

1988   Doctor *honoris causa,* University of Barcelona, Spain.

Doctor *honoris causa,* University of Cuyo, Mendoza, Argentina.

Awarded Special Recognition, ALDEEU.

Special guest of the Argentine Government. He again lectures in Buenos Aires and other cities.

1989   Inaugurates the Ferrater Mora Chair for Contemporary Thought, University of Girona, Spain.

1990   Directs summer school course, Complutense University of Madrid, Spain.

1991   Travels to Barcelona for the publication of *La señorita Goldie,* suffers heart attack, dies January 30.

Posthumous award, University of Santiago de Compostela, Spain.

JOSÉ FERRATER MORA'S WORKS

Only books are listed.

Cóctel de verdad, 1935.

Diccionario de Filosofía, 1941; 2nd ed., 1944; 3rd ed., 1951; 4th ed., 1958; 5th ed., 2 vols., 1965; 6th ed., 4 vols., 1979; 7th rev. ed., 1994 (ed. by Josep-Maria Terricabras).

España y Europa, 1942.

Les formes de la vida catalana, 1944; 2nd ed., 1955; 3rd ed., 1960; enlarged ed. with the essay "Catalunya enfora," 1980.

Unamuno: bosquejo de una filosofía, 1944; 2nd ed., 1957 (English version: *Unamuno: A Philosophy of Tragedy*, 1962; reed., 1982).

Cuatro visiones de la historia universal: S. Agustín, Vico, Voltaire, Hegel, 1945; 2nd ed., 1955; 3rd ed., in *Obras Selectas*, 1967; 4th ed., 1982 (Italian translation: *Quattro visioni della storia universale*, 1981).

Cuestiones españolas, 1945.

Variaciones sobre el espíritu, 1945.

La ironía, la muerte y la admiración, 1946.

El sentido de la muerte, 1947.

El llibre del sentit, 1948.

Helenismo y cristianismo, 1949.

El hombre en la encrucijada, 1952; 2nd ed., 1965 (English version: *Man at the Crossroads*, 1957; new ed., 1968).

Cuestiones disputadas: ensayos de filosofía, 1955.

Lógica matemática, 1955 (with H. Leblanc); 2nd ed., 1962.

Ortega y Gasset: An Outline of His Philosophy, 1957 (English version: *La filosofía de O. y G.*, 1958; rev. Spanish translation: *O. y G.: etapas de una filosofía*, 1958 [2nd ed., in *Obras Selectas*; 3rd ed., 1973]); 2nd ed., 1963.

Qué es la lógica, 1957; new eds., 1960 and 1965.

La filosofía en el mundo de hoy, 1959; 2nd ed., 1963 (English version: *Philosophy Today: Conflicting Tendencies in Contemporary Thought*, 1960; Catalan version: *La filosofia en el món d'avui*, 1965); rev. ed.: *La filosofía actual*, cf. infra.

Una mica de tot, 1961.

El ser y la muerte: bosquejo de una filosofía integracionista, 1962; 2nd ed., 1967; 3d ed., 1979; 4th ed., 1988, with a new "Prefaci" (English version: *Being and Death: An Outline of Integrationist Philosophy*, 1965).

Tres mundos: Cataluña, España, Europa, 1963 (includes *Las formas de la vida catalana*).

El ser y el sentido, 1968 (later *Fundamentos de filosofía*, cf. infra).

La filosofía actual, 1969; 2nd ed., 1970; 3rd ed., 1973 (rev. edition of *La filosofía en el mundo de hoy*).

Diccionario de filosofía abreviado, 1970.

Indagaciones sobre el lenguaje, 1970; 2nd ed., 1980.

Els mots i els homes, 1970 (Spanish version: *Las palabras y los hombres*, 1971; 2nd ed., 1991).

El hombre y su medio y otros ensayos, 1971.

Las crisis humanas, 1972 (rev. edition of *Las crisis humanas*, cf. supra); new ed. rev., 1983.

Cambio de marcha en la filosofía, 1974.
Cine sin filosofías, 1974.
De la materia a la razón, 1979; 2nd ed., 1983.
Ética aplicada. Del aborto a la violencia, 1981 (with Priscilla Cohn); 2nd ed., 1982; 3rd enlarged ed., 1985.
El mundo del escritor, 1983.
Fundamentos de filosofía, 1985 (reelaborates *El ser y el sentido,* cf. supra).
Modos de hacer filosofía, 1985.

Posthumous

Mariposas y supercuerdas. Diccionario para nuestro tiempo, 1994.

Novels and stories

Relatos capitales, 1979.
Claudia, mi Claudia, 1982.
Voltaire en Nueva York, 1985.
Hecho en corona, 1986.
Ventana al mundo, 1986.
El juego de la verdad, 1988.
Regreso del infierno, 1989.
La señorita Goldie, 1991.

Posthumous

Mujeres al borde de la leyenda, 1991.

Edition of works

Obras Selectas, 2 vols., 1967.

Correspondence

Joan Oliver-Josep Ferrater Mora: joc de cartes, 1988.
"Correspondència de J. F. M. — Antonio Rodríguez Huéscar," *Boletín de la Institución Libre de Enseñanza,* II, 16 (1993), 7–34; 17, (1993), 7–32.

Bibliography

Leopoldo Montoya, "J. Ferrater Mora's Published Writings" in the volume edited by Priscilla Cohn, *infra,* pp. 201–32 (complete to 1981).

Carlos Nieto Blanco, "Bibliografía de y sobre José Ferrater Mora," in the volume edited by S. Giner and E. Guisán, *infra*, pp. 335–46.

SELECTED BIBLIOGRAPHY ON FERRATER MORA

Monographs

Priscilla Cohn, ed., *Transparencies. Philosophical Essays in Honor of José Ferrater Mora*, 1981.

C. Nieto-Blanco, *La filosofía en la encrucijada. Perfiles del pensamiento de José Ferrater Mora*, 1985.

Special Issue of *Anthropos*, 49 (1985).

A. Mora, *Gent nostra. Ferrater Mora*, 1989.

S. Giner, E. Guisán, eds., *José Ferrater Mora: El hombre y su obra*, 1994.

Isaías Hernández León, *Cinco etapas evolutivas en el pensamiento de José Ferrater Mora*, 1994.

Selected Articles

Priscilla Cohn. "Tendiendo puentes: la teoría del sentido y el continuo en Ferrater Mora," *Teorema*, 11 (1981), 37–56.

A. Guy, "El integracionismo de Josep Ferrater Mora," en A. Guy, *Historia de la filosofía española*, 1985, cap. V, pp. 358–67.

J. Muguerza, "J. Ferrater Mora: de la materia a la razón pasando por la ética," *Revista Latinoamericana de Filosofía*, 15 (2) (1989), 219–38.

J.-M. Terricabras, "Josep Ferrater Mora: An Integrationist Philosopher," *Man and World*, 26 (2) (1993), 209–18.

Index of Persons

Alarcón, Pedro Antonio de, 23
Alfonso XIII (king of Spain), 27, 28
Aristotle, 93, 130, 181, 183, 186, 214, 219, 221
Augustine, Saint, 36, 53, 214, 242–243
Ayala, Francisco, 20
Aymé, Marcel, 242
Azorín (pseud. of Josep Martínez i Ruiz), 18, 19, 20

Balmes, Jaime, 22
Baroja, Pío, 18, 27
Bayo, Ciro, 18
Benavente, Jacinto, 18
Bergson, Henri, 32, 136, 152, 157, 158, 165, 180, 183, 246
Blasco Ibáñez, Vicente, 18, 29
Boethius, 229
Borges, Jorge Luis, 69
Bradley, Francis Herbert, 80, 153
Bruno, Giordano, 39, 43, 44
Buddha, 50
Bunge, Mario, 222

Caesar, Julius, 129
Cajetan, Cardinal, 53
Cassou, Jean, 75, 103
Castelar, Emilio, 23
Castro, Américo, 68, 69
Cela, Camilo José, 84
Cervantes, Miguel de, 71–74
Chestov, Leo, 37
Cohen, Hermann, 74, 138

Cohn Ferrater Mora, Priscilla (widow of José Ferrater Mora), v, 8
Costa, Joaquín, 18, 20, 23, 64
Curtius, Ernst Robert, 82, 103

Darío, Rubén, 79
Debussy, Claude-Achille, 133
Descartes, René, 140–141, 153, 159, 164, 181, 213
Dickens, Charles, 84
Dilthey, Wilhelm, 151, 158, 163, 164, 180, 186
Donoso Cortés, Juan, 22
Dostoevski, Feodor, 84
Eddington, Arthur Stanley, 221
Einstein, Albert, 129
Epicurus, 245

Faulkner, William, 84
Ferrater Mora, José, 1–8, 11
    Càtedra Ferrater Mora (Chair in his honor), 7–8
Fichte, Johann Gottlieb, 74, 165, 190, 219
Flaubert, Gustave, 84
Franco, Francisco, 1
Freud, Sigmund, 32

Galileo Galilei, 218
Ganivet, Angel, 18, 20, 24, 68
García Lorca, Federico, 248
Gide, André, 243–244
Giner de los Ríos, Francisco, 18, 23, 66, 75

Gladkov, Feodor, 84
Goethe, Johann Wolfgang, 71, 94, 167
Goya, Francisco de, 129
Greene, Graham, 84

Hartmann, Eduard von, 50
Hegel, Georg Wilhelm Friedrich, 33,
    34, 39, 43, 44, 61, 79, 80, 95, 97,
    130, 148, 154, 173, 181, 223
Heidegger, Martin, 4, 151, 180, 220,
    234, 244, 247
Heraclitus, 44, 165, 183
Horace, 243
Hume, David, 93
Husserl, Edmund, 4, 129, 136, 150, 180

Ibn Khâldun, 129

Jaspers, Karl, 234
John of the Cross, Saint, 140–141
Juan de Yepes. See John of the Cross

Kant, Immanuel, 2, 53, 58, 79, 82, 93,
    129, 139, 147, 148, 167, 173, 184,
    190
Kierkegaard, Soren, 34, 36, 37, 53, 59,
    93, 97, 101, 183, 247
Kline, George, 8
Krause, Karl Christian Friedrich, 138

Landsberg, Paul Ludwig, 230, 242
Leibniz, Gottfried Wilhelm, 97, 149
Lessing, Gotthold Ephraim, 55
Lorca, Federico García. See García
    Lorca, Federico

Mach, Ernst, 165
Machado, Antonio, 18
Machado, Manuel, 18
Maeztu, Ramiro de, 18, 135
Mann, Thomas, 251
Marcel, Gabriel, 235
Marcus Aurelius, 130
Marías, Julián, 84, 87, 104, 136, 163–
    164

Mauriac, François, 84
Mehl, Roger, 235
Menéndez y Pelayo, Marcelino, 18, 24,
    65–66
Meyer, François, 49
Mill, John Stuart, 130

Nabokov, Vladimir, 54
Neruda, Pablo, 248
Neumann, John [Janos] von, 222
Newton, Isaac, 148
Nicholas of Cusa, 39, 43
Nietzsche, Friedrich, 36, 46, 93, 148,
    149, 150, 152, 186, 224

d'Ors, Eugeni, 3, 20, 27, 28, 82, 135
Ortega y Gasset, Eduardo, 29
Ortega y Gasset, José, 1–5, 7, 20, 23,
    27, 28, 64, 67, 73, 74, 82, 84,
    127–190 (passim), 223, 228

Pascal, Blaise, 36, 53
Paul, Saint, 36, 53, 73
Pereda, José María de, 23
Pérez Galdós, Benito, 18, 23, 66, 84,
    88
Philip II (king of Spain), 65
Pi y Margall, Francisco, 23
Plato, 77, 93, 149, 216
Primo de Rivera, Miguel, 1, 28
Proust, Marcel, 129

Quine, Willard van Orman, 133

Renan, Ernest, 129
Rilke, Rainer Maria, 248
Romains, Jules, 238
Rousseau, Jean-Jacques, 152, 155
Ruiz Contreras, Luis, 18
Russell, Bertrand, 136, 149, 165, 247

Salmerón, Nicolás, 23
Sanz del Río, Julián, 138–139
Sartre, Jean-Paul, 223, 226, 228, 234,
    241, 244, 245

Scheler, Max, 4, 29, 180, 217
Schlegel, Friedrich von, 166
Schopenhauer, Arthur, 44, 50, 57, 94
Seneca, 246, 247, 248
Shaw, Bernard, 73
Silone, Ignazio (pseud. of Secondo
    Tranquilli), 84
Silverio, Lanza (pseud. of Juan Bautista
    Amorós), 18
Simmel, Georg, 145, 148, 149, 150,
    152, 158, 233
Socrates, 72, 154
Spengler, Ostwald, 158
Spinoza, Baruch, 49, 79, 102
Supervielle, Jules, 248

Tacitus, 79
Teichmüller, Gustav, 149
Terence, 35
Terricabras, Josep-Maria, 8
Theresa from Avila, Saint, 140

Thomas Aquinas, Saint, 53, 54, 214
Thucydides, 79
Torre, Guillermo de, 66
Toynbee, Arnold Joseph, 154
Trueba, Antonio de, 22

Unamuno, Miguel de, 1–5, 7, 13–104
    (*passim*), 135, 136, 140–141

Vaihinger, Hans, 149
Valera, Juan, 18, 20, 23, 24, 64, 66
Valle-Inclán, Ramón María del, 18
Vauvenargues, Luc de Clapiers, Mar-
    quis de, 248

Vergés, Joan, 8

Weber, Max, 137

Zola, Émile, 84
Zubiri, Xavier, 1

Index of Subjects

abstraction, 3, 33–35
anthropology, 2–3, 5. *See also* man
atheism, 45–46. *See also* God

becoming, 218, 224. *See also* being;
   existing
being, 179–86, 218–20, 224. *See also*
   becoming; existing
belief, 160–62, 174
biography, 131, 170. *See also* method
biologism, 151–52, 157, 215–18. *See*
   also life; materialism
buddhism, 50

Christianity, 58–60
circumstances, 146–47, 160, 228
concept, 147–48
culture, 217, 224

death, 5, 6, 230–35, 245–49. *See also*
   immortality; life; mortality
   three cases of, 235–42
   in literature, 242–45
   essence of human, 249–52
dialectical approaches, 39–40, 229
dualism. *See* integrationism; limiting
   concepts

ego, 166–68
empiricism, 94
essentialism, 7, 15
europeanizers, 4, 63–70, 139–40. *See*
   also hispanizers

existentialism, 179–80
   Unamuno's, 14–15, 34–35
existing, 218, 227. *See also* becoming;
   being

facts, 77–79
fiction, 89–91, 103. *See also* literature;
   reality

generation of 1898, 17–20
God, 41–47, 49, 224. *See also* atheism

hispanizers, 4, 102. *See also*
   europeanizers, quixotism,
   traditionalism
   the problem of Spain, 63–66, 139–40
   Spain as a conflict, 66–70
history, 4, 60–61, 68, 70, 162–64, 180–
   82, 216, 229

idealism, 36, 40–41, 72, 98, 141, 185
ideas, 35–37
   as different from beliefs, in Ortega,
   160–162
immortality. *See also* death; mortality
   hunger for, 47–50
   forms of, 50–54
   as a struggle, 54–56
   Christian concept of, 51–54. *See also*
   soul
individual, 33–35, 38–40
inside/outside, 215, 225–26. *See also*
   mind-body problem; soul

integrationism, 5–7. *See* limiting concepts
intellectualism, 4, 141
intrahistory, 57, 60, 63, 70, 90, 96
intralife, 57. *See* intrahistory
irrationalism, 15. *See also* rationalism

Kantianism, 138–39, 184
Krausism, 23, 100, 138–39

life, 164–70, 215–18. *See also* biologism;
 death
 tragic sense of, in Unamuno, 3, 33–
  35, 37
limiting concepts, 5–7, 49. *See* integrationism
literature, 78–80, 90. *See also* fiction;
 poetry; words
logic, 187–88

man, 2, 91, 101, 164–70, 213–14. *See
 also* personalism
 as selfhood, 220–22
 as property, 222–23, 226–27, 250
 definition of, 224–29
materialism, 45. *See also* biologism;
 spiritualism
memory, 57
metaphysics, 220. *See also* science
method, 130–31, 146, 159–60. *See also*
 biography
mind-body problem, 213–14. *See also*
 inside/outside; man
monism, 43–45
mortality, 229–30. *See also* death;
 immortality

newspapers, 135–37
nothingness, 50
novel, 83–91

objectivism, 4, 131, 138–43, 217. *See
 also* perspectivism

pantheism, 45
paradox, 26, 36–37, 41–42, 44, 67, 71,
 73, 80, 83, 229–31. *See also* tension
past, 56–57
personalism, 26, 45, 138. *See also* man

perspectivism, 4, 132, 142, 145–56. *See
 also* objectivism
philosopher, 2, 3, 4, 35–37, 77, 93–94,
 130–31
 the idea of philosophy, 186–89
Platonism, 43, 47–48, 50–53, 69, 74, 76
poetry, 81–82. *See also* literature
 poetic realism, 41. *See also* realism
politics, 26–28
pragmatism, 33, 35, 38

quixotism, 70–74. *See also* hispanizers

rationalism, 4, 15, 35, 37–38, 40, 43,
 72, 83, 142, 153. *See also* ratio-
 vitalism; vitalism
ratio-vitalism, 4, 132, 157–78. *See also*
 ratio-vitalism; vitalism
 vital reason, 157–64, 165–66
realism, 40–41, 80–81, 85, 87–88, 98
reality, 93–98, 217. *See also* fiction
regenerationism, 64–65. *See also*
 europeanizers

science, 220. *See also* metaphysics
scientism, 78
society, 170–76
soul, 47. *See also* immortality (Christian
 concept of); inside/outside; mind-
 body problem
Spain. *See* hispanizers
spiritualism, 45. *See also* materialism
State, 173
struggle. *See* tension
style, 4, 137–38
system, 7, 129–30, 139, 145

tension, 3, 38–41, 43–44, 52, 54–56,
 58, 69, 74, 77–78, 86–87, 97–98,
 101. *See also* dialectical approaches;
 dualism; paradox
traditionalism, 24–26, 139. *See* hispanizers

vitalism, 4, 34–35, 142, 154–55, 157–64.
 See also rationalism; ratio-vitalism

words, 75–82, 103. *See also* literature